Michel Luc
Bellemare

The
Structural-Anarchism
Manifesto:

*(The Logic of Structural-Anarchism
Versus The Logic of Capitalism)*

Blacksatin Publications Ltd.
©2016

Blacksatin Publications Ltd.
©2016

[ISBN: 978-09781151-3-5]

-[Textual Note]-

The chosen format of this text, i.e., the format of the manifesto, is deliberate and calculated in the sense that it is the logical outcome of a rational process of content refinement and elimination so as to arrive at the most poignant structural outline of the logic of capitalism and its antithetic substitute, structural-anarchism. The format of the manifesto permits a philosopher to jettison many conventions, conventions which are the product of the academic establishment in its effort to limit and control knowledge and intellectual advancement. Consequently, little to nowhere in this text will one find quotations, footnotes, chapters, a bibliography, paragraphs etc., and/or any other convoluted gibberish, which is traditionally found and localized in customary academic, textual outputs and standards. This was done on purpose so as to usurper the academic status quo. There are only two small footnotes in the text.

Of course, any reader familiar with the subject-matter, within this text, will find ideational connections throughout, links in concepts and lines of thought, possibly anticipated by someone else. However, this matter is of total indifference and is of no consequence as this is a manifesto, therefore, it is not an academic critique and/or measurement of how far the ideas expressed within, coincide with those of other thinkers. Notwithstanding, the ideas expressed within are on all accounts fresh, having refashioned a well-worn, overworked subject-matter in a new interesting manner, re-contextualizing many outdated concepts into a new perspective, a perspective that is more conducive to the post-industrial, post-modern age, we find ourselves within.

In consequence, the structure of the manifesto enriches academic autonomy and permits the greatest possible, academic textual freedom imaginable, both in its visual look and its ideational exegesis. The structure of the manifesto enables the philosopher to discard writing conventions, organizational conventions, and long historical explanations, without losing any poignancy in the meaning and understanding of the ideas and logic expressed inside. The manifesto permits the philosopher to arrive at the heart of the matter, surely, effectively, and accurately. As a result, these are all liberties, which a reader will find throughout this unorthodox text.

Moreover, and more importantly, the structure of the manifesto, permits the philosopher to construct a general abstract theory without delving too deeply, and broadly, into particular socio-economic phenomena. The structure of the manifesto, by its very nature, is design to be short and sweet, it is designed to simplify complex subject-matter to get to the point, quickly and poignantly, resulting in the maximization of its internal elucidations, ideational structures, and its effect on its specific readership. In fact, the manifesto is an invaluable tool for political philosophy in its efforts to expound logical structures, concepts, and processes, without having to resort to history and/or prior overlapping texts etc. Henceforth, the structure of the manifesto permits the philosopher to override, upend, and overturn, years of indoctrination, ideology, and academic bourgeois conformism. It permits one to throw the baby out with the bathwater, in one fell swoop, without remorse, and without rancor.

In sum, if this work has any value it consists in three crucial points: 1., its logical structure, which is designed to upend and overturn academic, bourgeois, conformist mediocrity, 2. the originality of the concepts and ideas expressed within. And 3., the rigor of the conceptual logical apparatus within, which introduces old concepts in a new light and explodes the thin, abstract-conceptual veneer of bourgeois-state-capitalism. Due to the fact, the logical apparatus in this text is constructed to ruthlessly expose bourgeois-state-capitalism, for what it is, a soft-totalitarian-state, a soul-sucking, military-industrial-complex, determined to expand, amplify, and realize its vampiric mercenary objectives, by any means necessary, at the lowest financial cost, as soon as possible.

CONTENT

-[Preface]-

First and foremost, this book outlines a new form of anarchism, i.e., structural-anarchism, which advocates for a series of micro-revolutions, designed to install an anarchist federation/patchwork of municipalities, cooperatives, and autonomous-collectives, devoid of capitalism and devoid of any federal state-apparatus. Specifically, structural-anarchism is a form of anarchist-communism. It is communism from below, rather than, the Marxist notion of communism from above, i.e., authoritarian-communism. Ultimately, the fundamental purpose of this unique book is to give certain movements an interpretative model or language of understanding and action, concerning the basic workings of our current, dominant, political-economic framework, i.e., bourgeois-state-capitalism. The purpose is to develop definitive conclusions separate of capitalist and Marxist ideology, whereupon, an anarchist micro-program of resistance, revolution and subversion can be implemented in the micro-recesses of everyday life. That is, a micro-program which can stimulate, subtle, refined, radical social changes, unrelated to the bourgeois-capitalist status quo. This book establishes the central workings of the logic of capitalism, including, the tenets of structural-anarchism. Therefore, the rationale for this philosophical exposition is an excavation of the fundamental basis of the logic of capitalism, based not on any Marxist framework, but, on a structural-anarchism framework. The logic of structural-anarchism is a new interpretive framework and language of analysis, which, although, sympathetic to Marxism and its commodity-form analysis, develops beyond Marxism into its own revolutionary program and political-economy.

In addition, this book explores the complications and the complexities of the basic fact that we are increasingly living within the confines of a disciplinary surveillance society, where, privacy is really based on an individual's ability to expose the surveillance mechanisms monitoring his or her private life. The assumption is that surveillance and discipline are now total and that most surveillance, punitive and disciplinary-mechanisms never attain the light of public knowledge and scrutiny. As a society, western democracies have moved beyond democracy into a new socio-economic formation, the formation/framework of the soft-totalitarian-state. A bourgeois-totalitarianism, where, Antonio Gramsci's notion and theory of "hegemony" is now obsolete, having dissolved into a type of soft, all-encompassing totalitarianism. No longer is there the full possibility of counter-cultures and alternative-cultures operating independent and outside of dominant-mainstream surveillance, discipline and culture. Counter-cultures and alternative-cultures are now subjugated, monitored, and disciplined, within the parameters of the dominant-culture of the soft-totalitarian-state, i.e., the military-industrial-complex. It is soft-totalitarianism in the sense that we as humans are not imprisoned, disciplined, and punished, akin to traditional hardline-totalitarian-states, but, we are monitored and under surveillance akin to traditional hardline-totalitarian-states.

Like hardline-totalitarian-states, surveillance is total and continually seeks to refine its totality and its mechanisms of information gathering. Today, through the inter-connectedness of the state, its institutions, corporations, and para-state organizations, surveillance and discipline are total, but, there is a litany of disciplinary, punitive and censorship mechanisms in effect which are soft in nature, capable of applying variable degrees of soft and hard punitive and disciplinary measures, depending on the situation, deviation and/or individual. What distinguishes the soft-totalitarian-state from the traditional conception of the hard-totalitarian-state is its ability to have nuances in its disciplinary measures, i.e., the ability to be as hard and as inhuman towards dissent and disobedience as hardline-totalitarian-states, and the ability to be pliable, lax, and nuanced, towards various degrees of dissent and disobedience. The soft-totalitarian-state is ruled, for the most part, by administrative micro-fascism networks/languages, i.e., oligarchies, which function and operate at the micro-levels of everyday life. That is, a slow creeping fascism, seeking to batter down and discourage all alternatives and differences to its rule at the micro-levels of socio-economic life, in favor of a generalized dispiritedness and a celebration of the bourgeois-capitalist status quo, as rightfully and legitimately the best.

This microscopic total war, embodying a plethora of micro-skirmishes and micro-fronts, is present in our homes, our choices, our daily routines, our relationships, our ideas and, most importantly, in our livelihoods etc. These ruling, administrative, micro-fascist, oligarchical networks/languages, present to various degrees in all western democracies, are not necessarily blatant, flagrant, highly visible, or without humor and understanding, like traditional hardline-totalitarian-states. Their type of morality/amorality is not by nature stern and obdurate, but it can be, it is a military-industrial morality/amorality, a type of morality/amorality focused on maximizing the accumulation and extraction of surplus value, that is, capitalist profit. The truth is that this military-industrial morality/amorality is the logic of capitalism, and it is encoded everywhere and on everything. Today, capitalism possesses humor, wit, and superficial understanding; while, it is able to exercise its disciplinary measures and totalitarian-indignities upon socio-economic nonconformities. Bourgeois-state-capitalism upholds a thin veneer of a seemingly democratic meritocracy, with nonchalance, a sarcastic half-smile, and a hearty handshake, knowing full well that it is always in control and the determining factor of merit. It is micro-fascism, a sort of pop-fascism. It is a celebratory monologues celebrating the capitalist marketplace, the capitalist warfare-state and the capitalist mode of production, ad nauseam. That is, all the individuals, groups, institutions, and contemporary art, which embrace its central logic, its pseudo-religiosity, its righteousness, and its call that we all be self-absorbed naval-gazers, basking in and competing for our own microscopic capitalist glory and marketplace brilliance.

Despite the thin veneer of seeming democratic meritocracy, the administrative micro-fascism networks/languages, like all traditional hardline-totalitarian-states, are comprised of interchangeable cogs, who are essentially expendable, due to the fact that all that is required to comprise these micro-fascism networks/languages/oligarchies is obedience and ideological congruity. Every cog and individual unit, within these governing, micro-fascist, networks/languages/oligarchies, can easily be replaced if need be, by the influx of university graduates and the unemployed which flood the marketplace and have reduced the job market to a form of debt-slavery and wage-slavery. These socio-economic conditions are not the result of chance and/or global market fluctuations, but, are the result of logical administrative design so as to maintain and facilitate control and governance of the workforce/population, by these ruling, micro-fascist, oligarchical networks. The objective is to safeguard, expand and amplify the socio-economic processes of the logic of capitalism in and across everyday life.

In the arts, any artist or any contemporary artifact is expendable and disposable. They are expendable and disposable as they are dependent on bourgeois-state-capitalism for their survival and meaning, bourgeois-state-capitalism now being the primary financial supporter of the arts. They are dependent on bourgeois-state-capitalism for their survival and meaning because these artists and artifacts are devoid of independent vision and independent meaningful substance, other than, the vision and substance manufactured by the bourgeois-capitalist status quo. That is, the rampant celebration and total submission that the soft-totalitarian-state disseminates and engenders in the name of bourgeois-capitalism. Consequently, any artist, or artifact, which embodies this essential quality, i.e., ideological congruity with the logic of capitalism, which is ready-made, readily available, and epidemic throughout bourgeois-state-capitalism, can easily become a celebrated, merit-filled nexus of the ruling, micro-fascist, oligarchical networks, which entwine the capitalist social fabric into a soft-totalitarian-state.

Notably, this author bears no illusions that structural-anarchism is viable in the current socio-economic landscape, or could even succeed, at the moment in replacing the current socio-economic formation of bourgeois-state-capitalism. As, the majority of citizens are adverse and/or oblivious to the notion of the implementation of a new political-economic framework and/or system. This is primarily due to years of indoctrination, fear, and living with and under, the precepts of false-consciousness, engendered by the dominant capitalist ideology. Better the devil you know than the possibility of another, better to live with the rampant exploitation and enslavement of bourgeois-capitalism than to attempt an unknown, untested, organizational-form of politics and socio-economics. However, this does not mean that one should abandon such a venture. As, it is such a venture that stimulates hope, inspiration, innovation and, most importantly, the idea that the current socio-economic system, already in place, which manufactures such divisions, discriminations, and inequalities, can be more intelligently organized and can function more equitably for the greatest number. The primary principle that makes the logic of structural-anarchism a viable option and a venture worth pursuing is its innate poly-rationality, analysis, and call for open-participatory-democracy. That is, the poly-rationality, analysis, and open-participatory-democracy, which logically, demonstrates that the current, socio-economic system, i.e., bourgeois-state-capitalism, can be more intelligently organized and can function more equitably via the implementation of the poly-rationality of structural-anarchism. That is, a political-economic framework, which is founded on the central, grounding praxis of flipping the logic of capitalism on its feet, right-side-up again, so as to dislodge, displace, and return the logic of capitalism, from where it came as a subordinate appendage of the workforce/population and nature. The praxis of the logic of structural-anarchism is revolution not reform. It is about returning the logic of capitalism to the level of subordinate, namely, as a socio-economic process by which the workforce/population, democratically, sates its basic maintenance requirements. The logic of structural-anarchism is about the total annihilation of the logic of capitalism. The modus operandi of the logic of capitalism, at the moment, is the logical apparatus by which a select few, proficient-proponents of the logic of capitalism, subjugate and dominate vast segments of the workforce/population, according to the profit imperative, so they can grossly, and over-abundantly, indulge their insatiable mercenary impulses for power and for capitalist profit. Therefore, the objective is to abolish bourgeois-capitalism in all its forms.

This marginalization of so-called, bourgeois-state-capitalism, may be a figment of the imagination, meant only for classroom contemplation and reflection, but, this revolutionary logic, i.e., the logic of structural-anarchism, is what is required to do away with capitalist exploitation, capitalist domination and capitalist enslavement. However, on a long enough timeline, that which is more logical always rises above that which is less logical, and that which is more logical invariably has greater worth for the greatest number, greater advantages for the greatest number, greater longevity for the greatest number, and finally, equals the greatest level of happiness for the greatest number. This is the long-term formula for the eventual displacement and overthrow of the logic of capitalism in favor of something more logical, more poly-rational, more plural, more horizontally organized, and thus, more objective, more balanced, more egalitarian, more transparent and, ultimately, more democratic.

This book outlines the idea that the logic of structural-anarchism is about understanding and engendering socio-economic re-configuration, radical social change, not solely destruction. According to the logic of structural-anarchism, critique, pragmatic re-configuration, micro-revolution, and democratic-dialogue are the mediums for radical social change, not violence, per se. However, due to the unwillingness of bourgeois-capitalism to let go of its contextual supremacy and governing power, inevitably means that the overthrow of bourgeois-capitalism will require expropriation, demolition and the willingness to use force against the structures, apparatuses and processes of capitalism on a mass scale. The political-economic framework of structural-anarchism is about engendering a socio-economic-system founded on poly-rationality, equality, plurality, and an idea of society, where, the socio-economic fabric and all private property, both mental and physical, is collectivized, more intelligently organized, and more rationally distributed among citizens than it currently is under capitalism. The objective of structural-anarchism is a version of anarchist-communism. As a result, the use of force is to be precise, structural and directed at the systems of capitalism, namely, the capitalist modes of production, consumption and distribution. Demolition is a must, before, reconstruction can begin.

Above all, this book is meant, 1., for revolutionary/evolutionary movements, those movements on the intellectual/material fringes, who might belong to the status quo or not, but who think and feel there is something inherently wrong with neoliberal, bourgeois-state-capitalism, but, cannot clearly articulate the exploitation and impoverishment generated by bourgeois-capitalism. That is, the capitalist micro-fascism present in the capitalist networks and capitalist languages, which dominate society. 2., This book offers a comprehensive analysis and a critical lens by which to understand the mechanics of post-industrial, post-modern, bourgeois-state-capitalism. 3., This book illustrates anti-capitalist techniques, strategies, and tactics, by which to empower enlightened citizens and socio-economic movements to oppose the logic of capitalism, that is, capitalist control and capitalist indoctrination. 4. This book is also meant as a new reading on the mechanics of capitalism, namely, as an alternative to Marxism. And 5., this book establishes the logic of structural-anarchism as a primary revolutionary mechanism, capable of leading to a more logical democratic form of socio-economic organization, while, living within the parameters of bourgeois-state-capitalism.

The logic of structural-anarchism is not bent on armed-revolution, per se. Instead, the logic of structural-anarchism is about promoting revolutionary forms of thinking and doing things, i.e., poly-rationality, in order to snap the elastic-band of capitalism, tethering the workforce/population to the capitalist mode of production, that is, capitalist forces and capitalist relations. The strength of the logic of structural-anarchism is its notion that radical social change is something which begins very small in the micro-recesses of everyday life, namely, microscopic revolutions, within the private and public spheres of everyday life, seemingly innocuous, innocent, and banal, yet, filled with anarchist revolutionary fervor. Namely, micro-revolutions of everyday life, pointing the way to a massive, overwhelming anarchist revolution, where nothing is left unchanged and where capitalism is finally deleted. Where, financial divisions between people are drastically reduced. Where, the pangs of capitalist nihilism are extinguished, along with debt-slavery, wage-slavery and, in general, economic slavery. Where, finally, a guaranteed set of socio-economic rights can buttress civic human rights, namely, the guaranteed right to a living income, regardless of labor-market fluctuations. And, the guaranteed right to open-participatory-democracy, that is, the right to participate, more effectively, in politics and the governance of one's own life.

The premise of this book is that: 1. Capitalism is a totalitarian logic, i.e., a totalitarian language. 2. Capitalism is a totalitarian logical apparatus, which houses an insatiable drive for ownership/knowledge, within itself. 3. This insatiable drive for ownership/knowledge is the will to power, innate in nature and the human species. 4. Capitalism can never be totally done away with, it can only be marginalized, minimized and decentralized, out of existence. Because, it is an outgrowth of the insatiable drive for ownership/knowledge, which cannot but produce surplus, that is, multi-varied surplus values of all types and kinds. 5. The only revolutionary logic capable of overthrowing the logic of capitalism, is the logic of structural-anarchism, namely, poly-rationality. The logic of structural-anarchism is the sole revolutionary logic because the logic of structural-anarchism is the limit of liberty, autonomy, collectivism, and pragmatic egalitarianism. Beyond the logic of structural-anarchism is total chaos, i.e., nothingness and barbarism. As a result, the logic of structural-anarchism is the next phase, the next stage of political-economic evolution and revolution, devoid of bourgeois-capitalism. The logic of structural-anarchism is the pragmatic poly-rationale of miniature insurrections, within the micro-recesses of everyday life, designed to decentralize, horizontalize, and democratize, decision-making-authority and private property, in service of all by all, in relative equal measure.

The adversary of the logic of structural-anarchism is capitalist micro-fascism. Micro-fascism is those discourses, languages, networks, and entities, who embody the tyranny of the capitalist logic, and exercise this despotic logic, without thought, compassion and notion of consequence. Unlike the Marxist notion of class, micro-fascism is a fanaticism, which stems from all cultural sectors, social sectors and economic sectors, it is a deep despotic impulse and fervor for bourgeois-capitalist rule. The sole purpose of micro-fascism is to asphyxiate all counter-logics to capitalism in order to prevent the advancement of everything and anything, which is different, collectivist and alternative to the bourgeois-capitalist status quo. Micro-fascism is micro-dictatorships, dotting the city-landscapes, exercising totalitarian rule, within limited miniaturized autocracies. Whether, it is a household, a small business, a corporation, a court-room, or a university department, etc., micro-fascism is tyranny, a one-way monologue, droning on and on at the micro-levels of everyday life, drilling fear, repression, and perpetual indoctrination, if there is divergence from the logic of capitalism and the bourgeois-capitalist status quo, namely, bourgeois-mediocrity.

In contrast, micro-revolution is the structural-anarchist term for all those moments of everyday life, where micro-tyranny/micro-fascism is usurped; where micro-dictatorships are defied, disobeyed, subverted, and overthrown. Micro-revolutions are all those moments, when and where, an individual is empowered with a sense of self-determination, collectivism and autonomy, which temporarily runs counter and contrary to the bourgeois-capitalist status quo. The micro-revolution of everyday life is the road to the anarchist revolution and the structural-anarchism-complex, it is the micro-strategies and micro-tactics, consciously or unconsciously, used everywhere to defy and usurper, the many micro-tyrannies manufactured by bourgeois-capitalism, both conceptually and materially. Micro-revolution is underground barter, free goods and guaranteed equality. Micro-revolution is absenteeism, graffiti, pop-up galleries, occupy movements, referendums, clandestine assemblies, property-damage etc., hence, this manifesto is well-designed to give form, structure, and a theoretical basis, for these conscious, or unconscious, seemingly unrelated acts and cries of liberty, autonomy, collectivism and self-determination, i.e., existential cries for pragmatic egalitarianism and greater pluralism.

If micro-fascism is the ruling ideas, ruling art, and ruling social groups of our epoch, then, micro-revolutionism is the revolutionary/evolutionary spirit, art, acts, and minds of our epoch, which strive for a more equal, transparent, democratic, collectivist, ideational comprehensive framework based on a greater egalitarian organization of the workforce/population. The anarchist-praxiacrat is the cognizant anti-thesis to the micro-fascist technocrat. Namely, those technocratic-cogs, which inhabit the vast, interrelated, micro-fascist networks of the military-industrial-complex. The anarchist-praxiacrat establishes greater liberality, autonomy, collectivism, poly-rationality, and self-determination, wherever he or she contextualizes, or usurps, the logic of capitalism, wherever, he or she establishes greater egalitarian organization, beyond the logic of capitalism and its fascist administrative-apparatuses.

Finally, this book is a critique towards a political-economy of contemporary arts. This book gives reasons why contemporary art has devolved into something bland, mediocre, and lame, i.e., into a tool of bourgeois-capitalism and its totalitarian pursuit of capitalist profit. This book explains how and why contemporary art has eroded the way it has in recent years and has fallen under the thumb of the ruling, micro-fascist, oligarchical networks, for its continued survival and sustenance, while, there is more art to be found throughout society than ever before in history. Everywhere, we find contemporary art, contemporary art professionals, and newly minted art institutions, burgeoning, and yet, nowhere is revolutionary art visible, understandable, and identifiable, having itself been submerged and crushed beneath the vast expanse of meaningless, nonsensical, artistic kitsch, present at all levels of bourgeois-capitalist art education, all levels of the capitalist marketplace, and all levels of the bourgeois-capitalist art world. Today, contemporary art, saturated everywhere, represents and reflects, the average tastes, average wants, average aspirations, and the average meaningless nonsense of average bourgeois herd-mediocrity, that is, the wannabe bourgeoisie. And this is no accident. It is an artificial construct of the socio-economic processes of bourgeois-capitalism, designed solely to, 1., subsume and marginalize revolutionary art, due to its revolutionary capabilities, that is, so as to render these revolutionary capabilities ineffective. 2., This is designed to control the arts, i.e., to control what is produced and ideationally disseminated. And 3., this is designed to congeal, ideologically, a standard tightly-knit mass of the workforce/population geared towards the accumulation and extraction of surplus value, i.e., capital. Art, subsumed in service of bourgeois-state-capitalism, no longer strives for revolution, creativity and innovation. To the contrary, it is now anti-revolution, anti-creative, anti-innovative, anti-art etc., its goal is now averageness, lameness, dullness, banality, mediocrity, triviality, standardization, and indoctrination. It is engendered this way so that art can facilitate its capitalist-circulation as a commodity, in and across the military-industrial-complex, and so that, it can embody the exact capitalist imperatives and micro-fascism, centralized in the logic of capitalism.

In sum, we shall not wake-up one day miraculously to the structural-anarchism-complex, since, revolutions require hard-work and sound commitment; but, the logic of structural-anarchism is, on all factual accounts, correct and the inevitable next step. As a result, the logic of structural-anarchism forever pulls the workforce/population towards its revolutionary logic, compelling it to revolt, riot and strike. In fact, the value of this revolutionary logic, poly-rationality, is that it can never be underestimated, ignored, and fully marginalized, for its inherent poly-rationality forever returns to the revolutionary vanguard. The reason is the logic of structural-anarchism and the structural-anarchism-complex correspond better with the needs of the workforce/population and nature. And, with every miniature insurrection, this fact is increasingly becoming self-evident. The fact is the logic of structural-anarchism is intrinsic within the insatiable drive for ownership/knowledge, along with the logic of capitalism. However, contrary to capitalism, the logic of structural-anarchism is the equalization-algorithm, encrypted in logical-rationality, itself, capitalism is merely an offshoot of this equalization-algorithm. As a result, the poly-rationality of structural-anarchism veraciously proceeds towards contextual supremacy, ad nauseam, thus, the gravitational-power of the logic of structural-anarchism over and above the logic of capitalism. In short, capitalism has an expiration date. And, the date is well passed. Consequently, the logic of capitalism is finished. And, it is only a matter of time.

MLB/2016

"Petrified social conditions must be forced to dance
by singing their own melody to them. . .History is thorough, and it
goes through many stages when it conducts... an archaic
[socio-economic] formation to its grave."

(Karl Marx, *Critique of Hegel's Philosophy of Right*.)

"*Society finds its highest perfection in the union of order with anarchy.*"

(Pierre Joseph Proudhon, *What is Property*?)

Section One:
(Introduction)

<u>The Central-Operating-Code And The Commodity</u>:

(Capitalism Is An Artificial Context For An Unrelenting Unitary And
Divisionary Force Inherent In Nature And Human Existence)

1.a) Matter is in essence and substance, collective-capital.

1.b) It belongs to all and no-one. Matter, in fact, is collective property and it has always been that way. It is of no concern, whether, this property is conceptual, intellectual and/or material. There is no legitimate reason, or rational argument, which can legitimate and justify the notion of private property, since, private property kills intellectual and material development, individual or collective. Private property does this by blocking accessibility for the vast majority to the means of life. Consequently, private property denies life, itself, human and nature. It negates all capacities to live, survive, and evolve, stifling existence in its tracks. Ultimately, private property impedes progress. It impedes progress by producing ever-increasing economic-financial inequality. As a result, there can never be true equality in the world, adhering to the logic of capitalism, as true equality and progress require, first and foremost, economic-financial equality and free accessibility to resources for all, without the harmful roadblocks of private property. Private property is fundamentally retrogressive and a disease.

1.c) Matter is quintessentially collective-capital because matter is the collective medium by which an insatiable drive for ownership/knowledge, plural/singular in nature, and housed in the sum of existence, transforms its intrinsic abstractions into concrete material utilities and surpluses; so it can transcend its own existential limitations. Consequently, matter is always raw collective-capital, unformed collective-capital, unlimited, collective value and surplus value in its natural state, needing only a certain level of physical and mental activity in order to achieve its raison d'être, specific types of collective-capital, which initially, belong to all and no-one. Therefore, everything in the universe, including the human species, can be capitalized upon and turned into some sort of capital, i.e., value and/or surplus value. All that is required is a certain level of activity in order for this activity to surpass the level of basic necessities, i.e., its own basic maintenance requirements, and in essence, transform matter into specific types of collective-capital, i.e., various types of collective values and surplus values, which initially belong to all and no-one, and furthermore beget, additional types of collective values and surplus values, ad infinitum.

1.d) It is the fanaticism of capitalism, i.e., the instrumental rationality of capitalism, which drastically reduces, dismembers, and rigs, collective-capital into a set of highly-constricted capitalist-regimes, i.e., regimes of private property, individualism, financial profiteering and money etc. The purpose is to deny, marginalize, and eradicate, all forms of collectivism in favor of radical capitalist hierarchy, both among people and across socio-economic existence, without exception. Capitalism destroys collectivism, i.e., collective-capital. It destroys the collectivism inherent in matter and the collectivism inherent in humans, that is, the collectivism expressed in the human species' inherent capacity to share, in relative equal measure. And, it replaces this collectivism with a radical individualism and a molecular capitalist fascism, which, like a virus, begins to spread and infect everything, converting everything into private property.

1.e) In actuality, however, matter is infinite, variable, and belongs to all and no-one; it is collective-capital, namely, a type of capital which everyone has legitimate claims upon. Moreover, collective-capital is much more complex and multi-varied than its current, narrow-minded, capitalist individualistic conception. In fact, the insatiable drive for ownership/knowledge, continuously produces utilities and extras of all sorts and types, beyond its own basic maintenance requirements. It is only the political-economic framework of capitalism, i.e., the instrumental rationality of capitalism, which reduces the multiplicity of collectivist values and surplus values to the narrow confines of financial quantifiable capital, i.e., monetary gain and private property. The political-economic framework of capitalism, expressing the madness of instrumental rationality run-amuck, hunts, traps, and eradicates, certain capitals in favor of other capitals, specifically, it cherishes only those forces, human or otherwise, which maximize and augment financial quantifiable capital, namely, money, profit and private property.

1.f) Notwithstanding, ultimately, matter is in(corporeal) as is collective-capital, meaning matter and collective-capital are first and foremost conceptual. Capital is first and foremost a conceptual construct of the mind and the same applies for matter. What is matter? Matter is whatever the mind, i.e., the insatiable drive for ownership/knowledge, deems is matter. What is collective-capital? Collective-capital is whatever the mind, i.e., the insatiable drive for ownership/knowledge, deems is a utility, sustaining its basic maintenance requirements, and/or deems is a surplus, extending beyond its basic maintenance requirements. Collective-capital can be a quantifiable utility such as food, water, shelter etc. It can be an unquantifiable utility such as love, communication, courage, friendship, education etc., all of which, replenish basic maintenance requirements. As well, collective-capital can be a quantifiable surplus such as a surplus of money, a surplus of food, a surplus of water, a surplus of collective-property etc., and it can be an unquantifiable surplus such as a cultural surplus, i.e., a book or film etc., or an emotional surplus, i.e., a surplus of empathy, or a knowledge surplus and/or a creative surplus etc. These are the characteristics of collective-capital. And matter supplies both the collective-capital of basic maintenance requirements and the extras for collective surplus, due to the fact that matter is inherently collective-capital. It is only the ideational comprehensive framework of capitalism, which places undue emphasis on financial quantifiable capital, namely, money, profit, and private property, while, denying the inherent existence, influence, and utility of collective-capital, i.e., collectivist values and surplus values, both quantifiable and unquantifiable etc.

1.g) Matter is use(full), meaning its uses are in essence unlimited, ergo, collective-capital has unlimited use(fullness), i.e., utilities and surpluses of all kinds, which permit mental and physical activity to have all kinds of uses and surpluses that can be utilized in all kinds of collective ways and forms, both quantifiable and unquantifiable, mental and physical. This unlimited usefullness inherent in matter can better humanity; but the logic of capitalism denies this fact in the name of capitalist profit and private property.

1.h) Matter and capital come to fruition via thought and action. If there is no thought and action then there is no matter or capital, thought and action, together, is the machine that manifests matter and capital as concepts and through concepts, i.e., as material and immaterial conceptualizations. This conceptualization process is in fact a capitalization process, i.e., the initial phase of utility and surplus. It is the unity of thought and action, as immaterial and material process, acquiring quantifiable and unquantifiable value, utility and surplus, through an inherent, insatiable compulsion and dialectical process, for ever-refined conceptualizations, which endlessly perfects ownership and knowledge, ad infinitum, both individualist and collectivist. Indeed, as matter presents itself as matter, i.e., as concept in the mind, so does capital present itself as capital, i.e., as concept in the mind, i.e., as a means of utility and surplus, beyond the initial characteristics of basic unrefined matter and collective-capital. Subsequently, collective-capital is both matter itself in its natural state and a refined product of matter, i.e., something inherent in matter that only comes to fruition via mental and physical activity. Collective-capital is both quantifiable and/or unquantifiable. Collective-capital is both conceptual-value and/or material-value, arrived at through mental and physical activity, possessing either the qualities of utility, that is, quantifiable and unquantifiable basic maintenance requirements, and/or the qualities of surplus, i.e., that which is over and above quantifiable and unquantifiable basic maintenance requirements. Matter and capital are inherently collective in nature, their essence and substance is collectivism, factually, belonging to all and no-one. Therefore, any attempt to exclusively possess what, in fact, belongs to all and no-one, including what specifically develops out of this collectivism, is sub-human and an act against nature. That is, it is a form of barbarism, thievery, and a self-induced, idealistic madness sodden in fanaticism and fascism, which can never be logically and legitimately validated in any reasonable manner. As a result, all forms of capitalist private property, capitalist profit-making, and capitalist radical individualism etc., which are fundamentally founded on the collectivism of collective-capital, i.e., the collective nature of matter, factually belonging to all and non-one, are fundamental errors in reason and in judgment. Making, capitalism but a series of dominance hierarchies constructed on ungrounded falsehoods, designed only to negate and deny collectivism through the enslavement, impoverishment, and degradation of the human species and nature. The logic of bourgeois-capitalism is despotic and narrow-minded.

1.i) Capitalism is about amassing and monopolizing power. It is an ideational comprehensive framework designed to accumulate power and centralize power into small epicenters. Namely, bourgeois-capitalism is a logical, unfounded structure of concepts and material relations, initially derived from matter via mental and physical activity upon matter, which has now attained a certain level of contextual supremacy in defining, describing, categorizing, and manifesting, a totalitarian notion of reality. Capitalism is a political-economic, comprehensive framework, which manifests a meaningful comprehensive interpretation, model, and paradigm of existence, which encompasses, all socio-economic phenomena. Despite being only a particular ideational comprehensive framework, capitalism strives to be totalitarian and all-encompassing, by eradicating the inherent nature of matter and collective-capital, i.e., collectivism. A particular, inherent, fanatic feature of the ideational comprehensive framework of capitalism is that it denies, and/or attempts to deny, or destroy, all other ideational comprehensive frameworks, all meaningful comprehensive interpretations, models, paradigms of existence, and socio-economic phenomena, other than its own. Due to the fact, different ideational comprehensive frameworks produce different definitions and parameters of reality. In this regard, existence and reality mean different things and are different things, depending on the ideational comprehensive framework. Consequently, hardwired into the ideational comprehensive framework of capitalism is a radical antipathy for collectivism and all other ideational comprehensive frameworks, which it sees as obstacles to its ruling contextual supremacy of existence and reality, including anything which might thwart its ever-expanding totalitarian domination.

1.j) Even so, despite the mental and physical tendencies of despotic capitalism, there is an automatic, equalization-algorithm lodged within the human species, collective-capital and the unfolding of history. This equalization-algorithm is poly-rationality. And the march of poly-rationality, the equalization-algorithm, invariably and veraciously proceeds out of capitalism back towards the supremacy of global collectivism, that is, collective-equalization and collective-capital. Whereupon, the insatiable drive for ownership/knowledge of the workforce/population will, once again, share in and benefit from collective knowledge utilities and surpluses, and collective ownership utilities and surpluses, in relative equal measure, together, on a global scale. Indeed, capitalism is a dead-end, a detour on the way to anarcho-collectivism. Of course, capitalism denies this fact. As a result, bourgeois-capitalism fights against this fact with every fiber of its being, hence, the ways it impedes the unfolding of history towards anarcho-communism, and unwittingly strangles itself into total obsolescence.

-[2]-

2.a) The foundation of capitalism is intellectual/physical activity. However, capitalism is only a man-made shell, a logical apparatus, housing an intrinsic code found in all existing entities, i.e., the will to power, or the instinctual/social drive for ownership and knowledge, namely, creative-power. The logic of capitalism, which is a product of intellectual/physical activity, is the direct application and administration of this instinctual/social drive for ownership/knowledge, within a certain socio-economic, comprehensive framework. The logic of capitalism is the logical structure that mentally and physically contextualizes the insatiable drive for ownership/knowledge, the workforce/population and nature, within a set of socio-economic parameters and logical processes, which deny collectivism and pragmatic egalitarianism. These socio-economic parameters and logical processes are fundamentally man-made and arbitrary, and comprise all the physical and conceptual properties of neoliberal, bourgeois-state-capitalism.

-[3]-

3.a) Initially, capitalism developed through mental and physical activity, i.e., the insatiable drive for ownership/knowledge, in a collective effort to satisfy the basic maintenance requirements for a vast collection of insatiable drives for ownership/knowledge structured in a collective egalitarian community. Through these collective mental and physical activities, capitalism developed into a definitive, ideational comprehensive framework, which came to dominate and regiment the insatiable drives for ownership/knowledge, i.e., the workforce/population and nature structured in these collectivist communities. On the backs of the workforce/population, including nature, a bourgeois-capitalist aristocracy developed, by fanatically promoting and disseminating the logic of capitalism. Today, the ideational comprehensive framework of capitalism dominates and regiments the insatiable drive for ownership/knowledge, i.e., the workforce/population, to such a radical extent that it is now the logical form of factual reality, itself. Once riveted in the mental and the physical activities of the workforce/population, including its brain, capitalism erases and deletes any sense of collectivism and any alternative, ideational comprehensive frameworks from memory and the face of the earth, other than its own. And, in their stead, capitalism installs its own despotic logic for the accumulation and extraction of surplus value, by any means necessary, at the lowest financial cost, as soon as possible. That is, it installs its own reductive capitalist logic, i.e., the capital/labor relation, which is programmed towards the expansion and centralization of private property, profit and capitalist wealth.

3.b) Through the inherent, existential refining process of the insatiable drive for ownership/knowledge, i.e., mental and physical activity, the workforce/population, unable to do anything else, and as well, unable to rid itself of the ideational comprehensive framework of capitalism, welded to its brain, simultaneously refines and develops capitalism against its will, in addition to its own specific virtuosity and creative-power. This is how the ever-refining process of intellectual and material activity, defined as the will to power, and predominantly localized in the workforce/population, continually produces and ameliorates the ideational comprehensive framework of capitalism, against its will. This is how the insatiable drive for ownership/knowledge of the workforce/population, perpetually develops and refines capitalist technology and the parameters for the accumulation and extraction of financial quantifiable capital, i.e., private property and capitalist profit. And, as well, through the artificially-constructed, false-consciousness of the ideational comprehensive framework of capitalism, the workforce/population continually relinquishes its surpluses, its creative-power, its ownership/knowledge, its decision-making-authority, its freedom, and its sense of egalitarian collectivism, against its will to the best representative-agents of capitalism, namely, the state-finance-corporate-aristocracy.

-[4]-

4.a) The insatiable drive for ownership/knowledge is plural, singular, and intrinsic within existence. It is hardwired in our genes and life, itself. It is the will to power or will to possess and know, both individually and collectively, conceptually and materially etc. It is creative-power, simple and pure. This will to power is something akin to a central-operating-code, functioning within humans and existence as a result of the power-struggle for survival, wherefore, what is most powerful, adaptable, creative, collectivist, and knowledgeable, is what is most apt to survive and thrive. The ideational comprehensive framework of capitalism is a linguistic construct of this will to power, structured, both materially and conceptually, into a totalitarian, political-economic framework, designed exclusively to extract and accumulate financial quantifiable capital, that is, capitalist profit, wealth and private property, while, eradicating all oppositional forms of collectivism, freedom and socio-economic organization.

4.b) The insatiable drive for ownership/knowledge is an intrinsic code at the center of socio-economic existence, human beings, and broadly speaking, nature, which is unfolding, towards pure collective refinement and collective totality. This central-operating-code is a code incessantly refining itself, ad infinitum. The central-operating-code, i.e., the will to power, cannot do anything else other than construct, demolish and reconstruct, both itself and its surrounding intellectual and material environment, since, it is the unstoppable force of ownership and knowledge. That is, an insatiable drive for ownership/knowledge, which has no goal other than constant amelioration and the accumulation of power, both individual and collective. The logic of capitalism is its current man-made shell. The logic of capitalism is currently the socio-economic casing of the will to power.

4.c) As a result, bourgeois-state-capitalism is simply the latest stage and framework of socio-economic development, manufactured by the will to power, which is currently and temporarily at the moment contextualizing this will to power, this central-operating-code, which began to function and operate with the start of world history.

4.d) Bourgeois-state-capitalism is the current logical context of this dynamic central-operating-code, which is embedded in existence, nature, and human beings, which is, as well, inherently programmed to perpetually construct, demolish and reconstruct, both itself and its capitalist gridiron shell now holding it, directing it and controlling it.

4.e) What stimulates capitalist profit-growth and capitalist refinement is contextualization, rationalization, and the suppression of the will to power, according to the logical necessities of capitalism, both mental and physical etc.

4.f) The will to power is always in operation, always functioning, both at the micro and macro levels of socio-economic existence in the form of logics and ideologies. And capitalism merely suppresses these wills to power according to a specific capitalist form of organization so as to reap the specific secretions of these wills to power, namely, financial quantifiable capital, i.e., surplus value, private property and capitalist profit.

4.g) The point is to maneuver the will to power, that is, the insatiable drive for ownership/knowledge in a manner by which it conforms to the dictates of the logic of capitalism. And, capitalism accomplishes this, by maneuvering the will to power, both softly and forcefully, into artificially-constructed, highly-competitive environments, which favor survival of the fittest, zero-sum outcomes. These artificial capitalist environments, which exist everywhere, in and across bourgeois-state-capitalism, are designed to intensify and magnify the coercive laws of competition in order to maximize the accumulation and extraction of capitalist surplus value, namely, capitalist profit, out of the will to power. Through the intensification of the coercive laws of competition, the will to power, that is, the insatiable drive for ownership/knowledge, is coerced both softly and forcefully to secrete a specific type of capitalist value, free of charge, which is ultimately transformed into capitalist profit, by bourgeois-capitalists, i.e., the agents of the logic of capitalism. In fact, as the artificial man-made shell of the will to power, the logic of capitalism is a mode of being, perceiving, interpreting and acting, imposed upon humans and nature, mentally and physically, softly and forcefully, solely, for venal capitalist ends.

4.h) All in all, the will to power is the basis and the starting point of Structural-Anarcho-Political-Economics. Since, the will to power, the insatiable drive for ownership/knowledge, is the fount of value and surplus value. It cannot do anything else than manufacture an incessant plethora of values and surplus values, both quantifiable and unquantifiable etc. Finally, the will to power is most visible and at work in the workforce/population and nature. Hence, the reason, the logic of capitalism incessantly seeks to subjugate and enslave, the workforce/population and nature, according to capitalist dictates and, most importantly, according to the profit-imperative at the center of bourgeois-state-capitalism.

-[5]-

5.a) The insatiable drive for ownership/knowledge, the central-operating-code, can be seen and understood, both simultaneously and ubiquitously, as a unified totality and/or a divided set of partialities. It is simultaneously and ubiquitously pliable and rigid, conceptual and material etc., it is constantly working its magic, secreting values of all types and kinds beyond the limited, constraining, parameters of bourgeois-state-capitalism. The insatiable drive for ownership/knowledge is inherently revolutionary, evolutionary and collectivist. It is the personification of creative-power.

-[6]-

6.a) The insatiable drive for ownership/knowledge, i.e., the code, in its partialities functions at different magnitudes and on different trajectories. Moreover, these differences influence the possibility of connection and synergy between the different parts of the insatiable drive for ownership/knowledge, namely, the workforce/population.

6.b) It is the logic of capitalism, i.e., the ideational comprehensive framework of capitalism, which determines, administrates, and manages, where, how, when, why, and which of the drive's partialities shall connect and/or synergize. Most of the time, synergy and connection is based on the accumulation and extraction of financial quantifiable capital, i.e., the logical necessities of the logic of capitalism. As a result, the logic of capitalism manufactures a specific type of social relation founded on exploitation, i.e., the capital/labor relation. The logic of capitalism manufactures this type of social relation, ad nauseam, according to its fundamental, totalitarian logic. It does this for the maximization of capitalist profit, by any means necessary, at the lowest financial cost, as soon as possible. It does this for the expansion and centralization of private property and financial quantifiable capital, placing private property, money, and profits, increasingly into the hands of a select few, namely, the state-finance-corporate-aristocracy.

-[7]-

7.a) The insatiable drive for ownership/knowledge is qualitative and quantitative, its individual parts possess varying degrees of qualitative and quantitative material and immaterial characteristics, whose value and worth are a matter of the specific ideational comprehensive framework. For the ideational comprehensive framework of capitalism, worth and value are, solely, based on the logical necessities of the logic of capitalism and capitalist profit.

7.b) Humans and their insatiable drives for ownership/knowledge, to varying degrees, once hardwired into the ideational comprehensive framework of capitalism, have a limited effect on the capitalist system, in general. However, the logic of capitalism tends to subdue humans and their insatiable drives for ownership/knowledge in a confusing web of false-consciousness, a litany of bureaucratic nonsense, irrelevant empty-spectacles, pointless tasks, and distractions, which are ultimately meaningless, soul-crushing, highly alienating, and highly nihilistic. The point is to kill collectivism, the initial state, concept and sentiment of human relationships derived from matter and collective-capital. That is, the sense of communally shared capital, initially generated in childhood.

7.c) Moreover, any ideational comprehensive framework, whatever it may be, is a structural form of understanding and comprehension. An ideational comprehensive framework is a logical apparatus designed to control, administrate and direct creative-power, that is, the insatiable drive for ownership/knowledge, both individually and collectively, mentally and physically, so that it can understand and comprehend reality, phenomena, and socio-economic existence, according to a particular point of view and/or perspective, excluding all other points of view and/or perspectives.

7.d) The will to power is a machine, in essence, i.e., a serial of logic, mental and physical, eternally developing itself and its creative-power, both individually and collectively. It is always applying its pressures and forces on the political-economic framework, which is contextualizing and managing its logical necessities for growth and development. At the moment, capitalism is subject to the pressures of the will to power. And capitalism is currently controlling and managing the growth and development of the will to power. There is a dialectics of force and power at work between capitalism and the will to power, designed to maximize capitalist profit and capitalist private property, since, capitalism now rules.

-[8]-

8.a) What stimulates growth in the insatiable drive for ownership/knowledge, i.e., the workforce/population, is the possibility for increases in intellectual and material activity, brought about by new material, or matter, and new areas of inquiry, knowledge, and acquisition, either collective or individual. Freedom and free access to new areas, new materials, new technologies, and new forms of socio-economic existence, stimulate growth in the insatiable drive for ownership/knowledge. Capitalism must satisfy this need in the workforce/population, if it wishes to maintain its contextual supremacy. Its socio-economic supremacy depends on it.

-[9]-

9.a) The accretion of collective-capital, i.e., all types of capital, cultural capital, financial capital, knowledge capital, relationship capital etc., is the fundamental purpose of the insatiable drive for ownership/knowledge. The insatiable drive for ownership/knowledge cannot help but manufacture all sorts of values and surplus values, beyond the narrow confines of capitalism. It is the logic of capitalism, which values only financial/economic capital and private property over all other forms of collective-capital.

9.b) The insatiable drive for ownership/knowledge is inherently multi-dimensional and plural, in essence. And, it is only the logic of capitalism, which incessantly attempts to streamline the will to power into a one-dimensional, singular capitalist process, denying and negating, its natural plurality and capacity for variation in favor of some artificial, repetitive, invariable capitalist process, i.e., a singular capitalist way of thinking and doing things. Capitalism impedes the natural plurality and collectivism inherent in the will to power, including all new collectivist developments and advancements that conflict with the narrow confines established by the logic of capitalism. As, nothing must stand in the way of the satanic drive for ever-more capitalist profit, private property and power, namely, the centralization of money and power.

-[10]-

10.a) The central-operating-code, i.e., the insatiable drive for ownership/knowledge, is embedded and impeded in all aspects of the capitalist system. And, as long as the political-economic framework of capitalism, i.e., the ideational comprehensive framework of capitalism, controls and dominates the insatiable drive for ownership/knowledge of the workforce/population, the workforce/population will never be free. Meaning, capitalism will remain the framework and context of the workforce/population and nature, indefinitely.

10.b) Of course, the will to power cannot be eradicated and controlled, indefinitely. If somehow stifled, the will to power can always recommence its inherent process towards collectivism, freedom, and socio-economic pluralism, due to the fact that collectivism, freedom, and pluralism is its inherent destination and goal. The will to power is based on the premise that no matter how much, or to any zero-degree, collectivism, freedom, and pluralism is stifled or destroyed, there will always be a drive and a need for collectivism, freedom, and pluralism. And, this drive and need for collectivism, freedom, and socio-economic pluralism will always re-ignite and strive towards collectivist totality, ad nauseam. More importantly, the will to power can learn its lesson, it can adapt, evolve and refine, itself, ad infinitum, as its essence is collective ownership and the acquisition of knowledge, both individual and collective. The will to power is communist and anarchist. The will to power is anarcho-communist in the sense that its creative-power is maximized via collective ownership, collective sharing, and collective knowledge, which increases its freedom, its power, and its communal relationships, in and across everyday life, ultimately, boosting its happiness, its fulfillment and its creative-power to the Nth degree. In fact, collective-sharing maximizes human advancement.

-[11]-

11.a) In contrast, capitalism is about the appropriation and contextualization of the insatiable drive for ownership/knowledge. That is, the technocratic management of the intellectual and material activities that the workforce/population performs. The point is to capitalize on the workforce/population and nature so as to enhance the capitalist logic and, in general, the political-economic framework of capitalism. The point is the expansion of the logic of capitalism. The point for capitalism is to emphasize the production and reproduction of capitalist private property and capitalist profit, by any means necessary, at the lowest financial cost, as soon as possible. And, the logic of capitalism accomplishes this, foremost, through hard and soft despotism and by satisfying the minimum maintenance requirements of the workforce/population through such things as a minimum level of freedom and egalitarian collectivism.

11.b) Capitalism gives the workforce/population minimum sustenance, purpose, meaning, collectivism, and freedom, because these things maximize profit, i.e., the accumulation and extraction of surplus value. And, the workforce/population acquires minimum sustenance, purpose, meaning, collectivism, and freedom, from capitalism, because it permits itself to be contextualized and dominated by capitalism. It submits to the given dictates of capitalism. And, as long as capitalism dominates the workforce/population, and does this, with the greatest logical efficiency, while, providing the workforce/population with the minimum level of sustenance, purpose, collectivism, and freedom, which it desperately needs, the logic of capitalism remains the artificial context of the workforce/population and nature. That is, capitalism remains the central organizing principle of society, including, all the social relations within this capitalist socio-economic formation.

-[12]-

12.a) Firstly, capitalism satisfies its own logical necessities. And then, secondly, it satisfies the logical necessities of the workforce/population, via the production, consumption and distribution of commodities, or products. That is, via a vast plethora of mental and physical commodities and products, which are produced, consumed and distributed, through the networks of capitalism, so as to satisfy: 1. the needs of the logic of capitalism, and 2., the needs of the workforce/population. The necessities of the logic of capitalism always come before the necessities of the workforce/population and nature. Meaning, the capitalist profit-imperative hardwired in the socio-economic processes of capitalism controls the creative-power of the workforce/population, commanding the workforce/population evermore to produce, consume and distribute these very same commodities and products, out of a survival necessity. This is a cyclical, intensifying, and expansionary process. It is the means by which capitalism accumulates and extracts financial quantifiable capital from the workforce/population and nature, and increasingly, develops its totalitarian logic into new areas of everyday life, deeper into the workforce/population and nature, via ever-expanding capitalist private property.

12.b) A commodity is a construct of intellectual activity and material activity, i.e., an extraction and accumulation of creative-power from the insatiable drive for ownership/knowledge, structured into a particular mental and physical format, so as to satisfy the logical necessities of the workforce/population and the ideational comprehensive framework of capitalism. That is, capitalism's unquenchable thirst for financial quantifiable capital, namely, capitalist profit. Commodities are ideological.

12.c) The format of a commodity, or product, is contingent on the political-economic framework of a society. Different political-economic frameworks will instruct the insatiable drives for ownership/knowledge of the workforce/population to construct commodities or products, differently, and along different ideational comprehensive lines, namely, according to varying formats, depending on the economic framework. For example, a commodity, within the political-economic framework of capitalism, is a composite of two characteristics, utility and surplus. First, a commodity is fundamentally a composite utility, i.e., it embodies a use or uses, meaning it is a useful object and/or concept, in some shape or form, fit for satisfying some type of basic maintenance requirement. It is important to note here that all social, political-economic frameworks must manufacture useful objects and concepts, first and foremost, in order to satisfy the basic maintenance requirements of humans, including their insatiable drives for ownership/knowledge, if these frameworks wish to maintain their socio-economic and contextual supremacy. This is imperative. Second, within the political-economic framework of capitalism, built on top of the basic commodity characteristic of utility, is the second commodity characteristic of surplus. Thus, a capitalist commodity is a composite utility and surplus, including the capitalist ideology.

12.d) Under capitalism, a commodity is a composite of surplus in the sense that it is a tradeable currency, meaning, it is an object and/or concept which has worth beyond utility as a thing that can be exchanged, either quantitatively through social commerce, and/or non-quantitatively via free forms of exchange such as a conversation or peer-sharing. The logic of capitalism values only what is quantifiable, i.e., utilities and surpluses, which are finite, constant, and scientifically quantifiable. Everything else is nonsense, nonexistent, and worthless, even if it contributes to the supremacy of the logic of capitalism. It is important to note here that financial quantifiable capital is the main objective of the logic of capitalism; it is its raison d'être. And financial quantifiable capital is produced and realized when the logic of capitalism intensifies and augments mental and physical activity beyond mere basic maintenance requirements, that is, utility, and pushes production, consumption, and distribution of commodities, into excessive/obscene surplus. This surplus is a tradeable currency, whose worth is ultimately established in conceptual-perception and through conceptual-perception, via such mechanisms as supply and demand for the currency/commodity, and/or on the amount of mental and physical creative-power it costs to manufacture, including arbitrary price-forms based on pure fancy. Within the political-economic framework of capitalism, the objective is always to maximize a commodity's tradeable currency, i.e., its quantifiable surplus, while minimizing its utility. A different society, based on a different ideational comprehensive framework, could reverse this polarity, focusing on the maximization of utility over ex-changeability, that is, surplus, as well as, economic financial equality.

12.e) For capitalism, a commodity is a receptacle of surplus value, i.e., a tradeable currency or financial quantifiable capital, it is the promise of a surplus of value, on top of its utility and its value-cost to produce, when there is a completion of a future trade between two values of different, yet, agreed upon value-measurements and utility. This exchange process, which realizes surplus value and augments surplus value, i.e., profit, is the nexus of the logic of capitalism. It is this business process, linked with the exploitative, controlling relationship between capitalism and humans, embedded within the larger more complex socio-economic processes of production, consumption and distribution, by which capitalism, cunningly and shrewdly exploits humans, and their insatiable drives, in its favor, appropriating what does not belong to it, namely, collectively manufactured surplus value. As the logic of capitalism attempts to satisfy the workforce/population, it in fact primarily satisfies its own mercenary objectives through the totalitarian medium of mental and physical capitalist activity, which it conveniently regiments and constructs according to its own logical necessities and parameters. Those capitalist entities, whose insatiable drives for ownership/knowledge lay claim and ownership to these fundamental, capitalist business processes, embedded in the larger, more complex, capitalist exploitation processes of production, consumption, and distribution, become the acting representative-agents of the logic of capitalism. And, depending on quality and quantity of the particular business process, i.e., the size of the surplus extracted and accumulated in relation to utility within these capitalist business processes, these acting-agents of capitalism, including their capitalist insatiable drives, increase in force, importance, influence, and wealth in relation to the rest of society and all the insatiable drives for ownership/knowledge of the workforce/population which interlace capitalist society.

12.f) Due to its dual nature, as both utility and surplus, a commodity is in essence a mental and physical monetary interface, within capitalism, between the multitude of particular insatiable drives for ownership/knowledge of the workforce/population, unified and divided, which interlace the social fabric of society. As a monetary interface, a commodity is a mirror and a means by which entities and other commodities are measured, weighted, ranked, filed and valued against, according to the arbitrary yet ruling value-standards of capitalism. These capitalist standards, which are devoid of inherent validity and/or verity, nonetheless, have artificial value and significance, but only within the parameters of the ideational comprehensive framework of capitalism. Outside capitalist parameters, these standards are worthless and meaningless. Commodities are ideological, their value/price is set via their ideological congruity with the ideational comprehensive framework of capitalism. Value/price is fundamentally set by the logic of capitalism.

12.g) Even so, a commodity is never complete but is continually in a universal process of refinement, evolution and revolution, i.e., development, just like all concepts, all processes and all political-economic frameworks, whatever they are. What a human sees as seemingly complete, static, obdurate and eternal is in fact a snap shot, a picture at a set time and place of an ever-refining and developing evolutionary/revolutionary process of a particular commodity and the commodity form and structure, in general, i.e., utility and surplus, ad infinitum. Likewise, the same applies for the totalizing logical apparatus of bourgeois-state-capitalism, i.e., the ideational comprehensive framework of capitalism, in the sense that capitalism is never complete, but is continually in a universal process of refinement, evolution and revolution, i.e., development, just like all concepts, all processes and all political-economic frameworks, whatever they are. What is seen as seemingly complete, static, obdurate, and eternal is in fact a snap shot, a picture at a set time and place of an ever-refining and developing evolutionary/revolutionary process, inherent in the logical apparatus of bourgeois-state-capitalism, itself. This process/force, which is in fact the creative-power of all insatiable drives for ownership/knowledge of the workforce/population, wrapped into one, is welded to the parasitic logic of capitalism. And as a result, this evolutionary and revolutionary process/force incessantly transforms the exterior and interior, structural composition of bourgeois-state-capitalism, when it incessantly transforms its own make-up and composition. Notwithstanding, despite constant and perpetual transformations, this evolutionary and revolutionary process/force never alters the intrinsic nucleus of the logic of capitalism. That is, the capitalist nucleus, which is logically programmed to accumulate and extract surplus value, by any means necessary, at the lowest financial cost, as soon as possible.

12.h) The commodity, as a totality, is a construct of parts that can be subdivided into smaller and smaller parts, ad infinitum. And, as the individual parts of the general commodity-form deteriorate, its general concept evolves and refines itself. That is, as the form and structure of an individual commodity becomes increasingly obsolete so the concept of this individual commodity and, as well, the general concept of the commodity in its most generalized form, is increasingly refined, purified, clarified and ameliorated. This increasing refinement of the commodity-form, both as a totality and a vast set of partialities, which is brought about by the physical and mental deterioration of individual commodities, stimulates the workforce/population, welded to the logic of capitalism, to forever replicate, improve, refine, and expand, the commodity-form, both as a particularity and as a totality. Therefore, the deterioration of the commodity-form, general or specific, stimulates the workforce/population, through an incessant capitalist coercion, to refine, replicate, and disseminate, commodities and the general commodity-form, ad infinitum. This incessant capitalist coercion is instigated by the logic of capitalism welded to the insatiable drive for ownership/knowledge of the workforce/population, which commands the endless reproduction of the commodity-form, both as an abstract totalitarian concept and as an interactive composite of countless commodities, forming a vast plethora of countless commodity-forms, forms which totally mediate and overwhelm all aspects of daily life.[1]

-[13]-

13.a) A commodity's and an entity's value/price is based on the ideational comprehensive framework. Value/price is conceptual. Meaning that as the ideational comprehensive framework changes, value/price is, as well, subject to conceptual changes. Value/price is conceptual in the sense that value/price is based and constructed in the mind, via the influence of an ideational comprehensive framework on the mind, namely, on conceptual-perception. Likewise, once adopted, an ideational comprehensive framework, through variations of situational time and space, influences the value/price which a commodity and/or an entity has within the particular political-economic framework. For instance, accumulations in exchange and trade influence value/price, supply and demand influence value/price, if something is consumed influences value/price. If a vegetable commodity rots over time, its value/price will deteriorate, accordingly. If the last man on earth is dying of thirst and is surrounded with all the gold bullion he could ever wish for, this gold is valueless/priceless, if it cannot be exchanged for a water-commodity. In this regard, value/price is based in and constructed through conceptual-perception, specifically, the influence of an ideational comprehensive framework on the mind and the influence of a particular, situational time and space on the mind.

13.b) So as situational time and space changes so does value/price, hence, the term that value and price fluctuate. Value/price, i.e., what something or someone is worth, changes and fluctuates with time and within different spaces. Value/price is not an all-definitive measurement and/or perception; it is in constant flux and subject to continuous re-assessment. Value/price is both quantifiable and unquantifiable, conceptual and material, exchangeable and non-exchangeable etc., value/price is an arbitrary fabrication.

13.c) In this regard, value/price is based on conceptual-perception, i.e., ideational comprehensive frameworks, plus time and space. As a rule, the more useful, definitive, precise, clear, and tradeable a concept or thing is, the greater is its value/price, within a specific ideational comprehensive framework, i.e., greater is its intellectual/material power over others in this particular society, which subscribes to this ruling, ideational comprehensive framework. As a result, the control of value/price is one of the fundamental objectives of capitalism and capitalists, alike, as value/price is a deep-seated expression of power, power over other humans, power over nature, power over socio-economic existence and power over reality, itself. The control of value/price is a primary mechanism in the accumulation, extraction and centralization of surplus value, namely, the appropriation and build-up of capitalist power and capitalist wealth. Value/price is arbitrarily set, by capitalists, through power-blocs in order to augment influence, profit and power in the hands of a select few, namely, the state-finance-corporate-aristocracy.

13.d) Indeed, this is why control is paramount for the logic of capitalism and the state-finance-corporate-aristocracy, since, high-levels of control, or absolute control,
----
1. Karl Marx. "The Commodity," Capital (Volume One). London, England: (Penguin Books, 1990) 125-139. (Note: The commodity section, in Marx's Opus, helped clarify certain aspects concerning the nature of the commodity, specifically, Marx's theoretical explanation of the commodity-form.)

permit a capitalist entity, whatever this entity or these entities may be, to artificially and arbitrarily set value/price, according to any capitalist whim and/or unreasonable impulse. That is, fundamentally, according to conceptual-perception. Ultimately, a high-level of control allows a capitalist entity to realize super-profits, namely, achieve a maximum level of accumulation, extraction and centralization of surplus value, i.e., capitalist profit. In fact, it is this maniac impulse to control value/price by any means necessary, in order to set value, price and profit, at will, within specific spheres of production, consumption and distribution, propels capitalists and the logic of capitalism ever-deeper into the micro-recesses of everyday life, in an effort to establish greater control over people, nature and conceptual-perception. In effect, the greater the control of certain spheres of production, consumption and distribution, whether, through written agreements or unwritten agreements, violence or non-violence etc., grants a capitalist entity, or entities, the ability to artificially and arbitrarily set value/price at any level, pending, there is no resistance and/or opposition from the workforce/population. The Control of specific spheres of production, consumption and distribution, controls the limits of choice and options, thus, manufacturing artificial scarcity and high-levels of effective demand. This scarcity and higher than normal effective demand permit capitalists to artificially-fabricate and arbitrarily-set erroneous values and prices, due to the fact, in the end, power and force ultimately determine all values and prices. That is, force and power arbitrarily and artificially shape conceptual-perception by normalizing erroneous values and prices in the minds of the workforce/population, because, artificially-constructed scarcity backed by force establishes all values and prices. As a result, maximum control of all aspects of everyday life, including all natural resources and the workforce/population, means super-profits for the state-finance-corporate-aristocracy. It means maximum levels of capitalist accumulation, extraction, and centralization of wealth, power, profit and private property. It means the domination of the workforce/population and natural resources, by capitalist power-blocs, which themselves increasingly amalgamate into bigger and bigger large-scale power-blocs in order to enforce erroneous values, prices and super-profits. And, this maniac drive for super-profits means capitalist totalitarianism.

-[14]-

14.a) All in all, what this means is that capitalism is stimulated, developed, augmented, and intensified, when humans and their insatiable drives for ownership/knowledge are: 1. maneuvered and controlled to transform matter into commodities, and 2., are maneuvered and controlled to consume these commodities both as a totalitarian singularity, i.e., the universal concept of the commodity-form, and as a vast pluralized network of specific commodities. This structuring and socio-economic organization of the insatiable drives for ownership/knowledge of the workforce/population, by capitalism, enables capitalism to extract, accumulate and develop, both financial quantifiable capital and the technological mechanisms, which manufacture and amass more financial quantifiable capital, i.e. profit, via the direct exploitation of humans, nature, and through the many exchanges of commodities, which occur in and across the economy and society, in general.

14.b) In addition, what this means for the workforce/population is that it is developed, managed, administrated, refined and intensified, by capitalism, according to a specific, man-made, artificial capitalist regime, i.e., the logic of capitalism, whose main purpose is: 1., to satisfy the minimum maintenance requirements of the insatiable drives of the workforce/population and nature so as to remain in power. And 2., to satisfy its own logical necessities for maximum capitalist development, accumulation and extraction. The goal is to deny, negate and control the natural plurality, collectivism and variability of all the insatiable drives for ownership/knowledge into one, singular, invariable, capitalist workforce, namely, an efficiently-organized, hierarchical, subservient, capitalist ant-colony. That is, an ant-colony centred on the accumulation, extraction and centralization of profit, private property and power into small epicenters controlled by the state-finance-corporate-aristocracy personifying the logic of capitalism.

14.c) It is the tensions and contradictions between these two fundamental ends, within the parameters of the bourgeois-state-capitalism, which both intensifies and augments capitalism's exploitative processes, and at the same time, threaten its stability and its rule as the central, political-economic framework for the unrelenting, divisionary/unitary force of the insatiable drive for ownership/knowledge, namely, the central-operating-code of workforce/population and nature.

Section Two:

The Logic Of Capitalism:

(Static-Formations And Dynamic-Formations)

15.a) Logics are ideational comprehensive frameworks. Logics permeate the sum of existence, from alpha to omega. The same applies for ideational comprehensive frameworks. Nothing and no one lies outside logic in general, as logic, i.e., an ideational comprehensive framework, is the essential platform for understanding and/or comprehension, itself. A logic and/or an ideational comprehensive framework is a will to power bolted down and self-molded into a logical configuration and/or mechanism. That is, a logic and/or an ideational comprehensive framework is a codified apparatus or mechanism of the will to power channeling, coding, and administrating other types of wills to power along specific predetermined pathways. Thereby, logics are the essential scaffolding inherent in all modes of being, perceiving, interpreting and acting, enabling consistency, regularity and reliability. As a result, there are no modes of being, perceiving, interpreting and acting, namely, ideational comprehensive frameworks or ideologies, whatever they may be, without logic and vice versa. Meaning, there is no knowledge, no know-how, no ownership, and/or being, whatsoever, without some form of logical order and sense such is logic and such is an ideational comprehensive framework. Logics and/or ideational comprehensive frameworks are modes of knowledge production, in the sense that they are productive in manufacturing certain thoughts, ideas, and information etc., specific to their organized frameworks of partisan understanding and comprehension. People are carriers of specific logics and/or ideational comprehensive frameworks. That is, people are informed by ideologies and apply ideologies.

15.b) Logics are both conceptual and material. And consequently, ideational comprehensive frameworks are both conceptual and material. Logics are conceptually reinforced, replicated and refined via material conditions and processes. And vice versa, logics are materially reinforced, replicated and refined via conceptual conditions and processes. The same holds for ideational comprehensive frameworks. Moreover, some material conditions and processes are natural, i.e., automatic conditions and processes of being human and existing in a certain type of natural environment, while some material conditions and processes are man-made and artificially manufactured by humans themselves. In addition, the same applies to conceptual conditions and processes in the sense that some conceptual conditions and processes are natural, i.e., automatic conditions and processes of being human and existing in a certain type of natural environment, while some conceptual conditions and processes are man-made and artificially manufactured by humans themselves. The point is that logics are both conceptual and/or material, both natural and/or artificial, both independent and/or dependent, both superior and/or inferior etc., and these features are the same for ideational comprehensive frameworks.

15.c) Humans manufacture logical order and sense, i.e., ideational comprehensive frameworks or logics, regardless, if they intend to or not. And moreover, logical order and sense, i.e., ideational comprehensive frameworks or logics, manufacture humans in turn, regardless if intended or not. Logics construct us just as we construct logics. In fact, humans are by nature logical entities, that is, beings inherently programmed and built to construct logical order and sense, i.e., ideational comprehensive frameworks. Simultaneously, ideational comprehensive frameworks are by nature logical arrangements, that is, logics inherently programmed and built to construct logical order and sense, i.e., logical entities, mediums, and/or adherents. This is the human condition, la raison d'être of the human species, or for that matter, all species and/or entities, namely, logic. Either/or, logics and ideational comprehensive frameworks fetishize phenomena, favoring certain phenomena in the world over others, bestowing higher significance on certain phenomena over others. Either/or, logics and ideational comprehensive frameworks are inescapably bias.

15.d) Ideational comprehensive frameworks are the logics by which humans and things function and operate; they guide them, inform them, stimulate them, and make them move in all sorts of ways and fashions, both conceptually and materially etc., since, ideational comprehensive frameworks are the logics by which humans and things acquire method, meaning and purpose.

16.a) Logics, i.e., ideational comprehensive frameworks, interlace all social relations, both conceptual and material, both cultural and economic etc., as logics fabricate all sorts of conceptual and material multi-verses and relationships for all sorts of usages and practical performances.

16.b) Logics, i.e., ideational comprehensive frameworks, lead and tether humans to specific, material and conceptual, modes of being, perceiving, interpreting and acting, devoid of freewill; and to such a radical extent that humans and their multi-varied wills to power are forever immersed in the logic of ideational comprehensive frameworks and the ideational comprehensive framework of logic(s), ad infinitum. Moreover, logics are pitted against one another in a multiplicity of fluctuating, mental/physical, antagonistic and/or mutual-aid relationships, vying for contextual supremacy. The result is a multiplicity of mental and physical vantage points, or ideational comprehensive frameworks, making sense and logical order of phenomena, plus one supreme central point which comprises the singular, unifying, ideational comprehensive framework, namely, the organizing principle of logical order and sense for the sum of logic and, in general, for all of society.

16.c) Logics, i.e., ideational comprehensive frameworks, achieve supremacy through maximum utility and maximum performance brought about by firm consistency, regularity, and reliability, combined with incessant material and conceptual reinforcement, replication and logical refinement. Through this antagonistic-refinement process, entities, human or otherwise, become logical mediums for the construction, replication and dissemination of specific clusters of ideational comprehensive frameworks, over-arched by the specific ruling language, namely, the specific unifying logic or ideational comprehensive framework. In brief, this is the history of the supremacy of the logic of capitalism.

16.d) The logic of capitalism is the logical result of a long historical process of antagonism, mutual-aid, and logical refinement, whereupon, the logic of capitalism assimilated, subjugated and/or eradicated a litany of other, competing, socio-economic logics and ideational comprehensive frameworks. It did this, by firmly adhering to the maxim of maximum utility and maximum performance thru firm consistency, regularity, and reliability, combined with incessant material and conceptual reinforcement, replication and logical refinement. The logic of capitalism is totalitarian and war-like.

16.e) Out of this long historical process of antagonism, mutual-aid and logical refinement, the logic of capitalism has fashioned, and continues to fashion, a plurality of disciplinary and punitive mechanisms, both conceptual and material, designed to replicate, disseminate and refine capitalist, socio-economic structures and processes, indefinitely, that is, the logic of capitalism, indefinitely. The prime directive is always the same: the maximization of profit, by any means necessary, at the lowest financial cost, as soon as possible, while, only satisfying the minimum maintenance requirements of the workforce/population, the fount of profit and capital. Notwithstanding, the logic of capitalism is a socio-historical construct, constantly susceptible to change, including, radical social change.

-[17]-

17.a) The logic of capitalism is a totalitarian language, with an in-built set of concepts, which manifest an artificial ideational/material reality, a framework of ready-made automatic, ideas, relations, opinions, and answers to all social, economic and/or existential problems. The logic of capitalism is an ideational comprehensive framework, which is both material and conceptual. It is a military-industrial morality/amorality, a code of conduct.

17.b) The logic of capitalism is a totalitarian language that designs copies of itself, ad infinitum, a vast array of ideological facsimiles, both material and conceptual, which disseminate the logic of capitalism in various concealed and unconcealed forms. The logic of capitalism is a linguistic mechanism, both conceptual and material, designed to subjugate and indoctrinate the workforce/population, both materially and conceptually etc.

17.c) The logic of capitalism is at its nexus a tautology designing tautologies, simultaneously, ubiquitously, and paradoxically, yet, at the same time as it is a tautology, the logic of capitalism is a contradiction, designing contradictions, simultaneously, ubiquitously, and paradoxically. The logic of capitalism produces its intrinsic profit imperative, in a variety of forms and formats that overlap with each other in a patchwork of antagonistic and mutual-aid relationships sustaining capitalist contextual supremacy.

17.d) As well, the logic of capitalism designs difference(s) simultaneously and ubiquitously as it is designing similarities; notwithstanding, these differences and similarities are always superficial and always in its own ideational image, namely, as mechanisms for capitalist development, that is, capital accumulation and capital extraction.

17.e) The logic of capitalism is a mental/physical language of unitary opposites and/or double standards. Depending on socio-economic conditions, the logic of capitalism functions and operates as if it has ethical standards or a moral concept, and/or as if it is composed of the contrary, namely, no moral concept or ethical standards. The logic of capitalism permits itself this double standard, i.e., this Janus-Face characteristic, because it is the ruling logic, i.e., the logic that must satisfy its own mercenary necessities, by any means necessary, and in turn, the basic necessities of the workforce/population, all the while, denying and regimenting the the natural plurality and variation of the insatiable drive of the workforce/population into a singular, capitalist, productive force and a singular, capitalist, socio-economic framework.

18.a) The logic of capitalism structures social relations between people via mental and physical models and commodities, which are social interfaces. The logic of capitalism is the ruling logical process and framework by which people relate to one another. And people are structured and mediated by the logic of capitalism via a plethora of state-capitalist-constructed-images, institutions, processes and commodities, which give direction, meaning and value to their insatiable drives for ownership/knowledge. These state-capitalist-constructed-images, institutions, processes and commodities establish a conceptual/material series of false-consciousness(es) between people, which is reflected in and buttressed in material and ideational terms. These conceptual and material false-consciousness(es) between people, structure their modes and relations of mental/physical production, consumption, and distribution, ultimately, enabling the logic of capitalism to permeate and to control these modes and relations of mental/physical production, consumption, and distribution, in its favor, in order to replicate, disseminate, and refine its logic. Hence, how the logic of capitalism dominates all modes and relations, both materially and conceptually. And, in the end, how the logic of capitalism determines the political-economic framework of society, in general.

18.b) The logic of capitalism is a political-economic framework, i.e., a linguistic set of ideational concepts, articulated in material terms, which permeate all socio-economic structures, mediums and entities within society. There is no outside to the logic of capitalism due to the fact that it has conquered for itself the central point of logical organization, that is, the singular, organizing principle for all ideational comprehensive frameworks. Consequently, in general, the false-consciousness of capitalism excludes those that have not adopted its false-consciousness/fallacies, and/or question its false-consciousness/fallacies, and includes, those that have adopted its false-consciousness/fallacies, and obey these fallacies without question.

18.c) In sum, the logic of capitalism is false-consciousness, i.e., it is a series of arbitrary beliefs, and/or a double-standard logic, which induces a suspension of disbelief in its participants. It is an ideational comprehensive framework reflected in material terms that functions on the basis of false-consciousness. It functions on the basis of precepts and concepts which are illusory and have importance only in the sense that 1. these concepts are organized as ideational, material structures, and 2., the logic is agreed upon by a community, specifically a ruling oligarchical network of a select few, which imposes this logic on society as a whole, either thru repression and/or propaganda.

18.d) For instance, money is in reality paper, nothing but paper, its value/signification is based on a socio-economic agreement, between a select elite group of individuals and socio-economic institutions, that this paper represents segments of accrued labor-time and/or a certain amount of monetary-power. This connection is a false-consciousness, i.e., an arbitrary construct, grounded in a select form of communal thinking, where socio-economic networks, both human and institutional, have adopted a false-consciousness, pertaining to certain types of paper in order to excluded all those other forms of trade and value/signification, which might challenge the status quo of the logic of capitalism.

19.a) An important linchpin of the logic of capitalism and the unlimited accumulation and extraction of surplus value, i.e., capitalist profit, is its permissible allowance and encouragement of the spiritual dimension, i.e., religious belief. Religious belief is the engine of a self-induced, suspension of disbelief, i.e., the necessary mechanism in order to establish the all crucial serials of false-consciousness for capitalist development and for the accumulation and extraction of surplus value, i.e., profit and power.

19.b) Religion is the product of escapism and infantile fictional belief, i.e., it is humans projecting unto the mental and physical world the best qualities they internally possess and manifest through their own intellectual and/or material activity, that is, their insatiable drive for ownership/knowledge. These projections of their fantasies and best internal qualities, unto nothingness, uncertainty, and phenomena, reflects back onto them as a meta-being, which is seemingly superior to them in every way. God is an internal manifestation derived from human beings, themselves. God is false-consciousness and a phantasm. Religious belief is false-consciousness, a false-consciousness, which allowed for the initial development and organization of the capitalist-nation-state. The idea of the capitalist-nation-state is founded on religious belief, namely, a totalizing unitary force capable of total national administration and organization, i.e., capable of god-like influence, here on earth.

19.c) The capitalist state is false-consciousness just as organized-religion is false-consciousness, however, both are the product of surplus value extraction and accumulation, albeit, different types of surplus values. Christianity has annexed and absorbed the surplus alienation, surplus dread, and surplus anguished, manifested by the will to power over the centuries, and constructed for itself a monolithic apparatus of spiritual/mental domination, indoctrination, and repression, called: "The Church". Likewise, the logic of capitalism has annexed, and continues to annex, financial quantifiable capital, i.e., capitalist property and profit, manifested by the will to power of the workforce/population, over the last two or three centuries, in order to construct, and to continue to construct, a monolithic apparatus of secular domination, indoctrination, and repression, called: "Bourgeois-State-Capitalism". Where Christianity and organized-religions are deemed the unitary spiritual/mental force of the people, the capitalist state is deemed the unitary practical/material force of the people. Ultimately, both seemingly exercise the people's will in the people's name, for the people's benefit. However, this is illusory nonsense as mental and physical enslavement is the goal of both.

19.d) In actuality, the capitalist state is comprised of a select few and exercises its rule in the name of the many but in benefit of a select few, i.e., the chosen few, which exemplify and enact the necessities of the logic of capitalism. Likewise, just as Christianity and organized-religions are comprised of a select few, i.e., a chosen few, who mediate and administrate the relations between people and God, Christianity and organized-religions organize and exercise their spiritual/mental rule in the name of the many but in benefit of a select few. In truth, both the capitalist state and Christianity, or organized-religions, are developments of specific types of surplus value and both strive for the continued development of surplus value, albeit, different types of surplus values. The capitalist state administers and controls the material and ideational relations between people for the maximization of capitalist profit, while, Christianity and organized-religions administer and control the material and ideational relations between people for the maximization of ideo-spiritual power. In many ways, Christianity and organized-religions feed-off the spiritual emptiness, alienation, and nihilism, which the logic of capitalism and its central, socio-economic relation engenders, namely, what the capital/labor relation, at the heart of the capitalist system, engenders. If religion is the opiate of the people, it is an opiate designed to appropriate, temper, and alleviate, the spiritual pain and angst, festering across capitalist production, consumption, and distribution, so as to keep capitalist production, consumption, and distribution, efficiently working, and more importantly, profitable. Christianity and organized-religions facilitate and assist the logic of capitalism, at the center of bourgeois-state-capitalism, because, Christianity and organized-religions have always been forms of domination, exploitation, and enslavement, like the logic of capitalism. Thus, today, they are extensions of the logic of capitalism.

-[20]-

20.a) Within bourgeois-state-capitalism, there are two types of formations, static-formations and dynamic-formations. These two types of internal formations are micro-formations, i.e., types of micro-socio-economic-frameworks, which are essential to the survival of bourgeois-state-capitalism and the logic of capitalism. These type of micro-formations are embodied in bourgeois-state-capitalism to various degrees and numbers, but, are not necessarily produce by bourgeois-state-capitalism and/or the logic of capitalism:

Static-Formations: are symmetrical, logical formations, where inputs and outputs, supply and demand of the socio-economic system are able to be predicted and monitored, past, present and future. These are capitalist socio-economic formations, where the will to power, is contextualized, constant and predictable. A static-formation is a mini-replica of capitalism, in general. It is a micro-capitalist formation.

Dynamic-Formations: are asymmetrical, illogical formations, where inputs and outputs, supply and demand of the socio-economic system are unable, or difficult, of being predicted and monitored, past, present and future. These are anti-capitalist socio-economic formations, where the will to power is un-contextualized, irregular and unpredictable. A dynamic-formation is the will to power of the workforce/population, extracting, accumulating, and developing, autonomously, outside of administrative-capitalist-control, on its own terms. A dynamic-formation is a mini-replica of structural-anarchism, in general. It is an anti-capitalist formation.

(Note: At its Nth degree, there are no dynamic-formations as a total dynamism is without comprehension. It is absolute socio-economic liberalism, liberating all into total nothingness or obdurateness, i.e., it is the reduction of the human species to a primitive and barbaric form of socio-economic existence.)

20.b) Dynamic-formations and static-formations have gradations, depending on their individual stage of organizational development. And, what energizes, i.e., fuels, dynamic and static-formations is the will to power, which, when organized into a formation, animates and structures, or de-structures, dynamic and static-formations, either, along the lines of the logic of capitalism and/or along the lines of the logic of structural-anarchism.

-[21]-

21.a) i) Dynamic-formations and static-formations are rudimentary socio-economic assemblies, manifested by the insatiable drive for ownership/knowledge, which may, or may not, create financial quantifiable capital and/or be connected to the overarching logical apparatus of bourgeois-state-capitalism, i.e., the logic of capitalism.

ii) Dynamic-formations and static-formations are the miniature moorings of bourgeois-state-capitalism, which is to state that dynamic-formations and static-formations comprise the multi-varied base of bourgeois-state-capitalism. Dynamic-formations and static-formations are dependent on, indirectly dependent on, and/or directly independent of the logical apparatus of bourgeois-state-capitalism, that is, the logic of capitalism.

21.b) Dynamic-formations are the small free and/or flexible socio-economic forces and structures of the insatiable drive for ownership/knowledge, which are producing, consuming and distributing, autonomously, according to their own volition and pragmatic egalitarianism. Dynamic-formations are founded on poly-rationality. They are poly-rational assemblies. In contrast, static-formations are the small unfree, rigid, socio-economic forces and structures of a small set of insatiable drives for ownership/knowledge, administering and organizing, socio-economic forces into quantifiable, organized, micro-cycles and micro-processes of mental and physical, capitalist production, consumption and distribution, at the base of bourgeois-state-capitalism. Static-formations are founded on instrumental-rationality. They are instrumentalist assemblies.

[Schemata A]

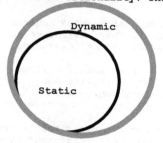

← (Static-Formation) →

[Schemata B]

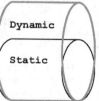

(<u>Note</u>: A static-formation is the page the schematic is written-on, and a dynamic-formation is the reader's free thoughts, which are slowly structured into an understanding of the diagram.)

(<u>Note</u>: Dynamic-formations are more fluid than the rigid structures of static-formations. As a result, dynamic-formations tend to flow in and out of the structures of static-formations. Dynamic-formations tend to envelop static-formations and, inadvertently, sheath and insulate the rigid structures of static-formations, including their inherent drive to control the plurality of insatiable drives for ownership/knowledge into the micro-processes of capitalist development and capitalist profit-making.)

21.c) <u>Static-Formations</u>: are the small, rudimentary, socio-economic, structures of bourgeois-state-capitalism, which allow for the quantification of capital and a small set of insatiable drives, so as to determine their projections and capitalist developments, via solid measurements. Static-formations are the small, congealed, socio-economic structures of bourgeois-state-capitalism, which organize newborn sets of specific insatiable drives into socio-economic processes, capable of accumulating and extracting surplus value. A child's lemonade-stand is a good example of the instrumental-rationality of a static-formation, which services the needs of bourgeois-capitalism.

<u>Dynamic-Formations</u>: are the small, rudimentary, socio-economic forces of the insatiable drive for ownership/knowledge, whose qualities are variable and arbitrary, difficult and/or incapable of organization and accurate determination. Dynamic-formations are the small, uncongealed, socio-economic forces of the insatiable drive for ownership/knowledge, which are producing, consuming, and distributing, in egalitarian fashion, independently of bourgeois-state-capitalism. Hide and go-seek,Peer2Peer Sharing-Economies, are good examples of the poly-rationality of a dynamic-formation, which fuels the logic of structural-anarchism.

21.d) <u>Static-Formations</u>: are in essence the objective side of the insatiable drive for ownership/knowledge. They are objective in the sense that bourgeois-state-capitalism can find a use for them and/or they are objective because they are material, i.e., measurable, consistent, quantifiable, and systematized into the logic of capitalism, that is, instrumental-rationality. A static-formation is small bundles of socio-economic processes, which are organized to accumulate, produce and centralize capitalist profit, power and wealth.

<u>Dynamic-Formations</u>: are in essence the subjective side of the insatiable drive for ownership/knowledge. They are subjective in the sense that bourgeois-state-capitalism has not found a specific material use for them, or bourgeois-state-capitalism has not discovered their use as of yet, and/or they are subjective because they are speculative, theoretical, experimental, and poly-rational. A dynamic-formation is small, variable bundles of socio-cultural, or socio-economic, processes which are freely and loosely organized to accumulate, produce and spread autonomy, liberty, wealth and egalitarianism.

21.e) <u>Static-Formations</u>: are small, hierarchies which generate large, instrumental-rational hierarchizations. They are rudimentary rigid orders, within parameters, aligned according to the instrumental-rationality of capitalism.

<u>Dynamic-Formations</u>: are without, or have small, horizontal-hierarchies. They generate large, poly-rational horizontalizations. They are rudimentary collectives, without parameters and/or within loose parameters, aligned according to the poly-rationality of structural-anarchism, not bourgeois-capitalism.

(<u>Note</u>: Both dynamic and static-formations are vital to accrue and extract capital. Both dynamic and static-formations create different types of capitals. Static-formations create quantifiable capital, what the logic of capitalism needs. And dynamic-formations create unquantifiable capital, what capitalism does not need, but nevertheless, what anarchist communism needs in the sense that dynamic-formations lead to communes, total equality, financial egalitarianism and structural-anarchism.)

21.f) Every industry, profession, grouping and/or large socio-economic system etc., embodies to various degrees small static-formations and dynamic-formations within themselves. This is due to the fact that dynamic-formations are the rudimentary formations of socio-cultural and socio-economic development, that accrue and extract immeasurable surplus value. And static-formations are the rudimentary formations of socio-cultural and socio-economic development, which accrue and extract measurable, capitalist surplus value. However, only static-formations align with the logic of capitalism, only static-formations ameliorate the logic of capitalism. Dynamic-formations tend to manufacture revolutions and the insurrectionary overthrow of bourgeois-state-capitalism, thus, dynamic-formations tend to be, most of the time, suppressed by the logic of capitalism. Dynamic-formations are expressions of the poly-rationality of structural-anarchism in rudimentary forms.

-[22]-

22.a) Static-formations are the primary, rudimentary, socio-economic systems, by which the workforce/population is regimented and disciplined to the rhythms and rational processes of physical and mental capitalist production, consumption, and distribution, in and across bourgeois-state-capitalism, from the time humans' are born and all the way to their deaths.

22.b) Static-formations shape behavior and thinking processes at the micro-levels of everyday life, along the lines of the logic of capitalism. Static-formations aim to eventually achieve the transformation of the workforce/population into robotic, unfeeling, and unthinking, atomized, capitalist entities, which are solely focused on the amelioration of the mental and physical, socio-economic processes of bourgeois-state-capitalism, i.e., capitalist profit-making. The goal is the production of instrumental-rational, technocrats.

22.c) Dynamic-formations are the primary, rudimentary, socio-economic systems, by which the workforce/population are made aware of their creativity, autonomy, independence, freedom, individuality, imagination, cooperation, equality, ingenuity, and most importantly, pragmatic egalitarianism.

22.d) Dynamic-formations liberate behavior and thinking processes at the micro-levels of everyday life, along the lines of the logic of structural-anarchism. Dynamic-formations aim to eventually achieve the realignment of the workforce/population into cooperatives, anarchist-municipalities, and autonomous-collectives, whose members mutually share decision-making-authority and the fruits of their labor in relative equal measure. The goal of dynamic-formations is the production of poly-rational, anarcho-praxiacrats.

(<u>Note</u>: Within post-industrial, post-modern, bourgeois-state-capitalism, dynamic-formations and static-formations oscillate between each other in a disequilibrium, dictated by capitalism. They constantly mutate in their attempts to annihilate their opposite. However, the logic of capitalism tends to side with static-formations because they are the logical off-springs of capitalism. Finally, for a well-functioning bourgeois-state-capitalism, there must be a type of uneven balance, between static and dynamic-formations, specifically in favor of static-formations. The logic of capitalism cannot do without this disequilibrium. Its supremacy depends on it.)

-[23]-

23.a) Static-formations and dynamic-formations in addition to being economic in nature are as well political, i.e., cultural, in nature. In fact, all politics stem from static-formations and dynamic-formations, as both represent contradictory logics and political visions within bourgeois-state-capitalism. Within bourgeois-state-capitalism, the foundation of all types of politics and economies stem from the rudimentary assemblies of static-formations and/or dynamic-formations.

23.b) Static-formations align with the instrumental-rationality of capitalism, while dynamic-formations align with the poly-rationality of structural-anarchism. Static-formations tend to be objective, superficial, formal, vertical, and bureaucratic, while dynamic-formations tend to be arbitrary, informal, horizontal, communal and cooperative.

23.c) The political-state is the result of the increasing complexity of the insatiable drive for ownership/knowledge of the workforce/population, namely, capitalist-society, in general. An increasing plethora of logical necessities, brought into existence via capitalist development, has led to the construction of the political-state so as to administrate this ever-increasing plethora of logical necessities. The political-state organizes necessities into static and dynamic-formations always in favor of the logic of capitalism. To administrate these burgeoning micro-formations and necessities, static and dynamic-formations are configured, by the political-state, into specific political-economic layouts, stationed in and across the micro-recesses of everyday life. These political-economic layouts are arranged on a political-economic-spectrum, from far-left to far-right.

-[24]-

24.a) i) At one extreme of the political-economic-spectrum, communism, for the most part, is a composite of static-formations based on the future promise of a plethora of dynamic-formations. Initially, communism quantifies, structures and controls the insatiable drive for ownership/knowledge in an effort to limit and terminate the logic of capitalism, via the future promise that such a socio-economic program will engender a vast plethora of dynamic-formations, i.e., an ideal communist utopia. However, communism quantifies, structures, and controls, the insatiable drive for ownership/knowledge to such an extent as to render the insatiable drive for ownership/knowledge, and all possibilities for dynamic-formations, null, static and stillborn. As a result, communism leads to socio-economic inertia, due to the fact that its dictatorship of the proletariat controls the insatiable drive for ownership/knowledge of the workforce/population to such an aggravated extent as to manufacture total, socio-economic inertia.

ii) At the other extreme of the political-economic-spectrum, fascism, for the most part, is a composite of extreme financial, dynamic-formations and extreme socio-cultural, static-formations. Its notion of economic de-regulation, de-quantification and uncontrolled capitalism, coupled with the extreme control and streamlining of cultural differences, evaporates all capitalist developments. Fascism de-quantifies, demolishes, and liberates capitalism to such an extent as to render capitalist development, chaotic, dynamic, and prone to extreme market-fluctuations and stagnation, not to mention socio-cultural fanaticism. Fascism leads to socio-economic and cultural extinction, via its inherent economic liberality and cultural intolerance, which results in uncontrollable, illogical, hyper-dynamic and hyper-static-formations, radical inflation/deflation, extreme economic divisions and extreme cultural homogeneity, i.e., fascist neoliberalism. Fascism simultaneously liberates and controls the insatiable drive for ownership/knowledge to such extremes as to force the insatiable drive for ownership/knowledge of the workforce/population, beyond any static inertia and into, complete and total, annihilation of itself, including all organized society.

24.b) On the political-economic-spectrum, conservatism is more moderate than fascism but is fundamentally on the side of fascism as conservatism and fascism's fundamental premise is to liberate, by any means necessary, the insatiable drive for ownership/knowledge so as to control the insatiable drive for ownership/knowledge, more effectively, towards capitalist development, via cultural and economic homogenization. Conservatism, like fascism, pursues the intensification and stimulation of the workforce/population, 1. by removing socio-economic securities which can temperate the workforce/population, and 2., by effectively negating and denying all the increases of plurality, autonomy and creativity of the workforce/population. The point is to transform all entities into a homogeneous, socio-economic labor-force, which is super-focused on capitalist development and profit-making. Conservatism unbalances the capital/labor relation in favor of capitalism in order to restrict the workforce/population, more effectively, for economic production, profit-making, and for socio-cultural homogeneity. That is, for the conservation of capitalist profits into the hands of a select few. Conservatism spends little and cuts lots. It regiments and intensifies capitalist relations and capitalist forces inside the capitalist mode of production.

24.c) On the political-economic-spectrum, liberalism is more moderate than communism but is fundamentally on the side of communism as liberalism and communism's fundamental premise is to control, by any means necessary, capitalist development, in order to liberate the insatiable drive for ownership/knowledge, from incessant capitalist development. The point is to satisfy, more effectively, the logical necessities of the workforce/population, i.e., to free the workforce/population, more effectively, from the pressures of incessant capitalist development. Liberalism, like communism, attempts to place limits on capitalist unlimited development, 1., by creating socio-economic barriers, taxes and placing security measures on capitalism, and 2., by encouraging the plurality, autonomy and creativity of the workforce/population, i.e., socio-cultural heterogeneity. The point is to free and moderate the workforce/population, so that it can catch its breath, pertaining to intensive capitalist profit-making. Liberalism balances the capital/labor relation slightly in favor of labor so as to free the workforce/population, more effectively, for economic consumption, income-spending, and for socio-cultural heterogeneity. That is, for the liberation of capitalist profits, out of the hands of a select few, in service of investment. Liberalism liberates profit-increases and spends these increases, both on the workforce/population and on capitalist expansion, so as to set the stage for the creation of a larger, more intense, capitalist development, via a new round of capitalist conservatism. Liberalism spends lots and cuts little. It accelerates and expands capitalist relations and capitalist forces inside the capitalist mode of production.

(Note: Both liberalism and conservatism work together in service of the logic of capitalism. They are the two-sides of the capitalist coin, i.e., its instrumental-rationality.)

-[25]-

25.a) The political-economic-spectrum, as a diagram, is structured like this:

The Political-Economic-Spectrum:

[LEFT-WING] AUTHORITARIAN-STATE-COMMUNISM   AUTHORITARIAN-STATE-FASCISM [RIGHT-WING]

COMMUNIST-STRUCTURAL-ANARCHISM \
(OPEN-PARTICIPATORY-DEMOCRACY)

LIBERALISM / \ CONSERVATISM

[THE POLITICAL-ECONOMIC CENTER]

25.b) The logic of structural-anarchism is not as radical as communism as the logic of structural-anarchism is not founded on instrumental-rationality, like totalitarian-communism. The logic of structural-anarchism exercises poly-rationality, i.e., multi-dimensional mode of understanding. Moreover, in contrast to communism, the logic of structural-anarchism permits limited ownership on the basis that ownership is a logical necessity of the workforce/population. The logic of structural-anarchism is not as radical as communism as the logic of structural-anarchism is not a dictatorship of the proletariat, i.e., a totalitarian monolith, but is a federation of municipalities, cooperatives and autonomous-collectives. That is, a plurality sharing, in egalitarian fashion, decision-making-authority, ownership, knowledge, and the sum of capital.

25.c) Looking more closely within the political-economic-spectrum, specifically within bourgeois-state-capitalism, politics is based on the notion that the majority rules, but decision-making-authority is a highly controlled, machinated affair, contextualized, and shared, between liberalism and conservatism. Politics is highly controlled and highly machinated, by ruling, micro-fascist, oligarchical networks, i.e., the best embodiments of the instrumental-rationality of capitalism, which severely limit, political-economic options/choices for the workforce/population.

25.d) Moreover, after political-economic options/choices are constrained and limited, by the ruling, micro-fascist, oligarchical networks, through various political parties and political-economic agreements, decision-making-authority is in essence a dictatorship of the bourgeois middle. It is a dictatorship of the most average common denominator, where the highly limited, decision-making-authority of the majority is shared by, or between, liberalism and/or conservatism. As a result, this highly limited, orchestrated politics is ruled by averageness and mediocrity, i.e., average intellects, average cultural tastes, average bourgeois art, average goals, average aspirations, averageness in all shapes and forms, which replicate and mirror the limited political-economic options/choices, determined and offered by the ruling, micro-fascist, oligarchical networks. In addition, the majority is localized where money congeals the most, at the most basic, average point, situated in the middle of the political-economic-spectrum.

25.e) For this reason, political voting, within bourgeois-state-capitalism, has been transformed into a superficial popularity contest, devoid of any substantial, decision-making-authority, due the fact that elite, micro-fascist, oligarchical networks, predetermine issues, policies, and political-economic direction, beforehand. Therefore, it is a superficial popularity contest in the sense that the person who best represents, in the best fashion, mediocrity and averageness, wins the heart and mind of the average majority, i.e., the herd. In sum, it is the person and/or political party, which seeks to meld with the herd most thoroughly, willing to express its herd-mentality, with greatest zeal and accuracy, for the longest period of time, which thrives politically. To succeed in capitalist politics, one has to appeal to the average majority and the average majority is only interested in its own average mediocrity, which are expressions, opinions and ideals of average intellect, average benign taste, average aspirations and average technical proficiencies. All that is commonplace guides the politics between the liberal left and the conservative right, within the parameters of bourgeois-state-capitalism. The political-authority-spectrum of bourgeois-state-capitalism is an even balance between extremes so as to encapsulate the greatest portion of the middle, i.e., the greatest average number. Nothing changes, or very little changes, in politics because liberalism and conservatism are two-sides of the same capitalist coin. One breaths-in and one breaths-out, the logic of capitalism, and vice versa, depending on who holds political power. The perpetual victor of every election, within bourgeois-state-capitalism, is the instrumental-rationality of capitalism.

25.f) This is the general framework of the political-authority-spectrum:

<u>The Political-Authority-Spectrum</u>:

Poor	Wealthy
Ignorant	Intelligent
Tasteless	Tasteful
Wasteful	Resourceful
Unsuccessful	Successful
Intolerant	Tolerant
Boring	Charismatic etc.

The Average Mediocrity,
i.e., the majority in the
in the middle

[The highest concentration of available money, profit, wealth, private property, political legitimacy, and political-economic-power is found where the majority resides in the middle.]

[This is the dictatorship of the center and the middle, namely, the wannabe bourgeoisie.]

(Note: It is in the meat of the curve, where the majority congeals. Notwithstanding, the majority congeals in averageness, average tastes, average intelligence, average employment, average aspirations, i.e., lame bourgeois mediocrity, par excellence. And, the political parties, buttressed by ruling, micro-fascist, oligarchical networks, forever pander to this bewildered mass, the wannabe bourgeoisie, despite knowing full-well, the choice has already been made for them, by another dictatorship of the center artificially-manufactured by the state-finance-corporate-aristocracy.)

25.g) The political candidate, or political party, which captures the greatest portion of the average middle within the limited, political election-context, constructed and machinated, by the ruling, micro-fascist, oligarchical networks, is victorious. He or she becomes the voice of the wannabe bourgeoisie, where the greatest level of decision-making-authority resides, but he or she, in actuality, becomes the will of the logic of capitalism, a morsel of capitalist power. Notwithstanding, the political-authority-spectrum explains why capitalist-politics is so dull, lackluster, and lukewarm, as the middle is uninspiring and very average. It is from the body of the wannabe bourgeoisie, wherefore the best capitalist civil servants germinate, according to the logic of capitalism, due to the fact that the wannabe bourgeoisie is soaked in the logic of capitalism. Illuminated, indoctrinated and appointed, the wannabe bourgeoisie, wholeheartedly, exercises the imperatives of bourgeois-state-capitalism upon the workforce/population, with utmost sincerity, all the while, double-speaking to the contrary, in the name of the many, but really in service of a select few, the ruling, micro-fascist, oligarchical networks, the source of their newfound morsel of capitalist political power. The wannabe bourgeoisie is the average base median, fully immersed, fully versed, and fully covered, from head to toe, with the logic of capitalism.

-[26]-

26.a) Above all, bourgeois-state-capitalism is structured akin to a pincer, where the workforce/population is pinched together from the conservative-right via mega-corporations and organized-religions, and from the liberal-left via unions, the state and its institutions. Ultimately, these two sides, which seem at odds, are in fact unified, in structure and in form, at the top of socio-economic hierarchies, where micro-fascist, oligarchical networks, increasingly rule society according to a totalitarian, political-economic framework founded on the logic of capitalism. These networks rule in the name of the many but in the service of a select few. As a result, the workforce/population is squeezed between pseudo-differences, the false-consciousness of liberalism and conservatism.

(Note: Workforce unions and associations are open-points, where the overthrow of the logic of capitalism is possible. It is through these open-points where the logic of structural-anarchism is visible, realizable and embryonic, unless these unions and associations should fall prey to the bewitching fake-dualism of liberalism and conservatism.)

26.b) Bourgeois-state-capitalism is a totalitarian, political-economic framework. It is a pyramid ruled by money and power, where ruling, micro-fascist, oligarchical networks, i.e., the best representatives and personifications of the logic of capitalism, circulate, regenerate, and propagate over and above the workforce/population. It is these ruling, micro-fascist, oligarchical networks, who imprint, implement, expand and exercise the logic of capitalism, through various cultural, political, corporate and state-institutional mechanisms and media. It is these ruling, micro-fascist, oligarchical networks, who regiment, discipline, and/or punish the workforce/population, both conceptually and materially, so as to make the workforce/population produce, consume, and distribute, wealth and themselves, according to the dictates of the logic of capitalism. The logic of capitalism has no outside. It is a soft totalitarian totality, designed to tether and press the workforce/population in service of ever-intensifying profit-making schemes and ever-greater sums of capitalist profit. The point is to maximize and centralized capitalist wealth and power into small epicenters, namely, a state-finance-corporate-aristocracy.

26.c) The socio-economic pyramid of bourgeois-state-capitalism is structured like this:

THE STATE-FINANCE-CORPORATE-ARISTOCRACY AND THE NEXUS OF UNITY

(THE UNITY OF LEFT AND RIGHT OPPOSITIONS AT THE TOP OF BOURGEOIS-STATE-CAPITALISM)

```
          +-------------[TOTALITARIAN-MICRO-FACIST-OLIGARCHICAL-NETWORKS ]-----------+
          |                               |                                          |
          |   LEFT                        |                        RIGHT             |
          v                         _____|_____                                   v
                                    |  THE WORKFORCE  |
          UNIONS,         +         |                 |                   + MEGA-CORPORATIONS
          THE         -------->[ THE WILL TO POWER] <----------- AND THE CHURCH
          STATE AND ITS +         |                 |                   + OR ORGANIZED
          INSTITUTIONS            |  THE POPULATION |                     RELIGIONS
          ^                       +-----------------+                                ^
          |                               |                                         |
          |                               |                                         |
          +--[STATIC-FORMATIONS]-- [THE LOGIC OF CAPITALISM]--[DYNAMIC-FORMATIONS]---+
```

26.d) The logic of capitalism informs and permeates all aspects of bourgeois-state-capitalism, in and across its political-economic framework. This framework in theory is a hardline-totalitarian-state, but in practical reality it is not. Notwithstanding, with the advent of post-industrialism, post-modernism, and sophisticated, mass communication technology, it is increasingly implementing its own form of totalitarianism, within the micro-recesses of everyday life, namely, within our everyday realities.

26.e) The unity of opposites at the top of the socio-economic hierarchies, i.e., pyramid, is the area where synthesis is most obvious and pervasive, between the left and the right, between the ruling, micro-fascist, oligarchical networks, that is, the state-finance-corporate-aristocracy.

26.f) The present political-economic system is structured akin to a pincer, where either the left or right of the pincer plays the good or the bad in relation to the other, and in relation to who holds the synthesis position, i.e., governing authority. Both sides of the political-spectrum are in fact one, in relation to the structure and form of the political-economic framework, in general. Liberalism and conservatism, within the confines of bourgeois-state-capitalism, are two oscillating sides of the same capitalist logic. When liberalism holds governing power, liberalism tends to strive to limit and slow capitalist development, while freeing the workforce/population, mildly, from the pressures of capitalist development. When conservatism holds governing authority, conservatism tends to strive to de-limit and augment capitalist development. It tends to stimulate and control the workforce/population so as to maximize capitalist development, namely, capitalist profit.

26.g) Within the parameters of bourgeois-state-capitalism, politics is a dialectic of dualities and reciprocities, between liberalism and conservatism, first and foremost, to satisfy the logical necessities of the logic of capitalism, by any means necessary, and secondly, to meet the minimum requirements, needed to satisfy the logical necessities of the workforce/population and nature, which tend to always come last.

    (<u>Note</u>: The minimum requirements are variable and tend to change when the needs and demands of the workforce/population increase, or decrease. Antagonism is imperative for the workforce/population in its relations with the logic of capitalism as it sustains its acceptable levels of basic maintenance requirements.)

26.h) Within bourgeois-state-capitalism, liberalism and conservatism are reciprocal manifestations of each other and magnify via each other's influence. Liberalism and conservatism comprise the necessary unity and the superficial duality necessary for the logic of capitalism to exercise the capitalist pincer, which enables it to contextualize the workforce/population, within a singular totalizing, political-economic framework. That is, a framework designed solely for the accumulation and extraction of surplus value, i.e., for the maximization of profit.

26.i) This political-economic unity, derived from the liberal/conservative duality, is the point where politics and the economy connect and constitute each other as a state-finance-corporate-nexus, a nexus designed for profit-making, by means of an ever-increasing domination and exploitation of the workforce/population thru the totalitarian logic of capitalism. Consequently, bourgeois-state-capitalism, for all its pomp as the best socio-economic formation for freedom and individual prosperity, only exists as a means to facilitate the extraction and accumulation of surplus value, both from matter and from the workforce/population. And those blessed few, who denote and perform the necessities of the logic of capitalism, with utmost devotion and pragmatic commitment, are 1. to maximize profit, i.e., capital, by any means necessary, at the lowest financial cost, as soon as possible, and 2., are only to accomplish the bare minimum, pertaining to the basic maintenance requirements of the workforce/population and nature.

26.j) This is the logical fulcrum of the logic of capitalism, to maximize profit, by any means necessary, at the lowest financial cost, as soon as possible, while, only satisfying the minimum basic requirements of the workforce/population and nature. It is this simple maxim, this simple morality/amorality, i.e., logical nucleus, at the center of the capital/labor relation, which has engendered the transformation of rudimentary societies into an all-compassing, high-tech, post-industrial, post-modern, gridiron edifice, called: the military-industrial-complex. As a result, the ideational comprehensive framework of capitalism, is constantly engaged in a totalitarian, dialectical movement, between its mental and physical micro-formations and manifestations, so as to augment, intensify, and refine, its capitalist mechanisms and profit-making processes, which reproduce, develop and intensify its exploitative capitalist-logic, evermore, in and across all the micro-recesses of everyday life. The all-encompassing, capitalist, military-industrial-complex is a technocratic concentration camp, based upon and revolving around the logic of capitalism, wherefore, workforce/population is constantly coerced, both seductively and forcefully, to work, consume and distribute, incessantly, in the name of capitalist profit and private property. Indeed, for the workforce/population, every moment inside the capitalist military-industrial-complex is an orchestrated capitalist moment, an artificially-designed moment, namely, a moment of capitalist production, consumption, and distribution without end.

26.k) The paradox of this is that the logic of capitalism is inherently despotic and favors the accumulation, extraction and centralization of quantifiable surpluses, i.e., financial quantifiable capital, at the expense of utility and the general well-being of all, that is, the basic maintenance requirements of the workforce/population and nature. As a result, the despotic capitalist-logic manufactures its own explosive demolition through its own operational logic. Because, every time it manufactures a litany of bizarre, illogical, capitalist schemes, which have nothing to do, or very little to do, with utility and the general well-being of all, and in fact, have everything to do with unlimited monetary gain, i.e., capitalist exploitation, wealth and private property, the logic of capitalism inadvertently brings forth its antithesis, the logic of structural-anarchism. Therefore, capitalism is stimulating its own collapse and its own antithetic replacement, i.e., the logic of structural-anarchism, the more totalitarian, tyrannical, and refined, its capitalist logic and its capitalist mechanisms/processes become. In short, the logic of capitalism carries within itself the logic of its own replacement and its own demolition, namely, the logic of structural-anarchism.

Section Three:

<u>The Military-Industrial-Complex</u>:

(Bourgeois-State-Capitalism Is A Soft-Totalitarian-State,
Exercising Micro-Fascism And The Logic Of Capitalism)

27.a) The logic of capitalism unfettered and unbound strives for an ironclad, authoritarian, bourgeois-state-capitalism, i.e., a military-industrial-complex. That is, a form of socio-economic organization where control, surveillance and work in the service of surplus value extraction, centralization and accumulation is paramount, highly functionalist, highly technocratic and highly regimented. The capitalist, military-industrial-complex is not a welfare-state. It is a warfare-state, both internally against its citizenry and externally against its perceived enemies. As a result, the military-industrial-complex is perpetually in a state of crisis. That is, crises of its own design to augment capitalist profits and unintended crises of retribution due to its tyranny and ever-increasing domination, both at home and abroad. Disequilibrium is the primary, socio-economic condition of the all-encompassing, military-industrial-complex. It is always in flux and in a state of constant antagonism, both internally and externally.

27.b) The military-industrial-complex is a technocratic-administrative society, where, military-organization and industrial-production are synonymous, stationed at the core of all socio-economic processes, apparatuses, and mechanisms, in and across bourgeois-state-capitalism. In an effort to maximize profit and harness greater portions of the insatiable drive for ownership/knowledge of the workforce/population, the logic of capitalism has engendered the industrialization of civilization and the militarization of civilization, in and across all levels of the military-industrial-complex. The logic of capitalism has done this so as to maximize interchangeability, standardization, utility, division, systematization, and time-management of the workforce/population, which results in greater levels of accumulation, extraction and centralization of surplus value. Moreover, the extension of the parameters and mechanisms of industrialization, in and across all sectors of everyday life, have also resulted in the extension of the parameters and mechanisms of militarization, in and across all sectors of everyday life, both human and environmental. The point is to enslave humans and their creative-powers in service of ever-increasing capitalist profits. And, the point is to enslave the environment and its resources in service of ever-increasing capitalist profits. Consequently, today, bourgeois-state-capitalism has militarized and industrialized the sum of human relations and human forces into a universal capitalist mode of production, in and across, the military-industrial-complex. Wherefore, this totalitarian, military-industrial-complex functions and operates solely in service of the logic of capitalism, specfically, for the accumulation, extraction and centralization of surplus value. As a result, industrial logics and military logics are central components of post-industrial, post-modern, bourgeois-state-capitalism. They work in tandem to enslave humans and nature in service of capitalist development. These capitalist logics permeate all the networks, institutions, and stratums of everyday life, regimenting socio-economic relations, socio-economic forces, and socio-economic modes, according to the underlying, logical necessities of the logic of capitalism, the logic of capitalism being the basic, logical pivot of the military-industrial-complex. Therefore, the logic of capitalism is constantly at war with all alt-logics and/or counter-logics. Whether, cold or hot, these microscopic wars are all about the contextual supremacy of capitalism, as well as, the unlimited accumulation, extraction and centralization of surplus value. Firstly, the standing military-army is concerned with the defense of the military-industrial-complex, from outside threats, and in addition, with waging war in order to expand the capitalist parameters of the military-industrial-complex. Secondly, the social para-military-army, i.e., the police-forces etc., are concerned with defending the military-industrial-complex, from inside threats, and in addition, with regimenting all internal deviances, according to the logic of capitalism. The social para-military-army is comprised of all the police-forces, judicial institutions, and the various surveillance apparatuses, directed at all the oppositional forces, in and across, the military-industrial-complex. Specifically, the anti-capitalist forces and the anti-capitalist logics, which might overthrow the logic of capitalism, both materially and conceptually. As a result, the military-industrial-complex is comprised of both mental and physical, punitive-mechanisms and disciplinary-mechanisms, which are designed to regulate, assimilate and/or terminate deviations, whether, softly or violently, in the name of the bourgeois-capitalist status quo and the logic of capitalism.

27.c) The military-industrial-complex is the pinnacle of capitalist development and the logic of capitalism. It can be infinitely refined and developed into a plethora of stratums with an emphasis on the expansion and amplification of the logic of capitalism, namely, the extraction, centralization and accumulation of surplus value, that is, capitalist profit, capitalist power, capitalist wealth and capitalist private property.

27.d) Notwithstanding, the military-industrial-complex is seemingly fragmented, but, in fact, is a connected series of micro-dictatorships, a network of networks, seemingly independent institutions, organizations, and mega-corporations, functioning in a dictatorial fashion, within the limited parameters of their autocratic influence. To work for a corporation is synonymous to working for a government institution, either/or, each functions in the same fashion, rewards, and disciplines, in the same fashion etc. These micro-dictatorships are like any communist dictatorship, a one-network or one-party rule, where, you have a board and a chairman dictating how the company, government institution and/or organization shall function and progress. Employees have relatively little to no-say and must find their own way to exist, survive and thrive under the rule of their cult-like, micro-dictatorial Leader/CEO/Minister, who, himself or herself, must conform to the logical necessities of the logic of capitalism, or perish, under the unstoppable juggernaut of the coercive laws of capitalist competition.

27.e) All the same, the plethora of micro-dictatorships embodied within the military-industrial-complex is over-arched by a set of micro-fascist, oligarchical networks, which fully embody the logic of capitalism and determine the majority of socio-economic decisions for society at large. This ruling set of networks is comprised of a multi-varied set of interconnected boards of director, CEOs, politicians etc., which are held together by the logic of capitalism. This a state-finance-corporate-aristocracy. And, it is organized to maximize profit, by any means necessary, at the lowest financial cost, as soon as possible, while, only satisfying the minimum basic requirements of the workforce/population and nature.

-[28]-

28.a) The military-industrial-complex as the contemporary socio-economic paradigm of all developed countries is best described as a giant, hi-tech, socio-economic ant-colony, which is both physical and mental, and which extends beyond the limits of our traditional understanding of the military-industrial-complex. That is, of what such a complex is and comprises of. This giant, all-encompassing, hi-tech, socio-economic ant-colony is a military-industrial-complex, i.e., a type of all-encompassing socio-economic organization that unites all mental/physical activities of civilization and organizes them according to the logical necessities of the logic of capitalism. It is a socio-economic form of organization, where militarization and industrialization sit at the heart of decision-making-authority, informing how everything is to be organized, i.e., education, politics, commerce, culture etc.; the point is to manufacture, both materially and conceptually, totalitarian, micro-fascist, bourgeois-capitalism, indefinitely. As a result, the military-industrial-complex has as its ideal the ant-colony in the sense that humans are free only to the extent that their insatiable drives for ownership/knowledge are organized, regimented and conform to the logical necessities of bourgeois-state-capitalism. Increasingly, the workforce/population is subjected to military-forms of organization akin to an ant-colony. As well, bourgeois-state-capitalism is increasingly dependent on free activity, or increasingly on smaller minimum wage activities in order to realize the inherent demands for maximum profit, commanded by the logic of capitalism. The military-industrial-complex is increasingly like a global ant-colony in the sense that in order to continually increase the accumulation and extraction of surplus value, it must increasingly regiment the workforce/population and abandon all forms of utility in favor of surpluses, namely, financial quantifiable capital, i.e., capitalist profit and private property. It must increasingly appropriate and control deviations of the workforce/population into its profit-making, socio-economic processes, while, increasingly minimizing free access to all basic maintenance requirements by the workforce/population. The military-industrial-complex is an open air prison, without walls, where humans are predominantly regimented mentally and organized physically, according to the dictates of capitalism. Humans are free to work, according to the dictates of capitalism; free to consume, according to the dictates of capitalism; free to express themselves, according to the dictates of capitalism; free to relate, according to the dictates of capitalism. Because, all thoughts and actions, seemingly free, are increasingly regimented along the acceptable lines of the bourgeois-capitalist status quo and the logic of capitalism. Not to follow guarantees marginalization, censorship, poverty, unemployment, discipline and punishment etc. That is, bureaucratic exclusion from any career advancement and decision-making-authority, due to the fact that all forms of socio-political deviations are increasingly intolerable to the micro-fascist, bourgeois-capitalist status quo. The logic of capitalism must be safeguarded, expanded, and refined, it must constantly increase capitalist wealth, nothing must impeded the logic of capitalist socio-economic development, nothing.

28.b) No longer are humans solely producers of commodities but humans are as well consumers, consuming the very commodities they produce on a mass scale for the purpose of realizing surplus value, a surplus value that only a select few benefit from. Useful commodities and services are increasingly cast aside in the name of immediate financial gain and quantifiable surplus.

28.c) Consumption is now a type of social work added to the human workday. The addition of physical consumption to physical production occurs, relatively, around the end of World War II, whereupon the military-industrial-complex expanded physical production to include physical consumption, which was attached to human activity, namely, the workforce/population. The 20th century added physical consumption to 19th century physical production. It was mass consumption added to mass production. However, early in the 21st century physical consumption and physical production have now, themselves, undergone an additional expansion and revolution, within the military-industrial-complex and the arrival of the digital information age. With the advent of the World-Wide-Web, and social media networks etc., roughly between 1993 to 2008, the military-industrial-complex established the capacity to totally incorporate the sum of human activity, i.e., the workforce/population, within the parameters of its totalitarian dominion, designed strictly for the accumulation and extraction of surplus value, i.e., capitalist profit.

28.d) Today, on the back of physical production and physical consumption has sprung mental production and mental consumption. Today, the military-industrial-complex has congealed, ossified, and universalized, itself, into an all-encompassing, soft-totalitarian-state, where all aspects of human life and the workforce/population are organized, monitored, and/or incorporated in sustaining, developing, and expanding, bourgeois-state-capitalism, i.e., the military-industrial-complex and the logic of capitalism.

28.e) The military-industrial-complex of bourgeois-state-capitalism is an amalgam of 4 types of mental and physical activity:

The Military-Industrial-Complex/The Global Workshop:

```
Mental Production   | Physical Production
-------------------------------------------
Mental Consumption  | Physical Consumption
```

Within, all-encompassing bourgeois-state-capitalism, conceptual production and conceptual consumption rest at the base of the military-industrial-complex in the sense that individuals must first and foremost brand themselves, i.e., produce themselves as concept and continually reproduce themselves as concept. Furthermore, humans must conceptually consume the individual brands/concepts of other fellow citizens in an effort to keep pace with the ever-changing mind-scape and body-scape of the digital information age and the police-state of the military-industrial-complex.

28.f) It is in this regard, that the logic of capitalism now functions and operates in the micro-recesses of everyday life, where the fronts of struggle are no longer on a mass scale as in the past. The many mass struggles of bygone eras have been fragmented into microscopic skirmishes across the stratums of bourgeois-state-capitalism. These micro-skirmishes present themselves in all sorts of systemic grievances such as the war of words that break out in the tweeter-sphere or occupy movements etc. All in all, these micro-skirmishes present themselves in the daily decisions and actions humans make every day in their daily lives across the stratums of the military-industrial-complex. These micro-skirmishes present themselves in the daily attempts by humans to realize the underlying logic of capitalism.

28.g) This twofold development in production and in consumption, from the physical to the mental has created a surplus of unemployment, i.e., a mass of individuals capable of high-tech., efficient and functional work, who have a desire to work, but cannot find work, due to the fact that physical production and physical consumption is no longer a central necessity for bourgeois-state-capitalism. The result is economic slavery and debt slavery of all types and kinds, the product of mental production and the post-industrial abolition of labor-time as the basis of value, price and wage.

28.h) The logic of capitalism puts individuals out of work to the extent that it increasingly needs individuals to enter the conceptual-workforce, i.e., to mentally produce and mentally consume conceptual-commodities, wage-free, hence the term economic wage-slavery and its aftermath, debt slavery.

28.i) Economic wage-slavery becomes increasingly the rule as the logic of capitalism puts humans out of traditional work to the extent that it overworks a select few, comprised in its traditional workforce. Economic slavery is the subjugation and domination of the workforce/population, piecemeal, so it has to work and sell its labor-power, regardless, either for a small wage and/or for free. Economic slavery is an appropriate term, when it is realized that only a fraction of daily human activities are considered to merit a wage, despite the fact that many of these zero-wage activities are vital to the contextual supremacy of capitalism, i.e., the accumulation and extraction of surplus value.

For example, the deliberate over-production of university graduates results in the fact that many graduates do not find traditional employment. As a result, these graduates fill-in the zero-wage activities of mental production and mental consumption, which are necessary for the accumulation and extraction of surplus value. For instance, someone must do the child-rearing during the traditional workday. Someone must watch the 24-hour television channels of capitalist indoctrination during the traditional workday. Someone must watch the commodity commercials during the traditional workday. Someone must tweet and/or face-book during the traditional workday in order to sustain social media popularity and profit making. Someone must shop-online and traffic through web-sites during the traditional workday etc. Subsequently, it is these zero-wage workers, central to post-industrial, post-modern capitalism, and the digital information economy, which mentally produce, consume, and distribute, the vast array of conceptual-commodities 24-7, researching conceptual-products, writing conceptual-product reviews, liking or disliking things, clicking on this or that, testing website functionality and being an unlimited source of information gathering etc. Post-industrial, post-modern capitalism, with its vast storehouse of zero-wage workers, is increasingly becoming the backbone of bourgeois-state-capitalism, due to its dependence on zero-wage activities. The vast majority of these activities, which are central to maintaining and developing bourgeois-state-capitalism, are free and devoid of financial benefits for the zero-wage workers. It is work, without financial benefit, and work, without social status, but, work which extracts and accumulates capitalist surplus value for a select few, hence, the socio-economic slavery in post-industrial, post-modern capitalism. That is, the zero-wage, mental/physical production, consumption and distribution supporting and developing the military-industrial-complex, free of charge.

28.j) When the parameters of this traditional, generative ant-colony and/or workshop, where, the wellspring of surplus value resides, were expanded into an all-encompassing military-industrial-complex, it is not a stretch to make the rational argument that the context of what activities merit a wage should as well have expanded beyond the traditional limits of the traditional, generative ant-colony and/or workshop. As, the wellspring of surplus value expanded, as well, should the wellspring of financial wages have expanded. Today, surplus value can come from any micro-sector of the military-industrial-complex, thus in turn, should a guaranteed living wage also follow suit.

-[29]-

29.a) Taking a closer look and descending into the epicenter of the all-encompassing military-industrial-complex, one sees every logical unit, human or otherwise, as processing material and/or as an embodiment/manifestation of the logic of capitalism, ready to be processed and/or ready to be plugged into the interchangeable systems of bourgeois-state-capitalism. Within the military-industrial-complex, each logical unit, or a specific, insatiable drive for ownership/knowledge, is designed and destined for the cyclical, repetitive, processes and patterns, which expand, sustain, and protect, capitalist accumulation, extraction and centralization, indefinitely.

29.b) Within the parameters of the military-industrial-complex, every logical unit has value only to the extent that these units supply the necessary processing materials for the capitalist system and/or are suitable plug-ins, or cogs, when other units/cogs deteriorate and/or malfunction, beyond the acceptable systemic standards of bourgeois-state-capitalism. These capitalist systems are both mental and physical.

29.c) Within the military-industrial-complex, the many humans, or insatiable drives for ownership/knowledge, are shaped and coerced, both softly and sternly, to work, i.e., to produce, consume, and distribute, mentally and physically, in service of capitalist accumulation, extraction and centralization. Everything and everyone is under surveillance, is regimented and/or is attempting to survey and/or regiment in order to construct and amplify his or her own authority in order to establish his or her own realm of capitalist influence and governing power. The military-industrial-complex is a competitive survival of the fittest arena. Where, those who embody and exercise the logic of capitalism to its fullest extent struggle to ascend to the level of the ruling, micro-fascist, oligarchical networks, which are composites of capitalist entities, who represent, own, plan, and enact, the logic of capitalism onto others, from high above, in the name of the man, but in benefit of a select few.

29.d) Privatization is the primary mechanism by which the logic of capitalism structures and intensifies the workforce/population, across the military-industrial-complex, due to the fact that privatization engenders artificial scarcity and competition. Artificial scarcity and competition are after-effects of privatization, i.e., primitive accumulation. Privatization is the result of the appropriation of matter and property, by the logic of capitalism, for its own purposes, via military conquest and/or economic conquest. Privatization engenders a state where the basic maintenance requirements of the workforce/population are wrestled away from it, by a set of capitalist entities. Subsequently, this set of capitalist entities, now victorious, then, capitalizes on the newly appropriated wealth, i.e., basic necessities, by holding these very basic necessities as incentives over a deprived workforce/population, forcing them to conform to the logic of capitalism, for their basic survival. Consequently, through privatization and the creation of artificial scarcity and competition, the logic of capitalism divides and organizes the workforce/population into a military-industrial-complex, bent on capitalist profit. That is, a large-scale, socio-economic formation, where members of the workforce/population are united and divided against each other, via ruthless competition, forced to capitalize upon socio-economic, profit-opportunities, in service of the logic of capitalism and their own survival. The logic of capitalism, and its material manifestation, the military-industrial-complex, are structured and designed to batter-down all oppositions to unlimited privatization, i.e., the extraction and accumulation of capitalist profit, the root of artificial scarcity and competition. The reason for this is to give, the best representatives and embodiments of the logic of capitalism, i.e., the ruling, micro-fascist, oligarchical networks, the opportunity to own everything and anything. Hence, the reason why the logic of capitalism seeks to incorporate all physical/mental forces, within the capitalist framework of privatization, artificial scarcity and ruthless competition. That is, so capitalist entities can satisfy the logic of capitalism, i.e., maximize profit, by any means necessary, at the lowest financial cost, as soon as possible. Privatization, artificial scarcity, and competition, perfect the military-industrial-complex. That is, they perfect the socio-economic processes of capitalism, namely, capitalist technology, capitalist-institutions, capitalist-mechanisms, and the capitalist modes of production, consumption, and distribution, in general.

29.e) The very notion of competition in society is the product of the logic of capitalism, where there must be competition, or warfare, between groups of the workforce/population in order to generate maximum profit. This warfare between groups is determined by the logic of capitalism, i.e., the logic, which holds contextual supremacy. And, the logic of capitalism divides the workforce/population along racial, gender, economic lines etc., or any other divisional manners it so chooses. The military-industrial-complex utilizes capitalist privatization, competition, and artificial scarcity, as its basic mechanisms for capitalist progress, expansion and refinement. In fact, capitalist privatization, competition, and artificial scarcity, manufacture new manifestations of capitalist privatization, competition, and artificial scarcity, continuously. This burgeoning of capitalist privatization, competition, and artificial scarcity, expands, validates, and legitimizes, also, the burgeoning bureaucratic, state-institutions of capitalism, which are forever called upon by the workforce/population to alleviate and administer capitalist privatization, competition and artificial scarcity. These constant petitions, by the workforce/population, to alleviate and administer capitalist privatization, competition, and artificial scarcity, are answered, by capitalism, with the minimum of basic maintenance requirements, nothing more. As a result, the military-industrial-complex has been bureaucratized, to such a radical extent and expanse, via capitalist privatization, competition, and artificial scarcity that the workforce/population is now totally organized, programmed, and hierarchized, in keeping with the perpetual amelioration and expansion of the military-industrial-complex, that is, the logic of capitalism. There is no longer an outside to bourgeois-state-capitalism. It is totalitarian. It is despotic.

-[30]-

30.a) In consequence, everything within the military-industrial-complex is based on interchangeability, standardization, utility, division, systematization, and the stop-watch, i.e., time-management. The point is to expand and refine, i.e., ameliorate, interchangeability, standardization, utility, division, systematization, and time-management, in and across all stratums of the military-industrial-complex so as to maximize profit, by any means necessary, at lowest financial cost, as soon as possible, while, only satisfying the minimum necessary requirements of the workforce/population.

30.b) The functional and operational moorings of the military-industrial-complex are:

1. The Principle of Interchangeability.
2. The Principle of Standardization.
3. The Principle of Utility.
4. The Principle of Division, i.e., hierarchy and dissection.
5. The Principle of Systematization, i.e., schematization and quantification.
6. The Principle of Time-Management.

30.c) These principles derive from the instrumental-rationality of capitalism which governs the military-industrial-complex. These principles shape and form all aspects of the military-industrial-complex via instrumental-rationality. Moreover, determining the success and/or failure in applying these principles, in and across the military-industrial-complex, is based on the instrumental-rationality of capitalism and the maximization of profit, by any means necessary, at the lowest financial cost, as soon as possible. The point is only to satisfy the minimum necessities of the workforce/population.

30.d) The success or failure of these principles is determined by the simple guideline: "whatever serves the logical necessities of the logic of capitalism best is right, regardless in the last instance, the means by which these ends are accomplished."

30.e) In order to achieve and maximize this simple guideline, bourgeois-state-capitalism has transformed itself into a military-industrial-complex, i.e., a soft-totalitarian-state, where, everything and everyone is increasingly molded, pressured and compelled to abide by the logic of capitalism in ever-increasing insideous manners of servitude, domination and enslavement.

–[31]–

31.a) The military-industrial-complex is a soft-totalitarian-state in the sense that, 1., it surveys, regiments, and controls, everything within its dominion down to its minute possible detail. 2., It exercises a variety of strategies and tactics to marginalize and neutralize any counter, and alternative, positions and/or viewpoints to its rule in an effort to regiment all deviations of the workforce/population into capitalist production, consumption and distribution. For the most part, the soft-totalitarian-state is not heavy handed, although it can be, if threatened enough, its disciplinary-mechanisms are soft and/or hard, depending on the degree of deviance from the capitalist status quo. Its surveillance is total but its presence is rarely overt as the soft-totalitarian-state has variable leeway, i.e., tolerance. This tolerance is not based on any generosity or understanding of the other, it is based on maximizing profit, due to the fact that the workforce/population requires a certain minimum leeway in order to function and operate, effectively, according to the dictates of the logic of capitalism.

31.b) The military-industrial-complex is a soft-totalitarian-state in the sense that it will not automatically incarcerate, or eliminate, outright oppositions to its rule, but it will go to various extents to censor, discipline, punish, neutralize etc., oppositions to its rule in an effort to reincorporate, deviant, elements of the workforce/population, back into the capitalist system. In reality, truth and fairness is inconsequential to the soft-totalitarian-state, its aim is always to retain contextual supremacy, increase political-economic control, and manufacture political-economic consent, at any cost. Truth, understanding and fairness is again not based on any generosity or understanding of the other, instead, it is based on a capitalist pragmatism, focused on maximizing profit. Meaning, the workforce/population is given certain minimum leeway because the workforce/population requires certain minimum leeway in order to function and operate, effectively, according to logical imperatives of the logic of capitalism.

31.c) The military-industrial-complex is a soft-totalitarian-state in the sense that, despite possessing the characteristics and mechanisms of hardline-totalitarian-states, it is flexible and able to vary its disciplinary measures, depending on the nature of the societal transgression and deviance.

31.d) The six factors for hardline-totalitarian-states are:

1.   There must be an official logic and/or ideology that must be obeyed, regardless of circumstances. This logic/ideology must embody the promise of social perfection.

2.   There must be a centralized network that controls the armed forces, both the social army, i.e., police-forces, and the standing regular army, i.e., the air force, ground force etc.

3.   There must be a centralized network that controls mass communication and mass dissemination within society.

4.   There must be a centralized network that controls the entire economy.

5. There must be a single political party, hierarchically organized and intimately interconnected with every aspect of the state's bureaucracy and its control of the workforce/population.

6. There must be a totalizing system of police-control and repression.[2]

These six qualities provide a basis for determining the extent of totalitarianism within a society. Although, not a hardline-totalitarian-state, per se, bourgeois-state-capitalism, nevertheless, exhibits many of the characteristics of hardline-totalitarian-states. In essence, it is a soft-totalitarian-state, embodying a military-industrial morality/amorality, exercised through a litany of bureaucratic fanatical processes and technocratic fascist applications, namely, processes and applications of micro-fascism:

1. There is an official logic and/or ideology within bourgeois-state-capitalism, which promises and strives for social perfection. This logic/ideology at the center of western societies is the logic of capitalism, which must be obeyed, regardless of circumstances. This logic/ideology promises and strives for social perfection across the globe. It is totalitarian, with totalitarian aspirations, designed to extend its dominion and its logic/ideology across all global territories.

2. There is a centralize network that controls the armed forces. First and foremost, within the parameters of the military-industrial-complex, the standing army is directly under the control of the state, i.e., an oligarchical network, which directs all-operations, all-workings and all-hierarchies of the standing army. Secondly in the past, the social army, i.e., the various institutional-police-forces, policing society internally were, more or less, loosely autonomous. However, since 2001 these various institutional-police-forces have been increasingly integrated into a cohesive unity, sharing information and hierarchy, both at home and abroad. More importantly, these institutional-police-forces have been integrated directly into a centralized state-political-apparatus, which is able to govern and survey everything itself, at the local levels, national levels and the international levels of the military-industrial-complex. The state, the social army and the standing regular army appear to be functioning and operating as a unitary totalitarian force, across western societies, communicating, coordinating, and manufacturing, a legal framework to legitimize, refine, and further extend, the global totalitarian influence of the logic of capitalism, including the total subjugation of humans, par excellence. Ultimately, this cohesive, totalitarian, police-state, based on the logic of capitalism, is in actuality a soft-totalitarian, military-industrial-complex, both unified and diffused, private and public, conceptual and material etc., which functions and operates across the stratums of everyday life, according to varying degrees of firmness. Notwithstanding, the objective of the soft-totalitarian-state is always to manufacture a litany of docile, obedient technocratic-ideological cogs, clucking together in unison, the latest state-approved platitudes, celebrating the capitalist, neoliberal status quo.

3. There is a centralized network that controls mass communication and mass dissemination systems within western societies. Since the 1970's there has been a continued refinement and whittling-down of independent, mass communication organizations and mass dissemination organizations. Today, there are roughly 5 to 20 mega-corporations. These mega-corporations are part of a centralized set of ruling, micro-fascist, oligarchical networks, which are closely interwoven with the state, permitting them to the control of the lion-share of mass communication and capital, i.e., capitalist profits and private property. Media convergence is term used to describe this increasing totalitarian control of the mass media.

4. There is not a centralized mega-network controlling the entire economy. There is a centralize set of ruling, micro-fascist, oligarchical networks influencing the entire economy. This is a small minority. Notwithstanding, there is autonomous, independent, economic opportunity, within the parameters of the military-industrial-complex, however, these opportunities are dwindling as surplus value accumulates in the hands of a select few nodes, points and centers, in and across the globe, namely, within the micro-fascist, oligarchical networks.

5. Western societies are not one-party-states. Instead, there is a set of political-parties, i.e., networks of two or more parties, who are hierarchically

----

2. Carl Friedrich and Zbigniew Brzezinski. Totalitarian Dictatorship and Autocracy. Cambridge, MA: Harvard U.P., 1965. (Note: This text supplied the 6 principles for defining a soft-totalitarian-state.)

organized, who share political power, and who are intimately interconnected with every aspect of the state-bureaucracy and its control of the workforce/population, which also includes the economy. For western societies, politics is a centralized set of ruling, micro-fascist, oligarchical networks, where voting is determined by the parameters set in place, beforehand, by the ruling, micro-fascist, oligarchical networks, whereupon, voting choice is limited, highly screened, and in many instances, predetermined by these ruling, micro-fascist, oligarchical networks, which governs the military-industrial-complex. The bourgeois-capitalist notion of one-person = one-vote, every 4 years, is a highly controlled state of affairs. Each citizen has the opportunity to vote for a party or representative; however, this is a highly limited choice, the choice of a select few engendered by a select few. Western democracies structure their political process akin to a choice between sodas, Pepsi, Coke, Orange Crush, Mountain Dew etc., whatever, the choice a citizen makes, this citizen is getting a soda, regardless. This is the political essence of the military-industrial-complex and, so-called, bourgeois-state-capitalism, i.e., limited choice packaged within the constructed illusion of democratic openness and democratic inclusion. It is in this regard that bourgeois-state-capitalism is a soft-totalitarian-state in the sense that its politics is un fait accompli, even before any election has transpired. Regardless, who wins or who loses, the maximization of profit, must go unchallenged, unquestioned, while, the minimum, basic, maintenance requirements of the workforce/population must remain as is or decrease. In fact, the political-economic framework of bourgeois-state-capitalism is engineered in such a way as to maximize profit, by any means necessary, at the lowest financial cost, as soon as possible, while, only fulfilling the minimum, basic, maintenance requirements of the workforce/population. That is, to pacify, placate and settle, at the lowest minimum levels, the basic maintenance necessities of the workforce/population, namely, there necessities for self-determination, community and pragmatic egalitarianism.

6. Like hardline-totalitarian-states, there is a totalizing system of police-control and repression, within the parameters of the military-industrial-complex.
Since 2001, there is an increasingly totalitarian system of police-surveillance and repression, in and across the stratums of the military-industrial-complex. Surveillance and repression are now theoretically total and full of nuances. Moreover, this surveillance and repression continues to be increasingly developed and expanded into, greater and greater, areas of everyday life. Police-control, surveillance and repression are continually being perfected and unified into a centralized state-apparatus. Notwithstanding, despite being totalitarian, capitalist surveillance and repression are multi-varied and based on the degree of deviation, from the status quo. There are now a multitude of disciplinary-mechanisms and punitive-mechanisms, in place, across the military-industrial-complex, able to exercise degrees of soft and hard corrective measures, depending on the nature of the transgression. The reason for this plurality in disciplinary-mechanisms and punitive-mechanisms is because the logic of capitalism must allot a certain minimum leeway to the workforce/population, so as to maximize capitalist production, consumption and distribution, through seemingly free-market exchanges and free-market transactions. The second reason for this plurality of disciplinary-mechanisms and punitive-mechanisms, including a guaranteed minimum leeway, is the fact that flexibility and leeway permits the workforce/population to function and operate, effectively, according to the logic of capitalism. It gives the workforce/population leeway to digest the logic of capitalism, according to their own specific, individual capacities, with abit of liberty, but, it is a highly-monitored and a highly-policed form of liberty.

32.a) Within the parameters of the soft-totalitarian-state, Antonio Gramsci's notion of "Hegemony" is no longer applicable in the sense that all aspects of society are now subjugated in service of bourgeois-state-capitalism. Today, there is no longer an outside to the logic of capitalism as a soft-totalitarian-state is a totalitarian form of rule. Albeit, this totalitarian rule is not totally obdurate. It is elastic. It is soft in nature, but it is still all-encompassing. In post-industrial, post-modern, bourgeois-state-capitalism, "hegemony" has mutated into a soft totalitarianism. This totalitarianism is like a rubber band, a rubber band, which encompasses the total sum of socio-economic modes, relations and forces, yet is still pliable and elastic in nature, capable absorbing the counter blasts of its anti-thesis, while, remaining fully intact. The soft-totalitarian-state bends but never breaks. It absorbs but never submits. It negotiates but never surrenders, due to the fact, its aim is an uneven balance between all positions and points of views, crushed beneath its overarching rule, beneath its essence, the capital/labor relation. Namely, the suppression and subordination of the workforce/population under the logic of capitalism, specifically, the agents of capitalism, i.e., the state-finance-corporate-aristocracy.

32.b) The reason a term like "hegemony" is outdated and that totalitarianism is a more appropriate term, is because within the confines of a soft-totalitarian-state everything is under surveillance and monitored, everything is subject to rationalization, exploitation, discipline and suppression. However, the difference between old forms of totalitarianism and the post-industrial, post-modern form of totalitarianism is that today totalitarianism is soft. Post-industrial, post-modern, totalitarianism is a framework of total knowledge, total surveillance and total discipline, like old forms of totalitarianism. However, unlike old forms of totalitarianism, the way the post-industrial, post-modern form of totalitarianism acts upon its total knowledge, total surveillance, and total discipline is soft and elastic in nature, subject to a variety of pliable disciplinary-mechanisms and punitive-mechanisms, which have various degrees of firmness. As a result, the soft-totalitarian-state is a state, where private life is under totalitarian surveillance, but is for the most part, subject to soft disciplines and soft punishments, depending on the deviation. Subsequently, the military-industrial-complex is not privy to "hegemony", it is a totalitarian form of socio-economic organization, which is soft and pliable, but nonetheless, it is unified, all-encompassing, and total. Soft-totalitarianism embodies a certain level of tolerance, but, only to better maximize capitalist profits.

–[33]–

33.a) Within the parameters of the military-industrial-complex, i.e., the soft-totalitarian-state, there are more punitive-apparatuses than ever before in the history of western civilization, there are more para-military organizations than at anytime in human history. Humans are more under scrutiny, surveillance and domination than any prior time and place in history. The Enlightenment promised the ideal that as people became more educated they would become more civilized and democratic. This has been shattered in the sense that as people have become more educated, they have become more suspect in relation to the workings of bourgeois-state-capitalism, the ruling, micro-fascist, oligarchical networks, and most importantly, their own neighbors. The reason is a strict emphasis on instrumental-rationality. As a result, humans have become more and more subject to domination and discipline, both by bourgeois-state-capitalism and their fellow citizens. In sum, the Enlightenment is totalitarian despotism and domination, par excellence.

33.b) All in all, the Enlightenment has not delivered on its promise that with specialized bureaucratic education, and a socio-economic emphasis on the logic of capitalism, society would shift, modernize, and become more humane, egalitarian and civilized. To the contrary, with increases in specialized bureaucratic education, technocratic science, and an emphasis on the logic of capitalism, society in fact has increased its militarization, industrialization, divisions, laws, punishments, bureaucracy, law-enforcement, punitive and disciplinary-mechanisms. And most importantly, there is an ever-increasing process of capitalist exploitation and domination, both concerning matter and concerning the workforce/population. Capitalist exploitation and domination has gone global and increasingly subjugates the micro-recesses of everyday life. In fact, the military-industrial-complex is the result of specialized bureaucratic education, technocratic science, and an emphasis on the logic of capitalism. Wherefore, the military-industrial-complex is now a totalitarian socio-economic formation, instrumentally engineered to maintain financial inequality, corporate feudalism, and the ruling, micro-fascist, oligarchical networks, i.e., the capitalist status quo, indefinitely.

33.c) In particular, science has degenerated to the level of technocratic-instrumental rationality. It has been subjugated and assimilated in service of the logic of capitalism and purged of all its Enlightenment ideals. And as a result, science is now primarily programmed to enhance systemic performance, meaning that it is programmed and organized to maximize technological development, technocratic development and the refinement of all the socio-economic processes of exploitation within bourgeois-state-capitalism. Science, subjugated to the logic of capitalism, functions and operates in order to refine and expand the principles of interchangeability, utility, standardization, division, systematization, and time-management, within the socio-economic processes of bourgeois-state-capitalism. It is programmed and organized for the quantification of the world and the amelioration of systemic performance. This is science's raison d'être within post-industrial, post-modern, bourgeois-state-capitalism. Performativity is its central criterion. As a result, individuality, identity and deep differences etc., are purged from the stratums and systems of bourgeois-state-capitalism in favor of superficiality, weightlessness, and the tabula rasa, par excellence, all of which is designed to enhance the performativity of bourgeois-state-capitalism. Wherever technocratic science dominates, it advances and manufactures nobodies, artificial superficialities, interchangeable units, disposable commodities, empty-individualities, empty-voices, empty-needs and empty-dreams, all streamlined into artificiality and superficiality, that is, state-approved constructs propagated, disseminated, and authorized, by the ruling, micro-fascist, oligarchical networks in service of the logic of capitalism. As a result, technocratic science has as its paradigm the maximization of systemic performativity so as to maximize the accumulation, extraction and centralization of surplus value.

33.d) Likewise, specialized bureaucratic education, technocratic science, and the socio-economic emphasis on the logic of capitalism, are making humans more authoritarian and machine-like in their thinking and in their actions. Beneath the veneer of perpetual political correctness, the language of speech and thought preaches tolerance, openness and acceptance, while, the language of action retains and enacts prejudices and bigotry as a systemic means for preventing individual, hierarchical, socio-economic advancement. For the political-economic framework of bourgeois-state-capitalism, socio-economic mobility must remain minimal and the status quo must remain unchanged, as much as possible, as socio-economic mobility and/or social change threaten the supremacy and stability of the ruling, micro-fascist, oligarchical networks, and ultimately, the logic of capitalism.

33.e) At the moment, the military-industrial-complex is organized and designed to prevent leaps of intellectual advancement and socio-economic advancement in favor of a degenerate, retrogressive, bureaucratic, average, capitalist status quo. Stasis is the preferable state of the military-industrial-complex and the logic of capitalism. Even, if stasis is in truth impossible, with the unstoppable progression of historical time, stasis is always the preferred condition for the logic of capitalism and the military-industrial-complex. Ultimately, the logical progression of things, the socio-economic order of things, must always remain the same. It must continue as is and in its current form in order to optimize the accumulation and extraction of surplus value. And if change should occur, as it inevitably does, due to the unstoppable progression of historical time, this change must be organized, administrated and managed, according to the logical necessities of bourgeois-state-capitalism, whether through an exceedingly slow and/or time-consuming bureaucratic process and/or a fast-pace bureaucratic process. Only social change that augments surplus value, the staying-power of the status quo, and in general, the logic of capitalism, in the immediate sense, is given permission to progress and/or to develop, unimpeded, at an accelerated pace. Contrarily, radical social change, which does not definitively and directly benefit bourgeois-state-capitalism, immediately, is consigned to the bureaucratic, disciplinary-mechanisms of the military-industrial-complex as expendable processing material, slated for processing, at a future date, when this type of social change is classified favorable and aligned with the instrumental-rationality of capitalism.

33.f) As a result, within the obdurate corridors of the post-industrial, technocratic, military-industrial-complex, the best and brightest do not necessarily rise, within capitalist hierarchies, due to the fact that the best and brightest of the workforce/population, by definition are unique, moral, creative, independent, and thus difficult to classify. They are different from the bourgeois-capitalist status quo, automatically, making these segments of the workforce/population suspicious and questionable in relation to the mechanical-workings of bourgeois-state-capitalism. In many instances, these divergent, atypical, segments of the workforce/population embody and produce radical social change, social change, which may not be necessarily favorable for the continued stability and contextual supremacy of bourgeois-state-capitalism. Consequently, these exceptional, segments of the workforce/population are continually subjected to the disciplinary and punitive-mechanisms of the military-industrial-complex, so as to limit and curtail their advancements, their independence, and their revolutionary capacities, which might possibly unsettle the ruling, micro-fascist, oligarchical networks, including the parameters of the military-industrial-complex. In sum, capitalism impedes mental and physical development.

-[34]-

34.a) Subsequently, in order to curtail the independence and the deviations of the workforce/population, the logic of capitalism has prompted the industrialization and the militarization of education and society, in general, along the lines of a mediocre bourgeois status quo. This was done to control the workforce/population, pertaining to the logic of capitalism. That is, to maximize profit and regiment the workforce/population, i.e., so many graduates per year, so many students per year, so many dollars per year, so many standardized tests per year, so many academic positions per year etc. The point is to fabricated and maintain a mediocre bourgeois status quo, ad infinitum. Consequently, the result is the radical functionalization, systematization and stratification of education and society, in general, according to dictates of bourgeois-state-capitalism, demanding conformity to the average, maudlin standards of bourgeois-capitalist mediocrity, i.e., the bourgeois status quo. As a result, there is the rampant development of a clear and definitive, capitalist set of pedagogic hierarchies, emphasizing bourgeois-mediocrity. In addition, this obdurate, capitalist set of pedagogic hierarchies have been given the administrative responsibility and duty, by the ruling, micro-fascist, oligarchical networks to eliminate from the capitalist system, in general, including the ranks and files of capitalist pedagogic hierarchies themselves, dissent, free thinking, critical thinking, academic autonomy, creativity, originality, and all knowledge advancements, which do not conform to the functional and ideological necessities of the military-industrial-complex, namely, the bourgeois-capitalist status quo. Ultimately, this is a general extermination process, inherent in and across the capitalist system. In the academic spheres, the sum of all capitalist pedagogic hierarchies, in and across the military-industrial-complex, from kindergarten to university graduate-studies etc., have been transformed, and are increasingly being transformed, into functional-ideological, rote-learning edification, with an emphasis on maintaining a lackluster bourgeois-mediocrity across all stratums of everyday life. The point is to fulfill the military and industrial requirements of the military-industrial-complex, i.e., the logic of capitalism, while, eliminating anything which might upset the mediocrity of the bourgeois-capitalist status quo.

34.b) The consequence of functional-ideological, rote-learning edification, i.e., education, is both radical specialization and micro-fascism in and across the military-industrial-complex:

1. Functional-ideological, rote-learning edification, manufactures an infinitely specialized workforce/population, technocratic-cogs, programmed with the logic of capitalism, who rightly and visibly understand that obedience is intelligence and intelligence is obedience. And, who with exceeding efficiency and resolve, eliminate all emotions, empathy, critique, dissent, and/or moral conflict within the socio-economic processes of the military-industrial-complex. Devoid of the capacity for critical thinking and independent thought, and innately programmed with the logic of capitalism, these micro-fascist technocratic-cogs concern themselves only with reinforcing the rules, the regulations, and the traditional status quo of bourgeois-state-capitalism, par excellence. Obedience is career advancement while critique is career suicide, the tell-tale sign of systemic disrespect and/or systemic disillusionment, all of which, must be eliminated from the socio-economic processes of bourgeois-state-capitalism. These technocratic-cogs are so completely stunted, so rooted in tradition, that these cogs seek to eradicate and extinguish all new intellectual and creative developments in the name of bourgeois-mediocrity and the bourgeois-capitalist status quo. These technocratic-cogs are the precious manufactured commodities of the bourgeois pedagogic hierarchy, well-versed in double-speak and ideological babbling. Indeed, these technocratic-cogs are designed to be ever-ready to be plugged into the socio-economic systems and processes, dotting the military-industrial-complex, ever-ready to pacify and pass judgment on truth and change in order to keep the workforce/population working, consuming and believing in the moral supremacy and the inevitability of the logic of capitalism and bourgeois-mediocrity.

2. Functional-ideological, rote-learning edification, manufactures micro-fascism, which is also a by-product of radical specialization in the micro-recesses of everyday life. Micro-fascism is the litany of small fanaticisms, within the socio-economic processes of bourgeois-state-capitalism, which are engaged in mini-skirmishes and administrative maneuvers to purge and streamline the conduits of the military-industrial-complex of all dissonance, emotions, empathy and/or critique. Ultimately, micro-fascism is about homogenizing the workforce/population, according to the logic of capitalism, into an ironclad, obdurate bourgeois status quo, i.e., bourgeois-mediocrity. Also, micro-fascism is an after-effect of radical specialization. That is, the radical specialization of work and life into smaller and smaller units of time and tasks at an ever-increasing speed. Compounded by the intensification of time-management, utility, interchangeability, standardization, division, and systematization, upon work and life, radical specialization manufactures a plethora of obdurate micro-fascisms, in and across everyday life, and in and across, the bodies of the workforce/population. These formal relationships are increasingly becoming hard-line, administrative, and machine-like, in their technocratic-instrumental rationale, in their performances, and in their relations to one another. The goal is always the same, conformity, obedience, and the extraction, accumulation, and centralization of surplus value, i.e., capitalist profit, private property and power.

34.c) Micro-fascism arises with the Über-Fordist organization of everyday life, where, the radical fragmentation of daily life, according to the logic of capitalism, engenders a military-industrial mindset in the workforce/population, where one must defend what capital one has accumulated, while, continually augmenting the sum and the influence this capital has upon others, in and across the military-industrial-complex. Radical specialization instills a subtle anxious paranoia over the workforce/population, an increasing pressure to keep up with the ever-changing, repetitive, capitalist cycles and phases of the soft-totalitarian-state, which are always designed to extract and accumulate surplus value, that is, to maximize capitalist profit and private property. If the workforce/population does not keep up, it risks its own obsolescence, both as a whole, via fully-automated technological machinery and artificial intelligence etc., or as a set of troublesome singularities, slated for idle unemployment, discipline, punishment and/or the abusive onslaught of bourgeois-herd mediocrity, i.e., those who obediently and mindlessly enforce the dictates of the state-finance-corporate-aristocracy.

34.d) The basis of the micro-fascisms', which dot the city-landscapes and work-stations of western capitalist countries, is the idea that every human is expendable and interchangeable, at any given moment. Due to the fact, there is an ever-increasing surplus of specialized unemployed workers, which, by their very existence, continually apply greater and greater pressures on the employed sectors of the workforce/population to conform to the fascist irrational dictates of bourgeois-capitalism.

34.e) Added to this, is the fact, there is an ever-increasing storehouse of technological mechanisms and machines encroaching evermore on the characteristics of work and life, which can render certain, specialized activities obsolete, if need be. These conditions, deliberately engendered by the socio-economic processes of bourgeois-state-capitalism, provide credence to the overwhelming pressure of the expendability and the interchangeability of workers. For example, closed-circuit-television could render the notion of a full-time university faculty obsolete, by the very fact that lectures on specific subject-matter could be given across provincial, national and/or international university campuses, by one or two state-approved professors, with an army of teaching assistants beneath them taking care of the daily, hands-on aspects of teaching etc. Students would only have to tune-in to their televisions on a weekly basis to receive their necessary course information and education, while, teaching assistants would take care of the rest. Consequently, these types of technological advancements, aspiring to eliminate troublesome sectors of the workforce/population, also inspire micro-fascism within the workforce/population, itself, which is increasingly positioned and thrown into survival of the fittest antagonisms. That is, capitalist forms of existence revolving around extreme competition and radical individualism. The reason is that the coercive laws of capitalist competition, increasingly short-circuited in the upper-echelons of the military-industrial-complex, due to crony-networking and an emphasis on bourgeois-herd mediocrity, are now evermore set free unto the workforce/population so as to grind-down the workforce/population evermore into micro-fascism and absolute docile obedience. Namely, a litany of microscopic hatreds and hard-line, right-wing, belief-systems, which ultimately, validate, buttress and legitimize neoliberal-state-institutions, including ever-greater encroachments into the micro-recesses of everyday life, by the military-industrial-complex, i.e., the bourgeois-capitalist-police-state. The objective is the production of orderly, docile obedience, in and across, everyday life by the workforce/population.

34.f) In general, micro-fascism is the zeitgeist and gestalt of post-industrial, post-modern, bourgeois-state-capitalism, where all functions and all operations, within the socio-economic formation/edifice, are increasingly designed to realize:

> an inhumane/inhuman age where there is an excessive totalitarian obsession with introducing ever new grades of rules, stratums, and regulations, while, enforcing the litany of rules, stratums, and regulations, new and outmoded, according to their exact and precise specifications, with a complete disregard for the individual and/or his or her well-being. For micro-fascism, all that is of consequence is the maximum performance of the logic of capitalism, the maintenance of the military-industrial-complex, the celebration of bourgeois-herd mediocrity, and the preservation of the ruling, neoliberal, bourgeois status quo, which includes, the capitalist-aristocracy. Consequently, micro-fascism impedes all developments, intellectual and/or physical, which might threaten, upset and/or run-counter, the neoliberal, bourgeois status quo, the capitalist-aristocracy and/or the logic of capitalism. In sum, micro-fascism is the underlying amoral-spirit, i.e., structure of feeling, unifying, all the capitalist processes, structures, and hierarchies, which prevent and/or stifle the free flow of information, institutional transparency, individual privacy, forward-thinking knowledges, freeing knowledges, collectivism and egalitarianism. Namely, all positive, radical social changes, which might liberate the workforce/population from capitalism and the tyranny of the military-industrial-complex, that is, the state-finance-corporate-aristocracy.

34.g) Micro-fascism is machine-like bureaucracy, processing mental and physical material through its computational-network-institutions without pity, without conscience, and without thought, with only the preservation, expansion and legitimacy of bourgeois-state-capitalism, i.e., the military-industrial-complex, and the ruling, bourgeois aristocracy as its basic end, and as end-in-itself. Micro-fascism is the anti-thesis to knowledge development and creative-power. It stifles instead of promoting.

34.h) In fact, micro-fascism is against all forms of knowledge development and creative-power, as knowledge development and creative-power are a threat to the supremacy and stability of bourgeois-state-capitalism, because, they represent radical social change. As a result, micro-fascism champions and celebrates re-statements and re-assertions of tradition and the bourgeois status quo. In contemporary art, this boils down to the celebration and the re-creation of past outmoded art-forms, i.e., neo-abstract-expressionists stuck in 1950's abstraction, re-creating 1950's abstractions in the 21st century etc., yet, hailed as innovators and leaders of contemporary, neoliberal bourgeois art, by the administrative bourgeois-institutions of contemporary art, despite being, in reality, retrogressive, conservative, artistically conformist, and utterly outdated. In a way, micro-fascism engenders cultural and historical amnesia, re-introducing the same old as new and revolutionary, via the shiny new branding and packaging designs and mechanisms of post-industrial, post-modern, bourgeois-state-capitalism.

34.i) Micro-fascism is false-consciousness, the process of thinking, saying and acting according to the immediate necessities of bourgeois-state-capitalism. In essence, micro-fascism is centrist conservatism, devoid of purpose, lest that purpose be simply to fashion the military-industrial-complex into an obdurate streamlined, socio-economic, hi-tech, generative ant-colony, homogenized and ideologically unified as one. Micro-fascism is technocratic-capitalist ideology, an arbiter of reality and factuality that taints the world of facts in order to turn everything into doubt, surplus value and/or in favor of the logic of capitalism and bourgeois-herd mediocrity.

34.j) Micro-fascism pragmatically constructs a reality based on nihilism, self-absorption, self-entitlement, self-aggrandizement and, most importantly, private property, radical individualism, profit and money. All in all, micro-fascism advances endless facsimiles, endless televised repetitions of its false-consciousness, examples to follow, heroes of the bourgeois-capitalist status quo, emblems of corporate-technocracy and the redundant pedagogic hierarchies of bourgeois-state-capitalism.

34.k) Ultimately, as zeitgeist and gestalt, micro-fascism is the zeal and the sardonic celebration, embodied in the self-glorification, self-legitimization and monologue of bourgeois-state-capitalism, ceaselessly duplicated and replicated at the micro-levels of everyday life, contaminating the workforce/population for its own mercenary capitalist benefits. If knowledge development and creative-power expenditures are to proceed, under micro-fascism, they must do so according to the logical necessities of the logic of capitalism. The contextual supremacy of bourgeois-capitalism must be maintained, expanded and obeyed, pure and simple, at any cost.

34.l) Micro-fascism can mutate into macro-fascism, given the right socio-economic conditions, due to the fact that bourgeois-capitalism is fundamentally a religious belief system, based on the maximization of profit, by any means necessary, at the lowest financial cost, as soon as possible. And, macro-fascism is an extreme manifestation of this bourgeois-capitalist religiosity, where everything and everyone must be subjected to the capitalist profit imperative, that is, exploited, administrated, and dominated in the name of capitalist profiteering. This capitalist profit imperative is often times interpreted in extreme forms, along racial/gender lines and legitimated and validated by the fact that capitalism commands and demands discrimination of all types and kinds. Fascists, micro and macro, are extreme capitalist zealots, who have broadened the capitalist profiteering imperative into all sorts of areas, both mental and physical, outside the economy. Namely, they are heroes of the bourgeois status quo, who have widened the capitalist profit imperative into cultural areas, in and across, the stratums of everyday life. German Nazism expressed a version of macro-fascism, which developed out of the dire, socio-economic conditions of the early 20th century, in and across Germany. German Nazism sought to regiment the sum of everyday life into a bourgeois-capitalist tyranny, i.e., totalitarian-bourgeois-capitalism. Ultimately, micro-fascism is more conducive to the logical necessities of bourgeois-state-capitalism. It fuels, effectively, the accumulation and extraction of surplus value, i.e., the maximization of profit, with certain religious zeal and devotion, required by the logic of capitalism, without fully-devolving into hardline macro-fascist totalitarianism. Micro-fascism is a military-industrial morality/amorality, manifested by the logic of capitalism, functioning and operating, in and across the socio-economic formation of the soft-totalitarian-state, softly and obdurately, setting-up socio-economic conditions for the centralization and maximization of private property, profit and power.

35.a) In consequence, as zeitgeist and gestalt, micro-fascism is hardwired into the mental and the physical circuits, systems and processes of the military-industrial-complex. Micro-fascism is the pragmatic rationale and structure of feeling of the ruling, micro-fascist, oligarchical networks, which permeates the stratums of the military-industrial-complex, and is sometimes mimicked in the micro-recesses of everyday life by some envious members of the workforce/population. Micro-fascism is present and operational wherever obedience is intelligence, ignorance is profitability, fear is respect and network-cronyism is meritorious. In fact, these maxims comprise the armature of micro-fascism and form the meritorious hierarchical standards of bourgeois-state-capitalism. Indeed, the armature of micro-fascism is utilized to measure the level of servitude and compliance of the workforce/population in relation to the logic of capitalism. The armature of micro-fascism is utilized to measure the level of servitude and compliance of the workforce/population in relation to the bourgeois-capitalist status quo, namely, all socio-economic hierarchies of the military-industrial-complex, commanding absolute conformity with bourgeois-mediocrity. Finally, the armature of micro-fascism outlines the dialectical-staircase, which leads to the ruling, micro-fascist, oligarchical networks, the armature of micro-fascism are the safety-valves and check-points safeguarding the ruling, micro-fascist, oligarchical networks, from revolutionary explosions and crisis.

35.b) The armature of micro-fascism is the general structure of feeling inherent across the stratums of the military-industrial-complex, it outlines the capitalist forces, the capitalist relations, and the capitalist mode of production, with certain obdurate fanaticisms, bigotries and jingoisms. The armature of micro-fascism is illustrated like this:

The Armature of Micro-Fascism

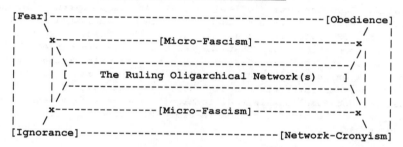

This framework is the means by which the ruling, micro-fascist, oligarchical networks of bourgeois-state-capitalism rule the military-industrial-complex, manufacture and control the workforce/population, disseminate the logic of capitalism, and accumulate and extract surplus value for their own selfish benefits. All movements up or down bourgeois-capitalist hierarchies, within the military-industrial-complex, by anyone and/or anything, is measured and analyzed by the inherent, systemic, armature of micro-fascism, which safeguards and supports the logic of capitalism and its ruling, micro-fascist, oligarchical networks, i.e., the best representatives and best material embodiments of the logic of capitalism from harm, crisis and/or revolutionary explosions.

35.c) 1. Network-cronyism is the means by which the ruling, micro-fascist, oligarchical networks rig socio-economic relations in their favor, for their own benefits. Network-cronyism is the means by which the ruling, micro-fascist, oligarchical networks override the parameters of capitalist-inclusive-democracy. Network-cronyism is the means by which the bourgeois-capitalist status quo is maintained and perpetuated, via collusion and machination, which assures the rightful winners are always stringent supporters of the bourgeois-capitalist status quo. Network-cronyism is a transparent glass ceiling, where visible illusions of career advancement are in fact highly controlled, micro-fascism processes, measuring, ranking, and/or purging the creative manifestations and surplus values of the workforce/population, according to the systemic necessities of bourgeois-state-capitalism.

2. Obedience is the means by which the ruling, micro-fascist, oligarchical networks, measure and determine intelligence and skill in relation to the acceptable, hierarchical standards of bourgeois-state-capitalism. Obedience is intelligence and intelligence is obedience in the sense that obedience and intelligence is a sign of reverence for the evident superiority of bourgeois-state-capitalism. And, obedience is intelligence in the sense that obedience and intelligence is a sign of understanding that time is money, and

that dissent and critique is expensive, wasteful, and not conducive towards the logical necessities of bourgeois-state-capitalism. As a result, obedience to the logical necessities of bourgeois-state-capitalism is indicative of intelligence and vice versa.

3. Fear is the means by which the ruling, micro-fascist, oligarchical networks determine respect for their supreme authority. Fear rivets the workforce/population to the logic of capitalism, fear focuses the workforce/population in service of bourgeois-state-capitalism, fear eliminates deviations in the workforce/population. Finally, fear is a product of propaganda, discipline, punishment, and the dramatization of reality, by the ruling, micro-fascist, oligarchical networks, so as to entrench bourgeois-capitalist ideology and bourgeois-capitalist versions of reality, within the workforce/population. Through fear, the ruling, micro-fascist, oligarchical networks entrench surveillance and police-mechanisms, ever-deeper into the micro-recesses of everyday life. The ruling, micro-fascist, oligarchical networks use fear to regiment, indoctrinate, and assimilate greater segments of everyday life and the workforce/population into the mechanical workings of the military-industrial-complex, utilizing these segments to benefit capitalism, in general. Fear of poverty, fear of unemployment, fear of marginalization and fear of death etc., rivet the workforce/population to the logic of capitalism, making sure revolutionary dissent and radical social change is minimized and, ultimately, extinguished.

4. Ignorance is the means by which the ruling, micro-fascist, oligarchical networks control the workforce/population. Ignorance is profitable in the sense that it is easily manipulated in the service of bourgeois-state-capitalism. It is easily indoctrinated, its reality is easily capable of being reduced to a black/white, right/wrong, yes/no, set of dichotomies. Consequently, the ruling, micro-fascist, oligarchical networks encourage ignorance, cherish ignorance, and champion ignorance, whenever and wherever, it is possible because ignorance is gullible, illiterate, radically specialized, suggestible, docile, passive, infantile, uncritical, quick to spend money, prone to doubt and, in many instances, can be instigated towards complete devotion for the logic of capitalism, i.e., religious micro-fascism. In fact, ignorance is such an important mode of control, that the radical specialization of all pedagogic capitalist hierarchies, and their increasing emphasis on functional-ideological, rote-learning edification, are all about manufacturing specialized ignorance, that is, radically specialized, obedient, technocratic-cogs. Specialized cogs, who despite their radically specialized and functionalist edification, are nonetheless, socially ignorant and unable to comprehend the broader bourgeois-capitalist processes organizing them, both mentally and physically.

35.d) The armature of micro-fascism permeates the military-industrial-complex and outlines the structures, the hierarchies and the socio-economic processes of bourgeois-state-capitalism, insulating the logic of capitalism and the ruling, micro-fascist, oligarchical networks, from revolutionary fervor and the pangs of the workforce/population, that is, the sum of the insatiable drives for ownership/knowledge embodied in the workforce/population, striving for collectivism, plurality, egalitarianism and post-modernism.

35.e) Micro-fascism is exactly what the logic of capitalism requires in order to construct, maintain and expand its influence and its profit-making machinery. This closed-system of fear, obedience, ignorance, and network-cronyism, freezing the workforce/population in its tracks, enables the development of systemic-control over greater sections of everyday life, by bourgeois-capitalism, while, at the same time, enabling the ever-increasing development of the logic of capitalism in and across everyday life, namely, all the capitalist mechanisms for the accumulation and the extraction of surplus value. In fact, via the paternalistic tutelage of micro-fascism, a dependent brainwashed flock of synchronized, babbling, self-entitled, ideological sycophants is manufactured and roams the earth. That is, a mindless herd of ape-like troglodytes, who are ever-ready to sing the praises of bourgeois-state-capitalism, while, being ever-ready to destroy all other socio-economic formations, which are antagonistic to, and/or differing from, the self-deluded perfection and spectacle-superiority of bourgeois-state-capitalism. The goal of these herds is to grind anything, or anyone, into bourgeois-herd mediocrity, wherefore, nothing ever changes and bourgeois-capitalism indefinitely remains.

-[36]-

36.a) In the arts, the armature of micro-fascism constructs connections and networks that congregate around publishing houses, art galleries, theaters, university disciplines etc., where nothing gets in or shown without the support and approval of the ruling networks. Today, great art, i.e., an articulate manifestation of the rational human spirit, is irrelevant, to be well-connected and good at networking is first and foremost. The eternal law is that "the network" must trump the rational human spirit in order for the workings of bourgeois-state-capitalism to persist and to expand. As a result, today, all contemporary art is filtered through state-endorsed networks which control the nodes of dissemination and presentation, and purge contemporary art of its revolutionary capabilities, capabilities which may threaten the status quo. The result is a litany of average, meaningless, lame, and bland art, which reflect the neoliberal tastes of bourgeois-state-capitalism and its administrators, who, due to the pressures and intensities of socio-economic production and capitalist consumption, have now become the neo-liberal peddlers of contemporary art. And because bourgeois-state-capitalism adheres ardently to the logic of capitalism, art is thus no longer adventurous, cutting edge and/or progressive in any manner. As a result, contemporary art has devolved into mediocrity even as it is saturated like never before in and across the stratums of everyday life.

36.b) Bourgeois-state-capitalism is solely designed to maximize profit, by any means necessary, and to meet the minimum necessary requirements of the workforce/population. As a result, contemporary art is merely a means and/or a tool, for bourgeois-state-capitalism, to maximize profit and to satisfy the minimum necessary requirements of the workforce/population. Subjugated in service of the military-industrial-complex, contemporary art becomes an indoctrination mechanism to maximize the logic of capitalism.

36.c) Today, contemporary art-networks, for the most part, buttress bourgeois-state-capitalism and are designed for bourgeois-state-capitalism purposes. They are designed to filter artistic critique, artistic dissent, politicization, artistic directness and revolutionary capabilities in favor of the status quo, that is, temperate artistic moderation, de-politicization, ambiguity, entertainment and, most importantly, network-connection. For instance, the jury process in the visual arts, although seemingly based on merit, is network based. It is pseudo-merit fashioned by bourgeois-capitalist networks for the benefit of those that comprise the inner sanctums of the ruling, micro-fascist, oligarchical networks, whereupon, a set of state-sponsored artistic networks select proponents from its networks for the jury and simultaneously for its winners. The end is always the same: 1. To advance and to buttress the logic of capitalism. And 2., to engender the approval, the support and the sponsorship of bourgeois-state-capitalism and its ruling, micro-fascist, oligarchical networks, by bestowing merit and accolades among the central nodes of the art-networks. That is, to those which display acceptable devotion and commitment, both to the temperate, neoliberal, tastes of bourgeois-state-capitalism and the essential bureaucratic-necessities of the logic of capitalism.

36.d) In fact, the administration of the arts is primarily composed of state-sponsored artists of one sort or another, who cannot make a living with their art outside the parameters of state-sponsorship and state-financial-support. Consequently, why would a state administrator support or champion avant-garde art, i.e., art that runs contrary to bourgeois-state-capitalism and its notion of art, when his or her job is on the line. The result is bland uninspiring art, average art, art that will not upset the status quo, but will buttress the status quo, offering just another banal, self-indulgent, cryptic, nonsensical, mildly entertaining expression of alienation brought about by the mental and physical production and consumption of commodities and capitalist ideology. Art administrators are conservatives, seeking to preserve the status quo so as to not upset the status quo, a status quo, which is the basis of their financial well-being and their careers. These administrators are dull nodes within the dull, bureaucratic, art-networks, civil servants, who for the most part have never lived or experienced any form of revolutionary avant-gardism. As a result, revolutionary avant-gardism appears to them as foreign, as suspect, as something to react against, due to the fact that it is not in-tuned with the logic of capitalism and the military-industrial-complex. What is truly cutting-edge is alien to the status quo, and where the status quo is concerned, it is art that must be negated. It is art that must be suppressed in order to maintain the status quo and its network supremacy within the art world. Such is the contemporary art world, networks upon networks, paralleling the logic of capitalism and its military-industrial-complex, geared to suppress avant-garde art in favor of neoliberal capitalist art, i.e., state-sponsored and state-approved art, i.e., temperate, non-revolutionary, bourgeois art.

> (<u>Note</u>: In every epoch, the ruling art denotes the ruling ideas and tastes of that epoch's ruling network(s) and its ruling ideology.)

36.e) This epoch's ruling art is bourgeois-state-capitalism art, i.e., neoliberalism art, which is based on and embodies 5 properties to varying degrees:

1. The Property of Ambiguity, i.e., Nonsensical Puzzlement.
2. The Property of Superficial-Entertainment, i.e., Empty-Spectacle.
3. The Property of Temperate-Moderation.
4. The Property of De-Politicization, i.e., The A-Political.
5. The Property of Network-Connection.

1. These 5 properties are comprised in all neoliberalism art to varying degrees and emphasis.

2. It is these 5 properties by whch any institutional art education is based upon and is designed to indoctrinate its pupils into.

3. Emphasis on these 5 properties, by bourgeois-state-capitalism, annihilates contemporary art of its capacity for revolutionary avant-gardism and its capacity for greatness and radical social change.

4. Emphasis on these 5 properties, maximizes that contemporary art will adhere to the inherent principles that govern capital circuits and cycles across the military-industrial-complex, i.e., interchangeability, standardization, utility, division, systematization, and time-management.

5. Emphasis on these 5 properties, facilitates the systematization of contemporary art as a commodity and as a means for expanding the logic of capitalism, i.e., the accumulation, extraction and centralization of surplus value, including as a means to stimulate the workforce/population to work and consume, while, only fulfilling the minimum maintenance requirements of the workforce/population.

6. Finally, the focus on these 5 properties, by bourgeois-state-capitalism, results in contemporary art being dull, cryptic, nonsensical, open-ended and conventional, namely, disposable empty-spectacle for the bewildered masses, where, artistic success is simply a matter of an individual's network-connections, pertaining to the ruling, hierarchical, art-networks, administering the bourgeois art-world. Ultimately, these bourgeois properties assure that artistic careers are based on network-connection rather than artistic production, where, the focal point of power and influence remains based on "The Network" rather than in any singular, rational, human spirit, or specifically, creative-power.

-[37]-

37.a) In the arts, saturation of the marketplace, due to universities, has resulted in arbitrary and radical specialization between emerging, mid-career and established artists. This arbitrary and radical specialization has nothing to do with enriching the quality of art that is produced as an emerging artist is as capable of producing a masterpiece as is an established artist. This division is designed solely to manage and to control the arts in service of the logic of capitalism. This arbitrary division has to do with indoctrination and the protection of the bourgeois-state-capitalism and its ideology, i.e., the logic of capitalism. This arbitrary and radical specialization allows bourgeois-state-capitalism to marginalize any art-form that might threaten its rule and to promote any art-form that might increase its governing power and its rule. This arbitrary and radical specialization enables bourgeois-state-capitalism to skew the meaning and the value of various art-forms for its own purposes. Most often than not, naive art-forms, that are totally oblivious to state-control and other capitalist modes of control, are allowed to flourish beside more informed art-forms. The point is to diffuse the revolutionary capabilities of an anti-capitalist art-form. Moreover, the administration of the arts has depoliticized the arts, moderated the arts, obscured the arts, and standardize artistic modes of expression. Today, art, when done well, is at best a sequence of beautiful nonsense, meaningless, disposable, empty-spectacle, entertainment, which flatters and amuses a misinformed public, rather than, inflaming it and prompting it to revolutionary action and/or consciousness.

37.b) Today, contemporary art, under state-control and capitalist modes of control, is devoid of meaning, coherence and vision. It is predominantly nonsensical but with all the flare of the spectacular. Contemporary art is now comprised of a vast array of empty-spectacles that entertain and bedazzle, but lack meaning and/or value so as to circulate freely within the profitable art-networks of bourgeois-state-capitalism. Contemporary art, under the control of state-administrators and capitalists, is now produced for state-administrators, that is, for the indoctrination and administration of the workforce/population, i.e., to control the mental and the physical activities of the workforce/population, via incessant bewilderment and capitalist shocks.

37.c) Today, established artists are rewarded for their long-term loyalty to the state, based on emeritus awards, which have more to do with their devotion to state-ideology and their quantitative years of ideological production rather than with the quality of work that is done. Emerging artists are rewarded based on the level of ignorance and obedience they demonstrate towards bourgeois-state-capitalism and its ideology. They are rewarded 1. by their ability to remain unaware and unsullied by the ideological machinery of bourgeois-state-capitalism, and 2., by their efficacy in obeying the state-sponsored administrators of contemporary art, i.e., curators, professors, instructors, arts coordinators, juries, gallery directors, submission rules etc. These arbitrary systemic standards of bourgeois-state-capitalism, concerning the arts, are manufactured by the armature of micro-fascism which outlines the socio-economic processes of the military-industrial-complex. Micro-fascism, which is designed to measure obedience, fear, ignorance and network-cronyism, specifically concerning the arts, as well measures these in relation to the 5 properties of neoliberal capitalism art. Together, these micro-fascism measurements and correlations are designed to maximize the principles of interchangeability, utility, standardization, division, systematization, and time-management, pertaining to artifacts and artists, allowing them to maximize capitalist profits as they circulate through the socio-economic, art-networks of bourgeois-state-capitalism.

37.d) Within the military-industrial-complex, intelligence is obedience and obedience is intelligence. In fact, obedience is what is rewarded and what matters most in the contemporary state-administrated art world. In religious times, artists obeyed the clergy, hence why the arts were filled with religious fervor, piety and religious imagery. Today, artists obey state-administrators, civil servants, and state-educators, hence, why the arts are filled with dullness, ambiguity, nonsense, indifference, and in most instances, empty-spectacles, which buttress bourgeois-state-capitalism, by celebrating its self-glorifying monologue and its cherished capitalist marketplace.

37.e) When art forgoes or abandons or suppresses its essence, social change, its reason for being, it loses all meaning, energy, and reason for being. Art becomes post-modern-kitsch, solipsism, and empty-entertainment, reflecting the lukewarm, subdued sentiments of state-bureaucrats. Purged of substance, contemporary art is mediocrity personified, such is the state of contemporary art. Art, to be art, must be able to speak truth to power and ignite radical social change. It must communicate the radical social change inherent in all insatiable drives for ownership/knowledge. True art, is the expression of an intrinsic need for radical social change. It is where the revolutionary capacity of the the workforce/population finds itself and expresses itself. When art achieves its raison d'être, its ceases to be meaningless decoration and becomes its essence, an expression and a vehicle for genuine, radical social change.

-[38]-

38.a) Meritocracy, the corner-stone of the state-sponsored art world and the military-industrial-complex, in general, is a fallacy and a bureaucratic construct. Meritocracy is false-consciousness in the sense that the same select few always decide and reward the same select few, namely, the devotees of the logic of capitalism and its ruling, micro-fascist, oligarchical networks.

38.b) What is forever rewarded within bourgeois-state-capitalism is state-supporting discourses, state-supporting art-forms, state-supporting individuals, and state-supporting products, never what is genuinely revolutionary and/or progressively avant-garde. In every state-sponsored, jury-type competition/examination, the same civil servant or servants, chosen by and representing the ruling, micro-fascist, oligarchical networks, hand-pick the jury and select the jury from the same pool of so-called state-sponsored experts, year after year. Then, this hand-picked jury is assigned to select from the same pool of so-called state-sponsored, state-approved proponents, those proponents who best exemplify the same state-sponsored, ruling, micro-fascist, oligarchical networks. That is, the ruling institutions, the ruling personnel, and the ruling ideas, which are in accordance with the hand-picked jury and the logical necessities of bourgeois-state-capitalism, i.e., neoliberalism. In this manner, all deviations from the neoliberal status quo are excluded and marginalized, while, all the proponents of the neoliberal status quo are celebrated and championed as worthy of bureaucratic merit. Beneath the thin veneer of merit, the point is forever the same, to continually perpetuate the bourgeois-capitalist status quo, by having the best possible state-supporting discourses, art-forms, products, and entities, selected and celebrated, as emblems of the evident superiority of bourgeois-state-capitalism, that is, the logic of capitalism. Notwithstanding, this is nothing but an ideological, self-serving, self-glorifying, capitalist monologue, whose conclusion is always rigged beforehand, by which the logic of capitalism praises and celebrates itself, by proxy and by force.

38.c) Subsequently, merit, the idea that what has the most merit should be most celebrated and encouraged is a state-constructed notion, veiled within a carefully constructed illusion of democratic openness and transparency. What, or who, has the most merit, within the soft-totalitarian-state, is the person, discourse, and/or the product, which is most useful and conducive to the capitalist ideology and the expansion of the bureaucratic-structures of capitalism, i.e., the logic of capitalism. In the arts, capitalist meritocracy has resulted in the saturation of the arts, across all the stratums of everyday life, and resulted in the radical purging of the revolutionary spirit, within the arts, so that the arts can conform to the logical necessities of bourgeois-state-capitalism. Contemporary art, in service of capitalist bureaucracy, is art without politics, art without edge, art without meaning, art without purpose, and most importantly, art without revolution. It is art which is moderate and subdued. Moreover, the only requirement for art to be state-approved, neoliberalism art, is that it be disposable empty-entertainment, for the bewildered workforce/population. That is, that its meaning be ambiguous, a-political, nonsensical, temperate, and finally, that its merit be solely based on state-supportive, network-connections, the art-networks sanctioned by the neoliberal status quo, namely, micro-fascism. Contemporary neoliberal art is the dissemination of bourgeois-capitalist values and micro-fascism.

-[39]-

39.a) The armature of micro-fascism constructs an artificial reality, which is always conducive to the logic of capitalism. This is its raison d'être. Consequently, like contemporary art, all information and commodity-images circulating within the parameters of the military-industrial-complex are highly filtered, purified and artificially constructed via the mediated processes and indoctrination mechanisms of bourgeois-state-capitalism. The point is always to display the logic of capitalism and the military-industrial-complex in the best light, preferably as a morally superior entity and socio-economic formation, which is the most just, inclusive and sympathetic to the necessities of the workforce/population. The point is always to display the political-economic framework of bourgeois-state-capitalism as incessantly fighting the good moral, honorable fight against morally degenerate adversaries and/or unacceptable, unjust situations. Mega-corporations, state-institutions and news agencies, seemingly independent, are mechanisms linked culturally, politically and economically to each other. They are parts, comprised within elite, micro-fascist, oligarchical networks. These seemingly, independent, impartial capitalist entities, who are in fact, intimately, inter-connected to overarching micro-fascist, oligarchical networks, support and buttress each other at arm's length, in agreement that they, and the military-industrial-complex, be portrayed in the best light. And in addition, that any counter-networks, logics, information, commodity-images, knowledges, viewpoints, and/or art-forms, which contradict the capitalist status quo and its rule, are in turn ignored, marginalized, misrepresented and/or eliminated.

39.b) Propaganda, disinformation, fake-news, bias editing, constructed ideological images, false-consciousness, and micro-fascism, continue to be the primary mechanisms of indoctrination and streamlining, within the parameters of the military-industrial-complex. Bourgeois-state-capitalism, both subtle and flagrant, undertakes to structure the thought and the behavioral patterns of the workforce/population. It does this by providing, ready-made, ideological lenses, ready-made sets of images and ready-made modes of being, perceiving, interpreting and acting, pertaining to all social events and everyday life, which, coincidentally, always parallel the ideological principles and practical needs of the military-industrial-complex, that is, the logic of capitalism.

39.c) An art-form, an idea, a revolutionary project and/or a news story's success and saturation throughout the media networks of the military-industrial-complex, is dependent on how, and how much, this art-form, this idea, this project, and this news story etc., is profitable and coincides with the logic of capitalism, i.e., the ruling principles and capitalist ideology of the military-industrial-complex. What best serves bourgeois-state-capitalism is most visible, most exposed, most discussed, most celebrated, most circulated, most disseminated, and thus most profitable.

39.d) Artificiality and superficiality is the objective of media technologies and media institutions, which appear seemingly independent and separated, but, in fact are unified and interconnected, because they all function and operate, according to the underlying, instrumental-rationality of bourgeois-capitalism. The techno-rationale of capitalist media industries, including the sum of the military-industrial-complex, is the rationale of systematic domination, that is, the indoctrination of the workforce/population to the ideological dictates of bourgeois-capitalism. Consequently, any real history is crushed, filtered, and re-fabricated so as to parallel bourgeois-capitalist prejudices, and the bourgeois-capitalist, order of things. Wherefore, even the sum of history comes to reflect a glittering, monstrous, pseudo-history, a fabricated history, which is best suited for bourgeois, capitalist, profit-making. As a result, via capitalist media technologies, the imagination of the workforce/population is calcified, atrophied, truncated, and neatly organized into the state-approved, ideological, molds of the capitalist status quo. That is, all those mind-numbing molds engineered to produce, consume, and distribute, capitalist commodities, both conceptual and material, for the administration and augmentation of capitalist profits. Everything down the smallest details is dissected, organized, and manipulated, according to the instrumental-rationality of bourgeois-capitalism. Media technologies are totalitarian. They are capitalist tools, where the celebration of difference, displayed, across the screen, is solely the superficial, ideological packaging, by which capitalist ideological homogeneity permeates, across the capitalist media industries and the micro-recesses of everyday life. Everyone can seemingly join-in the celebration, and be a merit-filled nexus of bourgeois-capitalism, distinguished, honored, and cherished, for an unwavering, capitalist devotion. Everyone is free, under bourgeois-state-capitalism, free to follow or be left behind, fully ostracized, as not to conform means to be labeled a disgruntled malcontent, slated for powerless obsolescence. In concert, capitalist media technologies repeat the same, over and over again, in ever-new, novel, programming methods and ideological formats, messages of obedience, compliance, and business, namely, the totalitarian business of capitalist profit-making, ad nauseam. Whereas, fact and fiction admix seamlessly between the fuzzy boundaries of all the capitalist facsimiles, engendered by the capitalist media industries. That is, capitalist facsimiles engineered to infest the stratums of everyday life and produce a litany of meaningless insatiable needs, in and across the workforce/population, all of which, can be reduced to one, single, generalized need, the need for more capitalist instrumental-rationality, i.e., capitalist profit etc. The point of capitalist media industries is always uniform, to repetitively engineer, both conceptually and materially, the workforce/population to compliantly live as if the sum of its existence was un fait accompli, and real history was nothing but a capitalist epic, motion picture. Whereupon, the cathartic, happy ending is, as always, a continual reaffirmation of the logic of capitalism and the need for a greater, more powerful form of totalitarian-capitalism, that is, the need for greater capitalist systemic barbarism and empty-vacuous consumerism.

-[40]-

40.a) The armature of micro-fascism also constructs an artificial concept of justice within the military-industrial-complex, namely, bourgeois-justice. This bureaucratic construct is military-industrial-justice. Military-industrial-justice concerns itself with exercising and imposing the logic of capitalism, embodied in the socio-economic processes of bourgeois-state-capitalism, onto any deviating physical/mental forces, circulating within the micro-recesses of everyday life. All laws, rules and regulations are based on manufacturing and safeguarding a coherent, legally framed workforce/population, which functions and operates, consistently, and wholeheartedly, in service of the logical necessities of bourgeois-state-capitalism. The law is an artificially constructed, arbitrary legal framework, designed to be applied stringently to the workforce/population and designed to be applied mildly, or not at all, to those capitalist entities which best embody the logic of capitalism, such as capitalist-corporations etc.

1. Within the parameters of the military-industrial-complex, bourgeois-justice is industrialized in the sense that bourgeois-justice is about manufacturing a totalizing, seemingly coherent, legal framework, which mentally and physically regiments the workforce/population to the workings of bourgeois-state-capitalism. All deviations, by the workforce/population supply the judicial system and its disciplinary-mechanisms with the necessary materials for legitimacy and its ever-refining judicial processes, which are designed to construct and maintain, an all-encompassing legal framework, by force and/or indoctrination. That is, a legal framework, which has been designed, and is being continually refined, to better serve and financially benefit the logical apparatuses of bourgeois-state-capitalism, specifically, the logic of capitalism. This means that the law is something that is applied rigidly to the workforce/population, specifically, the entities of the lower stratums of society, while, in contrast, the law is something which is open-ended,

loose, and flexible, when it concerns bourgeois-capitalist-entities, which best embody the logic of capitalism. The workforce/population tends to be continually victimized by bourgeois-law. The workforce/population tends to be continually caught in a catch-22 via bourgeois-law. Meaning, the workforce/population is continually trapped in a double-bind, wherefore, its judicial claims tend to be continually deprived of authority, liberty and a voice, pertaining to its victimization, while, the exemplars of bourgeois-state-capitalism, have full access to the mental and physical mechanisms of dissemination, government and capital. For the workforce/population, victimization is always accompanied by the loss of means to prove its very own victimization. The bourgeois-justice-system is designed to obscure and remove means, both judicial means and/or socio-economic means, from the workforce/population.

2. Within the parameters of the military-industrial-complex, justice is militarized in the sense that justice is about eliminating deviations from the socio-economic processes of bourgeois-state-capitalism. Secondly, it is about appropriating violence, from the workforce/population, and enacting this violence on all societal deviations in the name of the workforce/population, yet, always in benefit of bourgeois-state-capitalism, that is, the logic of capitalism. The workforce/population is continually deprived, via bourgeois-law, from the means to express its grievances, whether this is through legitimate violence and/or non-violent maneuvers and/or proceedings.

40.b) The guideline that underlies the legal/justice-system is the idea that "what best conforms to the logic of capitalism is what is most just". What best serves the logical necessities of bourgeois-state-capitalism is what constitutes justice. All verdicts, all judgments, all laws, pertaining to the bourgeois-judicial-system and society, in general, are founded on serving the logic of capitalism, first and foremost, i.e., to manufacture a hierarchical, all-encompassing legal framework that enshrines a definitive, functional workforce/population, which is completely subjugated and organized in service of bourgeois-state-capitalism. All the theatrics of the judicial-system, all the hierarchies of the judicial-system, are based on manufacturing, expanding, and maintaining, an all-encompassing legal-bourgeois-framework so as to enshrine a definitive, functional, workforce/population, which is completely subjugated and organized in service of the logic of capitalism. All legal frameworks, within bourgeois-state-capitalism, are founded on and tethered to the logic of capitalism. Despite its claims of equality and impartiality, bourgeois-justice is, in effect, a two-tiered justice-system, two different legal frameworks, one for capitalists, and one for the workforce/population, specifically, entities of the lower stratums of society. Whereupon, capitalism always wins and is always favored and safeguarded in all legal bourgeois proceedings. The point of the first-tier of military-industrial-justice is to confine and condemn the workforce/population to function and operate according to the logic of capitalism. And, the point of the second-tier of military-industrial-justice, the most important, is to legalize capitalist exploitation, that is, manufacture an ironclad, legal framework, which supports legalized capitalist thievery, capitalist private property, capitalist usury and capitalist fraud etc., namely, the foundation-stones for any capitalist profit-making.

40.c) All judicial processes and legal-mechanisms are pragmatic instruments, in service of bourgeois-state-capitalism, constructed and designed to regiment the workforce/population to the behaviors, thought processes, and codes of conduct of the logic of capitalism, specifically, for the accumulation, extraction, and safeguarding of surplus value, i.e., capital and profit. Whenever a member of the workforce/population is out of the ordinary and/or deviates from the moral and/or legal status quo, i.e., bends or breaks average conception and average conduct, then, the supremacy of bourgeois-state-capitalism is threatened. And thus, this non-standardized member of the workforce/population opens him or herself to military-industrial-justice and its vast array of bourgeois disciplinary and punitive-mechanisms. It all depends on the degree of the deviation. If a segment of the workforce/population deviates from the logic of capitalism, greater is the risk of running-up against military-industrial-justice. The irony is that every member of the workforce/population possesses an instinct whose specific ethic, to a certain extent, always deviates from the capitalist standards set by military-industrial-justice. As a result, every member of the workforce/population is a potential subject, and potential material, for judiciary procedures, i.e., the disciplinary/punitive processes and regulatory mechanisms, which enshrine, and are founded on, this two-tiered legal framework manufactured by the logic of capitalism. The fact that all members of the workforce/population have innate, natural deviations embodied within, stimulates the surveillance, the policing, and the judicial regimentation of all members of the workforce/population. The point is to make the workforce/population increasingly conform to the ever-pressing, logical necessities of bourgeois-state-capitalism. Moreover, this need for greater and greater surveillance, policing, discipline, punishment, and justice, derives from the innate natural deviations, housed in the insatiable drive for ownership/knowledge, which are essentially infinite. As a result, this need to police is essentially infinite because deviations from the capitalist status quo is an existential fact within all segments of the workforce/population. Likewise, this need to police, which is housed in the insatiable drive for ownership/knowledge, is intensified into a mania, via the logic of capitalism, propelling a never-ending development and refinement of surveillance, policing, and legality, i.e., disciplinary/punitive processes and regulatory mechanisms. That is, disciplinary and punitive processes and mechanism, central to the continued contextual supremacy of the military-industrial-complex, i.e., the logic of capitalism. And these burgeoning surveillance and policing-apparatuses are primarily directed and imposed upon the workforce/population, while in contrast, those capitalist entities, who best represent the logic of capitalism, are given free-reign, pertaining to their inherent capitalist deviations, which make profits through capitalist exploitation, thievery and network-cronyism, etc.

(Note: Military-industrial-justice, i.e., bourgeois-justice, is an outgrowth of the logic of capitalism. Its only claim to universal truth and any sense of justice is that it efficiently serves the logical necessities of bourgeois-state-capitalism, namely, the logic of capitalism and its state-finance-corporate-aristocracy. Meaning, it must help to maximize capitalist efficiency and profitability. Therefore, the primary concern of bourgeois-justice is the safeguard of private property, capitalist power, capitalist individualism, and capitalist profits, namely, the state-finance-corporate-aristocracy built upon these principles.)

40.d) Military-industrial-justice is organized and structured according to a network-logic, i.e., a state-sponsored grid of mutually state-supporting nodes that function and operate in unison to satisfy the judicial necessities of bourgeois-state-capitalism. This judicial-network-logic is not necessarily a reasonable logic, hence, the reason for much of the dissatisfaction today with military-industrial-justice. Notwithstanding, it is a logic that coincides with the logic of capitalism, i.e., to maximize profit, by any means necessary, at the lowest financial cost, as soon as possible, while, only satisfying the minimum basic requirements of the workforce/population. What is reasonable and logical, from a singular standpoint, is inconsequential to military-industrial-justice as it is the logic of the governing, micro-fascist, oligarchical networks, which sustains its authority and its legitimacy that matters. This is what matters for bourgeois, military-industrial-justice. Subsequently, the logic of capitalism is what preoccupies military-industrial-justice in the sense that the logic of capitalism, in essence, comprises its full attention and its underlying interest, due to the fact that military-industrial-justice owes its material and conceptual existence to the logic of capitalism.

40.e) Military-industrial-justice is about manufacturing the semblance of justice for the many and manufacturing genuine justice for the benefit the select few, i.e., the best representations and embodiments of the logic of capitalism. As a result, a member of the workforce/population, centered out for military-industrial-justice, becomes a locus and processing material, nothing more, for military-industrial-justice. This member of the workforce/population becomes processing material and a locus, for military-industrial-justice, so it can enact and exercise its judicial pageantry, namely, its necessary logical processes upon in the name of the many, but, in benefit of the select few, the logic of capitalism and its ruling, micro-fascist, oligarchical networks. Military-industrial-justice is a composition of judicial networks and hierarchies, which exercise the armature of micro-fascism, within an all-encompassing, two-tiered, legal-bourgeois-framework. The point is to purge the socio-economic processes of bourgeois-state-capitalism of dissent, imagination, and deviation, so as to maximize interchangeability, utility, standardization, division, systematization, and time-management, within the military-industrial-complex, in order to accumulate, centralize and extract surplus value, from the workforce/population, with little or no resistance.

-[41]-

41.a) Finally, the military-industrial-complex is a complex socio-economic formation, where "Man" as the basic measurement of all things and as the grounding principle of social relations, knowledge, ownership, and generally speaking society, has been subverted and dislodged from its central, modernist, socio-economic position in favor of a new central concept and principle, i.e., "the network". No longer is "Man" the measure of all things within society, it is "the network", which is the measure of all things. Today, the universal concept of "Man" only exists as a universal concept by the good grace of "the network", which brings it forth, from time to time, out of nostalgia as an ancient artifact from a by-gone era. The concept "Man", which was the mooring of modernity and the Enlightenment, has degenerated into subservience under the current universal concept of "the network". Today, "Man" is a tool, a device, utilized to buttress "the network", namely, to empower legitimacy and to enhance the network's governing power over total ownership and total knowledge in and across the military-industrial-complex, including the citizenry.

41.b) Notwithstanding, the universal concept of "Man" has not totally disappeared from the central socio-economic narrative, but, this concept has been relegated to the periphery and/or a secondary consideration in relation to the new universal concept of "the network". "The network" is now the measure of all things, not "Man".

41.c) "Man", i.e., the rational human spirit and the former central mooring of modernity, has been dislodged from its central position both within western knowledge and within the political-economic framework. "Man", the rational human spirit, is no longer the determining factor of truth and socio-economic justice. Our epoch is no longer a modernist epoch but something other. It is an epoch whose central concept and mooring is instead, "The Network". "The Network" is the ruling organization of intellectual/material forces and representations, where humans' are interchangeable and powerless, when, disconnected from the ruling-networks of power, in and across, bourgeois-state-capitalism.

41.d) The network's sole purpose is both 1. to control the workforce/population and 2., to develop the logic of capitalism, i.e., to maximize profit, while, meeting the minimum basic requirements of the workforce/population.

41.e) As an assemble of ideas, behaviors, perceptions, and ways of life, the network manifests a unified, synthetic, manufactured reality, i.e., a composite of fragmentary realities fused together as one, who process realities, people and situations now according to the logic of capitalism.

41.f) All ruling, micro-fascist, oligarchical networks are types of thinking-behaviorist machines, which are both pluralities and singularities, both mental and physical, that produce automatic meaning and automatic solutions to perceived empirical and ideational data. These networks are iron cages that house ready-made ideas, solutions, behaviors, statements, and most importantly, understandings, pertaining to all situations, phenomena and/or people, which are always in-line with the logical necessities of bourgeois-state-capitalism, i.e., the logic of capitalism.

41.g) "The network" trumps "Man" in almost every instance as "Man" is relegated to a secondary consideration. In fact, "Man" is now a product of "the network", the network brings "Man" forth like the carrot on the stick in order to stimulate humans to think and behave in specific bourgeois-state-capitalism fashions and manners. Today, individual humans have been subjugated and humiliated to the level of sub-humans, unter-mensch(es), fleshy fragments of the human species, who only achieve, temporarily, the level of human beings, "Man", as participant nodes, within the logical networks of bourgeois-state-capitalism. "The network" has appropriated the concept of "Man" for itself and now dishes it out as a reward, a perk, for network support and capitalist participation. The individual is no longer a unity but a confluence of material and ideational network-like forces, which produce and consume him or her as a singularity, for the purpose and benefit of extracting, centralizing, and accumulating capitalist surplus value. As a result, disconnected from his or her network an entity loses all relevance and power to influence his or her categorization and/or individuality. He or she becomes flickering, spectral-metaphysical nothingness, due to the fact, power and influence are no longer localized in the singular individual and/or the rational human spirit, they are now localized in "the network", as a whole. "The network" is a web of many rational human spirits that produce and consume the individual as a locus of power and influence, when, this individual is plugged into "the network". It is in this regard that today unemployment is a no-man's land between significance and insignificance, identity and non-identity, populated by fragmentary ephemeral entities, searching for network approval and support to re-animate and re-individualize themselves. This important shift from "Man", the rational human spirit, to "The Network", an amalgam-set of many rational human spirits, or power-relations, whom, together, comprise the primary deciding element in any decision-making-authority, is now the crux of the new post-modern paradigm. "The Network" is the new episteme and the new political-economic framework. "The Network" is the military-industrial-complex, whereupon, capitalist networking is the basis of post-industrial, post-modern, bourgeois-state-capitalism, including the logic of capitalism. In fact, the logic of capitalism demands and commands networking, the construction of webs upon webs of crony-relations and collusionary forces centered upon maximizing capitalist profit and ever new autocratic forms of the capital/labor relation.

-[42]-

42.a) By and large, the military-industrial-complex is a type of falsehood. It is a despotic form of bourgeois-state-capitalism resembling a soft-totalitarian-state. It is a digital-technocratic ant-colony, where work, commerce, ownership and knowledge are central, and fundamentally localized into various series of micro-dictatorships, i.e., a set of ruling, micro-fascist, oligarchical networks, which provide credence to the illusion of transparency and democracy, when, in fact, the opposite is true. Granted, these ruling, micro-fascist, oligarchical networks, dotting society, seem divided, due to the fact that they are, technically, engaged in microscopic warfare inside themselves and against one another, throughout the military-industrial-complex, in an effort to possess and control greater portions of the economy, but, this is false-consciousness. It is false-consciousness in the sense that their seemingly endless divisions are nevertheless unified on one crucial point, the logic of capitalism. What unifies these seemingly independent, antagonistic, capitalist entities, and networks, is the overarching logic of capitalism. The logic of capitalism loosely organizes these divisive, capitalist entities and networks into a network of networks, where decision-making-authority is focused and localized on the basis that these divisive, capitalist entities, and networks, best represent and embody the logic of capitalism. Consequently, seemingly divided and at war, these micro-dictatorial networks and capitalist entities, nonetheless, work in unison, akin to a school of predatory fish.

42.b) Like a school of piranhas, capitalist-enterprises work together and not necessarily together, so as to maximize profit, both for themselves, individually, and for capitalism, in general. Like a school of blood-thirsty piranhas, capitalist-enterprises are individualistic and collectively-driven, simultaneously. They are organized simultaneously as a unitary force, like a school of piranhas, and individualistically as a set of divisive forces, always ready to pounce on those capitalist-enterprises that lag behind. To ensure their survival and to ensure their development, capitalist-enterprises build relations, i.e., economic networks, among themselves, founded on the logical imperatives of capitalism. They build these economic networks both to stave-off the brute force of the unadulterated coercive laws of competition, which will surely result in their destruction if they are too isolated. And second, they build economic networks in order to dominate the global marketplace in their favor. Namely, through economic networks they artificially-fabricate values, prices and wages in their favor, according to the arbitrary vagaries of their own selfish desires. As a result, capitalist-enterprises work together without seemingly appearing to do so in the sense that, by networking together, these capitalist entities unwittingly fulfill the totalitarian ambitions of the logic of capitalism. Meaning, by executing and realizing their own mercenary ambitions for profit, they manufacture a police-state, i.e., totalitarian-capitalism. In essence, these socio-economic predators, i.e., piranhas, only coalesce as a unified force in their fundamental core directive: to maximize profit, by any means necessary, at the lowest financial cost, as soon as possible, while, only satisfying the minimum maintenance requirements of the workforce/population, the fount of multi-varied surplus value. However, this enough to manufacture widespread capitalist authoritarianism in all sorts of shapes and forms, which invariably, ends in the imprisonment of the workforce/population into debt-slavery and wage-slavery.

Section Four:

The End Of Bourgeois-State-Capitalism:

(Towards The Political-Economic Framework Of Structural-Anarchism)

43.a) The end of the logic of capitalism is logically incapable of being fully realized as the logic of capitalism is a force intrinsic and hardwired within the insatiable drive for ownership/knowledge, i.e., it emanates from specific insatiable drives for ownership/knowledge. In fact, it was the insatiable drive for ownership/knowledge, itself, which constructed the logic of capitalism in an attempt to satisfy its own basic maintenance requirements, i.e., its own insatiable drive for ownership/knowledge. Consequently, to completely destroy the logic of capitalism is to completely destroy the insatiable drive for ownership/knowledge, since, both are intimately intertwined. It can illogically and theoretically be done, but, at the terrible cost of life and existence, itself. As a result, the end of the logic of capitalism is logically incapable of being fully realized as a collective universal totality, since, its nucleus forms the will to power encoded within humans and nature. However, it is possible to destroy vast areas and territories, where, the logic of capitalism dominates, but despite, this destruction, the logic of capitalism, being highly resilient and intrinsic, within the workforce/population, holds within its capitalist logic the capacity to reanimate and germinate, once again, without end, stronger and denser than it ever was before.

43.b) No historical civilization, or political-economic framework, is ever completely annihilated, there are always traces and elements which survive into proceeding historical civilizations and political-economic frameworks, informing them. For example, ancient Roman civilization and its political-economic framework inform contemporary civilization and the contemporary, capitalist, political-economic framework, in various ways. Medieval feudalism as well survives within, and informs, contemporary civilization and the contemporary, capitalist, political-economic framework. As a result, no historical civilization, or political-economic framework, can be completely destroyed, but they can be marginalized and displaced from their obvious centrality. That is, all previous historical civilizations and political-economic frameworks exist in marginalized forms, within the current, ruling, contemporary civilization and political-economic framework. And, the fact that all historical civilizations and political-economic frameworks eventually fall into marginalization and obsolescence, means that capitalism, itself, will eventually fall into marginalization and obsolescence, giving rise to a new political-economic framework and civilization. Namely, an anti-capitalist, political-economic framework and civilization, founded on the logic of structural-anarchism. Contrary to Marxists, there is no higher stage of communism or socialism, where the stamp of former socio-economic formations, or civilizations, do not in some shape inform the current, ruling, socio-economic formation, or civilization. The past always informs the present and future. History always informs the present and future.

43.c) Furthermore, the fact that the workforce/population cannot but manufacture surplus, i.e., multi-varied surplus values of all types and kinds, beyond its basic maintenance requirements, denotes that capitalism is incapable of being eradicated from the face of the earth. The reason is the workforce/population embodies the logic of capitalism, within its constitution. That is, it embodies the possibility of capitalist exploitation and domination, in-itself. As a result, members of the workforce/population are endlessly being tempted by the abundance of surplus values, they manufacture. They are endlessly tempted to activate, animate, and initiate, the logic of capitalism, encrypted upon the insatiable drive for ownership/knowledge, i.e., the will to power, to appropriate violently, or through agreement, the excess communal surpluses in a manner which increases their power and their influence over others and the community. This means, the logic of capitalism is a constant threat and an inherent antagonism to any anti-capitalist, antithetical framework, regardless how much capitalism is eradicated.

43.d) Notwithstanding, despite the fact that the logic of capitalism cannot be completely abolished, the logic of capitalism can be decentralized, dislodged, and displaced as the central nexus and organizing principle within society, that is, the parameters of the military-industrial-complex. The logic of capitalism can be dislodged and displaced in the sense that its supremacy can be overthrown, marginalized and decentralized. The logic of capitalism cannot be completely destroyed, but the logic of capitalism can be rendered and relegated to the socio-economic periphery of society, it can be decentralized, displaced and subordinated as a secondary consideration in decision-making-authority and in all socio-economic processes, within a new political-economic framework. Granted, the logic of capitalism may never outright vanish, but it can be decentralized, displaced, minimized and deactivated, within all socio-economic modes and relations in and across the micro-recesses of everyday life, including, in general, society and civilization.

44.a) The first primary factor that will result in the dislodgement and displacement of the logic of capitalism and its material manifestation, the military-industrial-complex, is its own innate, ever-intensifying, circular, unreasonable logic. It seems that only if capital belongs to all and is shared by all is the logic of capitalism capable of finally incorporating all in its ardent enterprise for total developmental maturation and mercenary control, i.e., collective universal totality, over the sum of everyday life.

44.b) Herein lies the problematic enigma: capital, i.e., the logic of capitalism, in order to achieve its inherent enterprise, for collective universal totality and total domination, must decentralize, democratize and defuse itself to attain total domination and collective universal totality. The logic of capitalism must be everything to everyone. Consequently, it must be to a certain extent anarchism if it wishes to encompass and subdue the logic of structural-anarchism. And, in order to do this, capitalism must allow radical egalitarianism, collectivism and communism to flourish within its parameters:

1. It must do this to infiltrate, penetrate, and regulate, the micro-recesses of everyday life, i.e., the miniature time-frames and microscopic spaces, where the workforce/population deviates from the main in all sorts of anarchist ways.

2. The logic of capitalism must do this in greater and greater magnitudes in order to accumulate, extract, and realize, greater and greater amounts of surplus value, i.e. profit. That is, regiment ever-increasing sectors and elements of the workforce/population in service of the logic of capitalism. Due to the fact, it is the creative-power of the logic of structural-anarchism, which opens up new areas of capitalist exploitation and capitalist profit-making, including, new liberating technologies.

3. In consequence, the logic of capitalism inadvertently forces greater and greater segments of the workforce/population into the networks and circuits of its antithetic replacement and substitute, i.e., its anti-capitalist anti-thesis, as it cannot be everything to everybody. It cannot be anarchist and/or communist.

4. Therefore, capitalism structures and organizes, unwillingly, its antithetic replacement and the substitution to its own capitalist logic, via its incessant attempts at collective universal totality. Through the intensification and the narrowing of its regulatory law-like standards, upon the workforce/population, in order to achieve collective universal totality, the logic of capitalism increasingly excludes and impoverishes greater and greater portions of the workforce/population, driving them towards the antithetic substitute, the anti-capitalist logic, namely, the logic of structural-anarchism.

5. Moreover, this intensification process increasingly restricts and narrows the logic of capitalism, itself, i.e., its abilities to accumulate, extract and centralize surplus value, in the sense that there are increasingly less and less areas available, for annexation, regimentation, accumulation and extraction. Also, this intensifying process increasingly limits and extinguishes all revolutionary capabilities, the exact revolutionary capabilities the logic of capitalism needs to expand and to refine itself, so as to extract and accumulate maximum capitalist profit from the workforce/population. That is, in order to accumulate, extract and centralize greater portions of capitalist wealth, profit and power into ever-smaller epicenters, capitalism has to regiment and police the workforce/population to greater and greater extents, which is simultaneously stifling creative-power, namely, the exact creative-power the logic of capitalism needs in order to intensify and magnify the accumulation, extraction and centralization of capitalist wealth, profit and power. Consequently, it is in this regard that the logic of capitalism is unwittingly strangling itself into total obsolescence.

6. Finally, and most importantly, all of this fashions a peculiar paradox specific to the logic of capitalism, itself. This paradox or catch-22 is initiated by the very own logic of capitalism and its own totalitarian mercenary devices. This paradox or catch-22 is an intensifying snare, propelling, the logic of capitalism evermore towards decentralization, horizontalization and democratization in order to solve the paradox.

44.c) This paradox ever-more intensifies because the logic of capitalism, in its incessant attempts at collective universal totality, centralizes and concentrates capital and its socio-economic processes into ever-diminishing, select centers of hoarded capital, where, the logic of capitalism is most obdurate and concentrated. This concentration and intensifying pressure on those few centers of capital, including the workforce/population, which is increasingly squeezed into misery, is manufacturing a pressure-cooker ever-ready to explode at any moment.

44.d) Ultimately, the logic of capitalism, by focusing pressure strictly on these centers so as to relieve the pressure in other areas, due to the tightening noose of the paradox, forces these capitalist centers, via increasing pressure, both from the tightening noose and the antagonism of the workforce/population, to decentralize, horizontalize, and democratize, or risk total capitalist collapse due to a lack of creative-power, the primary lubricant of bourgeois-capitalism.

44.e) Therefore, both to solve the paradox and to achieve collective universal totality, the logic of capitalism is propelled ever-more to give up its contextual supremacy to its anti-thesis, the logic of structural-anarchism. Because, if it does not do this the result will be large-scale socio-economic explosions, in and across all capitalist processes, networks and apparatuses, derived from the antagonism of the workforce/population and this internal Catch-22 of capitalism. Moreover, in an ironic twist, solving the paradox, means the logic of capitalism will no longer itself, but, something other, namely, the logic of structural-anarchism, hence, the inescapable paradox in the logic of capitalism.

44.f) In sum, the logic of capitalism will fail because it is fundamentally unreasonable. Capitalism is an unsustainable as a socio-economic formation in the sense that it creates increasing inequality, devastation, and misery, in and across the workforce/population and nature, while, it increasingly narrows the options for finding equitable capitalist solutions to its inherent micro-vortex catch-22. As a result, capitalism is slowly hardening into an unyielding form of high-tech totalitarianism, wherefore, capitalist machinery, processes and apparatuses are slowly grinding to an abrupt halt, due to a lack of flexibility, creative-power and adequate personnel. This calcification of capitalism is increasingly making revolution and insurrection the only viable option for the amelioration and advancement of global society , including, the global workforce/population. Time is running out as capitalism is set to fail due to its inherent fatal nucleus.

44.g) In logical practice, the unrelenting systemic pressure at the center of capitalism, namely, its incessant attempts at collective universal totality, estranges and excludes greater and greater portions of the workforce/population, manifesting the ever-intensifying logical tension, or paradox, within the logic of capitalism. This ever-intensifying tension presents itself in everyday capitalist practices through the capitalist profit imperative, commanding the maximization of profit, while, minimizing production costs.

44.h) Contrary to Marx, within post-industrial, post-modern, bourgeois-state-capitalism, capitalists do not lower commodity-prices when they decrease their production costs. The reason is capitalists are obliged to maximize profit by any means necessary, thus to lower commodity-prices accordingly, runs contrary to the logic of capitalism. Instead, contrary to Marx, within post-industrial, post-modern, bourgeois-state-capitalism, capitalists, either keep commodity-prices the same or raise them slightly. To do otherwise, stimulates price-wars between capitalist competitors, which destroys capitalist profits, in general, when, in retaliation capitalist competitors lower their commodity-prices in turn in order to stave-off bankruptcy and retain their market share. Again, contrary to Marx, price-wars contradict the logic of capitalism, which is about the maximization of profit and the accumulation of economic capital.

44.i) Notwithstanding, this capitalist profit imperative, commanding the maximization of profit, while, minimizing production costs, does not force commodity-prices down, as Marx suggests, but, forces capitalists, within the spheres of capitalist production, to band together. Capitalists band together so as to expand capitalist production and their spheres of production. And, they band together to short-circuit the coercive laws of competition, which further maximizes capitalist profits. This is how ruling, micro-fascist, oligarchical networks are created and come to dominate much of the production spheres, within post-industrial, post-modern, bourgeois-state-capitalism. Even so, this lessening of the coercive laws of competition, by capitalists, does not eliminate competition from the military-industrial-complex, instead, competition is simply moved around the military-industrial-complex. Specifically, in a cruel twist of fate, the brute unadulterated force of the coercive laws of competition fall upon the workforce/population. The result is: 1., The workforce/population is increasingly fragmented, by the weight of competition on its shoulders, which magnifies division and divides the workforce/population increasingly against itself. And 2., the workforce/population is forced increasingly into economic slavery, i.e., stagnate wages, precarious work, unemployment, shit jobs etc., including rising debt slavery as the workforce/population increasingly has to pay more for less, pertaining to its basic maintenance requirements. All of which, magnify antagonism against capitalism and tighten the insurmountable paradoxical barrier inherent in the logic of capitalism.

44.j) Subsequently, as the logic of capitalism pursues to embrace all, be embraced by all, and realize its all, the logic of capitalism magnifies antagonism and ensnares itself, evermore, in its own vicious circular logic, which is increasingly spiraling out of its control. This is an intensifying circular logic, which increasingly displaces and dislodges the logic of capitalism, from its contextual supremacy, due to the fact that as the logic of capitalism incessantly enterprises to assimilate everything within its dominion, so as to reach the zenith of maximum capitalist profit, it is evermore frustrated this venture. It is frustrated in this venture because it cannot reach the zenith of maximum capitalist profit, unless it becomes completely another logic, an anti-capitalist logic, that is, the logic of structural-anarchism. Its level of frustration corresponds to the level of micro-fascism, permeating the military-industrial-complex. That is, the micro-fascism burgeoning across the soft-totalitarian-state, which expresses this capitalist paradox through intolerance, bigotry and jingoism, that is, increasing instrumental-rationality.

44.k) Ultimately, for the logic of capitalism to be omnipresent, omniscient and omnipotent, all capital, all ownership, and all knowledge, must belong to all and be shared by all, in relative equal measure, hence, the problematic enigma of the logic of capitalism. To attain collective universal totality, total domination and maximum profit, ad infinitum, the logic of capitalism must evermore negate its capitalist logic. That is, displace, dislodge, and extricate, itself, from its contextual supremacy, either by its own hand, via total socio-economic breakdown, or through, the hand of another, via revolutionary antagonism, i.e., universal anarchist revolution, generated by the workforce/population. Both these anti-capitalist processes, engendered by the logical paradox inherent in the logic of capitalism, negate the contextual supremacy of capitalism and organize an antithetic, anti-capitalist replacement to the contextual supremacy of capitalism, which can supplant the centrality of logic of capitalism. Finally, by the very fact that the logic of capitalism must continually nullify itself, with greater and greater efficiency, potency, and proficiency, so as to reach collective universal totality, total domination and the zenith of maximum capitalist profit, it invariably brings forth an efficient, potent, and proficient, antithetic, anti-capitalist, logical substitute, namely, the poly-rationality of structural-anarchism.

-[45]-

45.a) The second primary factor that will result in the dislodgement and displacement of the logic of capitalism and its material manifestation, the military-industrial-complex, is the constant and incessant focus, encouragement, and advancement, by bourgeois-state-capitalism, of measurement and the median, i.e., mediocre averageness, within all socio-economic processes and decision-making-authority. The logic of capitalism, knowing that the most politically robust, economically robust and the most profitable segment of the workforce/population is found in the middle, i.e., in averageness, the logic of capitalism focuses all its mechanisms and socio-economic processes in seizing, in fashioning and in capitalizing upon this averageness, i.e., the dictatorship of the middle. The decay of society and bourgeois-state-capitalism transpires because of too much calculation, computation and focus on averages, i.e., bourgeois herd-mediocrity.

45.b) Subsequently, the logic of capitalism utilizes a vast array of its resources and socio-economic processes so as to construct and fashion a base median. Human rights, laws, rules, regulations, and constitutions are tools for the fabrication, the study and the measurement of an average base median, or mediocrity. These are tools in the sense that human rights, laws, rules, regulations, and constitutions, under the dominion of bourgeois-state-capitalism, are methods by which bourgeois-state-capitalism identifies deviations from the capitalist status quo. For example, free speech enables bourgeois-state-capitalism to identify deviations in opinions, perspectives, and point of views. Deviating segments of the workforce/population, duped into freely expressing themselves, due to a false-consciousness in basic human rights, under bourgeois-state-capitalism, open themselves to the surveillance, the punitive and the disciplinary mechanisms of bourgeois-state-capitalism. Moreover, in contrast, free speech enables the celebratory monologue of bourgeois-state-capitalism to drone on and on through the seemingly, independent, voice-boxes of its manufactured average base mediocrity, i.e., the wannabe bourgeoisie, its mindless, indoctrinated, moronic herds, which obediently cluck the dictates of the bourgeois-capitalist status quo, on cue.

45.c) All in all, constitutional rights, and/or a charter/bill of rights, enable bourgeois-state-capitalism to identify, act upon and neutralize, to varying degrees, any deviations that exercise their so-called fundamental rights. The point is to level-down any deviations into the bourgeois-capitalist status quo. And, the point is to fashion, manipulate and exploit the median, i.e., an average base mediocrity, politically and economically so that the logic of capitalism can maintain its supremacy and embolden this supremacy. It is this crusty, indoctrinated, middle of the road, boorish base, wherefore, surplus value is measured, determined and compared in relation to an average base value, i.e., the inputs and outputs of an average sector of the workforce/population. Likewise, this average base value is utilized to further entrench and expand the parameters of the military-industrial-complex and to subject the workforce/population to greater and greater totalitarian, mechanistic, ideological influences, within their everyday lives. Calculation and average medians are the cornerstones by which the logic of capitalism maximizes interchangeability, standardization, utility, division, systematization, and time-management, in and across the stratums of the military-industrial-complex, so as to maximize capitalist profit. Calculation and average medians are the methods by which bourgeois-state-capitalism makes predictions, determinations, extrapolations, and plans, in the public sphere and in the private sphere, both in politics and in economics. As always, the point is to maximize the accumulation and extraction of surplus value, i.e., capitalist profit.

45.d) To determine what is a base value, and what is a surplus value, within socio-economic processes, bourgeois-state-capitalism must constantly establish, study, analyze, and maintain, an average median base, yet, any average median base is constantly shifting, is constantly subject to fluctuations, depending on all sorts of variable and/or invariable factors. In consequence, the administrative-power-structures of the military-industrial-complex are constantly engaged in technocratic-statistical analysis of all kinds so as to determine averages, medians, and ultimately, an average base median, namely, a solid, easily manageable, bourgeois herd-mediocrity. The goal of calculation and the establishment of average medians is to determine the mechanical-workings of the capital/labor relation. From these average base medians, the logic of capitalism calculates its development, its expansion, its workforce/population, and ultimately, its levels of capital accumulation and capital extraction, that is, capitalist profit.

45.e) When average medians are firmly realized at any level of socio-economic existence, surplus value extraction and accumulation is maximized, profit is maximized, control is maximized, obedience is maximized, homogeneity is maximized, and more importantly, the bourgeois status quo is ossified and maximized. The average medians permit the fusion of political-power, economic-power, and the greatest portion of the workforce/population, to blend to such a radical extent that, either/or, is indiscernible and imperceptible from each other. In fact, through the development of average medians, the bourgeois status quo and the average base mediocrity become one and the same, seemingly interchangeable and bent on disseminating, multiplying, propagating, and augmenting, the logic of capitalism, by any means necessary, at the lowest financial cost, as soon as possible.

> (Note: The construction and measurement of an ironclad average begins with the control of language. The state, and specifically the educational system, is the primary mechanism of linguistic ideational control. It is these sort of ideological-power-structures that define, categorize and classify the linguistic, ideational, bourgeois status quo and manufacture average mediocrity, many degenerate herds of bourgeois wannabes.)

45.f) Of course, average medians are in essence infinite and variable in the sense that averageness can be determined on a multitude of levels, based on gender, race, class, age, social group etc., and averageness is subject to mutate over time and in different spaces into new correlations. Fashioning an average median is a matter of context and contexts are variable. Consequently, averageness has multiple determinations, depending on the analytical context and lens one utilizes. This aspect of averageness, as infinite and as variable, prompts and stimulates the increasing micro-management of the workforce/population so as to pin down a relatively stable average base median, from which to determine stable calculations, projections, extrapolations and predictions. Due to this, the military-industrial-complex increasingly requires surveillance mechanisms, disciplinary-mechanisms and micro-management-mechanisms in order to stay current and remain in-tune with social, economic, and cultural fluctuations, which might put the ruling supremacy and legitimacy of the logic of capitalism in jeopardy.

45.g) It is for this reason that bourgeois-state-capitalism is increasingly totalitarian in the sense that it requires a totalitarian political-economic framework in order to continuously construct, measure and monitor an average base mediocrity. Even if this average base mediocrity has rights and freedoms, under bourgeois-state-capitalism, the exercise of these rights and these freedoms are about manufacturing, determining and measuring average medians, average medians that ultimately must be regimented, disciplined and/or organized, evermore to maximize the accumulation and extraction of surplus value. In sum, only a totalitarian political-economic framework can accomplish this, even if this totalitarian political-economic framework calls itself liberal, free and/or democratic. The point is always to exploit, to various degrees, the greatest possible median for the greatest capital return. That is, the point is to transform all ideational comprehensive frameworks and their agents into productive logics in service of the military-industrial-complex and the logic of capitalism.

-[46]-

46.a) Notwithstanding, its increasing emphasis and focus on averages, medians and middles is guiding the logic of capitalism towards its own displacement, decentralization and democratization. Its increasing emphasis on averages, medians and middles, by the logical apparatus of bourgeois-state-capitalism, is both propelling it towards the lowest common denominator, found in average medians, and towards total socio-economic inertia, paralysis, and stasis, i.e., the total breakdown of surplus value accumulation and extraction.

46.b) In its effort to maximize profit and its supremacy, the logic of capitalism ever-increasingly propels itself towards the lowest common denominator, where capital, authority and legitimacy is most robust, concentrated and abundant, namely where the majority resides. This means that all types of commodities are increasingly trite, pointless, disposable and/or identical. Whether politically and/or economically, all commodities are increasingly purged of substance, rareness, spirit and/or individuality so as to mimic the average stereotypes of the median majority and so as to maximize exchangeability. Differences are superficial, inconsequential, a matter of color, design, price and/or brand-name. The lowest common denominator located in the most basic average general median is the most profitable, the most powerful, and the most fixed position within the parameters of the military-industrial-complex. It is where the logic of capitalism resides in its purest abstract and concrete form as the ruling political-economic framework of society and social relations.

46.c) However, the lowest common denominator located in the most basic average general median is as well the most un-creative, the most obstructed and the most redundant position within the parameters of the military-industrial-complex. The lowest common denominator, located in the most basic average general median, is where bourgeois-state-capitalism is most inclined to breakdowns, impasses, cataclymsm, explosions, and obsolescence of all types and kinds, due to the fact, the lowest common denominator is so obdurate, fixed and ironclad, it is incapable of radical social change. Consequently, as the logic of capitalism increasingly becomes proficient, potent and efficient at pinpointing, measuring and manufacturing average base medians and the lowest common denominator within these medians, yes, it is increasing its supremacy, but, it is as well increasingly truncating its fundamental capacity, and its logical necessity, for radical socio-economic transformations. Therefore, with its ever-increasing regimentation, discipline and control of the workforce/population into basic average medians, in order to solidify its contextual supremacy, the logic of capitalism is ever-increasingly truncating the vital revolutionary/evolutionary capacities of the workforce/population, capacities, it sorely needs to grow and expand. That is, paradoxically, by manufacturing average base medians, bourgeois-state-capitalism is truncating all revolutionary/evolutionary capacities, capacities, it so desperately needs in order to continuously and radically transform its socio-economic processes, so as to accumulate and extract greater amounts of surplus value. By increasingly truncating the wellspring of surplus value, i.e., the workforce/population, in an effort to solidify an average docile median, which it sees as the root of its contextual supremacy and the basis for maximizing profit, bourgeois-state-capitalism is as well increasingly dooming itself into socio-economic stasis, paralysis and inertia. Its increasing proficiency, potency and efficiency, at encapsulating the lowest common denominator, which is, increasingly expanding and solidifying its contextual supremacy, the logic of capitalism is also demolishing its revolutionary/evolutionary capacities for greater accumulations and extractions of surplus value. The result is an ever-diminishing rate of profit and an ever-increasing rate of socio-economic breakdowns, stagnation and economic paralysis. As a result, this Catch-22 is prompting the dislodgement and displacement of the logic of capitalism by increasing socio-economic stasis, inertia, and paralysis, throughout the capitalist-system. In contrast, the antithesis of capitalism, structural-anarchism, is empowered and emboldened.

-[47]-

47.a) The third primary factor that will result in the dislodgement and displacement of The logic of capitalism and its material manifestation, the military-industrial-complex, is incompetence. In fact, bourgeois-state-capitalism is dependent on radical specialization for accumulating and extracting surplus value, that is, it is dependent on manufacturing a docile specialized workforce/population, which is highly technocratic yet is highly incompetent, outside its given specialization, concerning the mechanics of bourgeois-state-capitalism. As a result, this necessary dependence, inherent in the logic of capitalism, will eventually dislodge the logic of capitalism, from its central position as central organizing principle of the workforce/population. These incompetent technocratic-cogs, which are radically specialized, highly educated, and docile, are increasingly filling the upper-echelons of the military-industrial-complex, due to their technocratic specialties. These incompetent yet specialized technocrats are increasingly being stationed in the bureaucratic upper-echelons of bourgeois-state-capitalism, due to their specific submissiveness, and compliance with the logic of capitalism and the armature of micro-fascism. Consequently, these incompetent, yet specialized technocratic-cogs, who exercise the tenets of micro-fascism and the logic of capitalism with administrative efficiency, proficiency, and potency, on behalf of the ruling, micro-fascist, oligarchical networks, are nevertheless increasingly ill-equipped to handle and comprehend the ebbs and flows of bourgeois-state-capitalism and in sum the workforce/population. These incompetent, yet highly technocratic-cogs are increasingly, ill-equipped to adapt and comprehend the ever-changing, ebbs and flows of bourgeois-state-capitalism, and the workforce/population, because:

1. They have an ever-increasing necessity to increasingly conform to the logic of capitalism and its armature of micro-fascism in order to remain useful, important, harmonized, efficient and time-effective. This is a necessity precipitated by the logic of capitalism itself, namely, its own necessity to accumulate and extract greater and greater levels of surplus value, which increasingly magnifies the pressures on all the socio-economic processes within bourgeois-state-capitalism, including administrative-structural processes.

2. These incompetent yet highly specialized cogs are increasingly ill-equipped to adapt and to comprehend the ever-changing ebbs and flows of bourgeois-state-capitalism, and the workforce/population, because its necessity for radical specialization makes these so-called expert technocrats increasingly oblivious and illiterate to all social changes and deviations, which do not coincide with their highly independent, atomized, functional-ideological, rote-learning edification. They are increasingly blind to radical social change and deviations, within the workings of bourgeois-state-capitalism and the workforce/ population, which is increasingly augmenting the longevity and magnitude of socio-economic breakdowns, within bourgeois-state-capitalism, itself. Thus, these docile technocratic-cogs are increasingly destabilizing the contextual supremacy of bourgeois-state-capitalism as the only viable political-economic framework for any form of socio-economic organization.

47.b) Increasingly, these factors are destabilizing and displacing the logic of capitalism and its material manifestation, the military-industrial-complex. As the logic of capitalism increasingly stations an army of radically specialized yet incompetent docile cogs, in exceptional positions, across its soft-totalitarian-state, due to their systemic servitude and compliance with its core logic, it is as well increasing its own ineptitude and systemic failure. It is increasing its own ineptitude and failure because its armature of micro-fascism constructs and emboldens, mentally and physically, truncated sectors of the workforce/population, across the stratums of the military-industrial-complex, which are devoid of farsightedness, empathy, and backbone, other than serving the logic of capitalism with total devotion.

47.c) Moreover, this army of radically specialized, yet incompetent, docile technocratic-cogs, in exceptional positions, is slowly eliminating and degrading, socio-economic, risk-taking and socio-economic deviations, from bourgeois-state-capitalism, at the cost of its own inherent necessity for innovations and new discoveries. With its ever-increasing emphasis on the armature of micro-fascism and the principles of interchangeability, standardization, utility, division, systematization, and time-management, the military-industrial-complex is slowly eradicating innovation, renewal, and the search for discovery, from its processes, apparatuses and hierarchies. The military-industrial-complex is doing this in the sense that its emphasis on improving systemic performativity, across all its stratums, in service of the logic of capitalism, is increasingly driving it to reject all the sectors of the workforce/population, which might innovatively revolutionize and/or improve its logical mechanics. In consequence, its own emphasis on systemic performativity as the criterion for systemic success, within the military-industrial-complex, is eliminating all creative, innovative and anarchic elements, which it, paradoxically, requires in order to ameliorate its capitalist processes, capitalist apparatuses and capitalist hierarchies, namely, the politic-economic framework of capitalism. These revolutionary and/or evolutionary elements, generated by and housed in the workforce/population, increasingly being marginalized do to their revolutionary/evolutionary capacities, are in fact, the exact elements the military-industrial-complex needs so as to improve its lackluster, degenerating, logical mechanics. As a result, these mediocre yet highly specialized technocratic-cogs, situated in exceptional managerial positions, across the military-industrial-complex, are continually decreasing systemic performance over the long-run. That is, these technocratic-cogs are continually multiplying systemic incompetence and the possibility of grave systemic breakdowns across the capitalist system. These docile technocratic-cogs are decreasing systemic performance because they are not valuing qualification, intelligence, creativity and ability, instead, they are valuing obedience, conformity, appearances and ideological congruity in relation to the logic of capitalism, which is ultimately, manufacturing socio-economic conditions ripe for systemic explosions, explosions capable of blasting the whole capitalist edifice, sky-high.

47.d) They are increasing systemic incompetence and systemic breakdowns, by the very fact that, despite their prevalent mediocrity sheathed beneath their unwavering servitude and devotion for bourgeois-state-capitalism, these intellectually incompetent, yet highly, specialized technocrats are increasingly inept at anticipating and accommodating radical social change within the socio-economic processes of capitalism. Consequently, this ever-increasing ineptitude is as well increasingly impeding the accumulation and extraction of surplus value, and in addition, multiplying the possibilities for explosive socio-economic breakdowns across the military-industrial-complex.

47.e) Bourgeois-state-capitalism is a political-economic framework where the emphasis on an ever-increasing, specialized workforce/population is as well manufacturing an ever-increasing number of systemic breakdowns and systemic ineptitudes. Its ever-increasing emphasis on the armature of micro-fascism, i.e., obedience, ignorance, fear, and network-cronyism, as the basis for any decision-making-authority, means that bourgeois-state-capitalism will continue to manufacture an intensifying, insurmountable, pressure, within its own socio-economic processes, which will tear the whole capitalist edifice apart. This vortex-catch-22, i.e., intensifying no-win situation, or vicious circle, at the center of bourgeois-state-capitalism, is propelling bourgeois-state-capitalism to expand and to increasingly intensify, surveillance, punitive, and disciplinary-mechanisms, across the military-industrial-complex. It is doing this 1. to sheath the inherent incompetence within its socio-economic processes. 2. It is doing this to sheath the inherent incompetence of its ruling, micro-fascist, oligarchical networks. 3., It is doing this to sheath the ever-increasing possibilities of explosive systemic breakdowns. 4. It is doing this to shuffle socio-economic breakdowns around different socio-economic sectors within the military-industrial-complex. And 5., it is doing this in an attempt to regiment greater portions of the workforce/population in an effort to eliminate systemic dissonance and deviances, within capitalist processes, all the while, incorporating all it can in service of the logic of capitalism.

47.f) Mediocre, yet highly specialized technocratic-cogs, stationed in exceptional positions, by the ruling, micro-fascist, oligarchical networks, in service of the logic of capitalism, are increasingly stifling amelioration in the accumulation and extraction of surplus value, that is, capitalist profit-making. Average submissive people, with average submissive intellects, stationed in the administrative-power-structures of the military-industrial-complex, in exceptional positions, requiring exceptional intellects, are increasingly causing, magnifying, and multiplying socio-economic breakdowns, and increasingly extending the longevity and magnitude of these socio-economic breakdowns. It is the manner in which bourgeois-state-capitalism passes off mediocrity as superiority and superiority as mediocrity, in and across the military-industrial-complex, via micro-fascism, which is the primary motor and factor, propelling, bourgeois-state-capitalism towards its own obsolescence, overthrow, and demolition.

47.g) Its inflated sense of its own political-economic supremacy, as the only viable political-economic option for socio-economic organization, is propelling bourgeois-state-capitalism to demand ever-increasing rigid subservence from the workforce/population. Its increasing demand that the workforce/population conform to an ever-increasing set of complex regulations, rules, procedures, qualifications, and credentials, in order to function and operate successfully within bourgeois-state-capitalism, is alienating and detaching vast sectors of the workforce/population from the logic of capitalism. These vast alienated and detached sectors of the workforce/population, given the opportunity, would be extremely profitable for any socio-economic system and political-economic framework able to combine these vast sectors of the workforce/population into communal, anarcho-socialist, socio-economic processes. Of course, bourgeois-state-capitalism attempts to re-capture and re-incorporate this plethora of alienated and detached sectors of the workforce/population, via its socio-economic processes of mental and physical consumption. However, this is increasingly ineffective and prone to socio-economic breakdowns, due to the fact that consumption processes, themselves, generate their own amount of alienation and disillusionment in the workforce/population, in their attempts to stimulate higher levels of money-making-consumption. Consequently, in response, bourgeois-state-capitalism is continually increasing its surveillance, discipline and punishment, in and across the micro-levels of everyday life, so as to absorb and track the ever-increasing numbers of alienated disengaged deviants, increasingly multiplying in and across the workforce/population and the stratums of everyday life.

47.h) This alone is enough to result in the eventual demolition and/or displacement of bourgeois-state-capitalism. Notwithstanding, this is a slow demolitionist process, where, the compounding of specialized ineptitudes upon themselves, over a long period of time, in and across the many, inter-connected stratums of the military-industrial-complex, will eventually take its toll and result in accumulating socio-economic breakdowns. Of course, these systemic decompositions and displacements will initially appear in the guise and alibi that no one is singularly responsible for all this, but, nonetheless, everyone must bear responsibility and share the weight of a vast application of socio-economic austerity. All the while, the inter-connected stratums of the ruling, micro-fascist, oligarchical networks, superficially fragmented beyond repair, yet, innately always combined, will clandestinely attempt to reboot the logic of capitalism, once again, in their own image and for their own mercenary benefits. All in all, the primary cause of socio-economic breakdown is always the promotional, exaggerated, processes of bourgeois-state-capitalism, which, incessantly, favor docile obedience over intelligence, convention over innovation, banality over creativity, the 1% over the 99%, the bourgeois-capitalist status quo over any revolutionary social changes etc.

47.i) In consequence, no revolutions, no matter how sophisticated can out do the damage that mediocrity can inflict on its own socio-economic system, when, it is bestowed with a governing power that exceeds its intellectual capacity and its intellectual limits. Incompetence and ineptitude magnify and multiply over time and space, and eventually result in socio-economic breakdowns. Due to incessant exaggerations of competence, skill, intelligence, and worth, by bourgeois-state-capitalism, for all its subservient technocratic-cogs, which demonstrate high levels of conformity, compliance, and blind faith in the capitalist status quo, bourgeois-state-capitalism is, invariably, bringing forth its own gravediggers. Its own displacement, horizontalization, and democratization, will occur, not by any revolutionary proletariat, per se, but by an army of incompetent, inept, docile, capitalist bureaucrats of its own choosing, molded according to its own preferential criteria, which are laying the groundwork for a universal anarchist revolution. That is, a bunch of run of the mill capitalist zealots, in high places, who so eloquently express a highly specialized, technocratic-administrative, savoir-faire, yet are so completely mediocre, intellectually truncated, and outside the narrow parameters of their functional-ideological, rote-learning edification, these are the cogs, laying the groundwork for the revolutionary overthrow of totalitarian, bourgeois-state-capitalism. Because, these vast inter-connected networks of technocratic-cogs are increasingly unable to comprehend, anticipate, and incorporate, the ever-changing, multiplicity of collective expressions, deviations and pragmatic egalitarianism, spewing-out from the workforce/population. Therefore, the ever-narrowing, obdurate, socio-economic processes of bourgeois-state-capitalism are increasingly at a lost, and thus, are amassing a pungent insurgency, soon to blast the giant ant-colony to smithereens. This is the information-superhighway to the anarchist revolution, sounding the sirens, the demolition of the logic of capitalism and the military-industrial-complex.

-[48]-

48.a) The fourth primary factor that will result in the dislodgement and displacement of the logic of capitalism and its material manifestation, the military-industrial-complex, is universal nihilism. As the logic of capitalism expands and develops into new areas, new foreign markets and new sectors of the workforce/population, it increasingly demonstrates its essence, universal nihilism, and in addition, it increasingly manufactures its essence, universal nihilism. The logic of capitalism continually constructs and demolishes communities and ways of life, while, reconstructing them, according to its immediate needs and its needs for the foreseeable future, without any recourse to a basic truth and/or existential verity. Everything the logic of capitalism is, or does, is in essence without logical underpinning, other than, the vacuum of its own capitalist mercenary enterprise. Consequently, the logic of capitalism, or for that matter the mechanical-workings of the military-industrial-complex, are completely subjective, without solid foundation. There is no grounding fundamental rationality, or why things are the way they are. Everything about capitalism is founded on force. There is only the capitalist maxim to maximize profit, by any means necessary, for a select few, i.e., the best proponents of the logic of capitalism, which governs and informs thinking and behavior. The logic of capitalism has no recourse to any fundamental verity, and as a result, its foundation is completely vacuous. Its base is nothingness, complete uncertainty, that is, universal nihilism. Its only recourse to contextual supremacy is force, nothing more. Moreover, all its socio-economic processes manufacture vast amounts of nihilism, wherefore, all that is solid evaporates in the mechanical-workings of its defective capitalist logic. Universal nihilism is built into the structures of the military-industrial-complex, itself, and as a result, universal nihilism is comprised in everything that is produced by, disseminated by, and generated by the capitalist system as a whole. In fact, universal nihilism lies behind the thin veneer of all commodities, commodity-images, capitalist processes, capitalist structures, capitalist relationships, capitalist forces, and the capitalist mode of production, at the center of the military-industrial-complex. Power is all that matters, all that has significance in the eyes of capitalism, specifically, its ruling, micro-fascist, oligarchical networks.

48.b) The mechanical-workings of the military-industrial-complex function, operate, and manufacture, on the basis of universal nihilism, that is, on the pseudo-premise that physical and mental reality is devoid of timeless truth, validity, and ultimate value. Things and reality only have relative or subjective verity, validity and value as part of, or within, a particular governing, ideational comprehensive framework, or frame of reference, such as the ruling, ideational comprehensive framework of capitalism, that is, the ruling logical apparatus of capitalism. Consequently, the more the socio-economic processes of the military-industrial-complex accumulate and extract surplus value, and realize this surplus value, over and over, with greater and greater efficiency, proficiency, and potency, across vast areas of time and space, they as well amplify, expand, and refine, universal nihilism, within and across the military-industrial-complex.

> (Note: Alienation is a mild form of universal nihilism. Alienation is the stepping-stone to universal nihilism. Universal nihilism is total despair, worthlessness, and despondency, in the face of the way things are. That is, the way things are structurally organized never to fundamentally change, in any shape or form, despite constant change. Namely, the fact that things incessantly change, but nevertheless, remain forever, the same, superficial, artificial, trite and so listlessly bourgeois. Consequently, universal nihilism is a rational response, both conceptual and material, to the unhinging-effects of the capitalist system, wherefore, organic communities, identities, and old certainties are gutted, radically emptied-out of content, substance, and soul, so as to maximize the accumulation, extraction and centralization of surplus value, i.e., capitalist profit.)

48.c) This has grave consequences in that the by-product of universal nihilism is increasing disillusionment, estrangement, monotony, apathy, discontent, melancholy, deviation etc., which cause all sorts of manifestations of irrationality, stupidity and futility, like road rage, professional sports, organized religions, terrorism, suicide, mass murder, and generalized warfare etc. Notwithstanding, in all of this, universal nihilism, as well, increasingly organizes and emboldens the antithetic replacement to the logic of capitalism, as all sorts of sectors of the workforce/population begin to search, and rudimentary live, according to anti-capitalist, political-economic frameworks. Ultimately, this rudimentary, anti-capitalist, plurality of political-economic frameworks is articulated within the parameters of an advanced, political-economic framework. That is, a singular framework, which is more in-tune with the logical necessities of the workforce/population, namely, the political-economic framework of structural-anarchism, which is grounded in the poly-rationality of structural-anarchism.

-[49]-

49.a) Taking a closer look at the fourth primary factor, universal nihilism sheaths the socio-economic processes, mechanisms and apparatuses of bourgeois-state-capitalism:

1. Universal nihilism is present within the armature of micro-fascism, which permeates bourgeois-state-capitalism. It is present as the open-trapdoor that jettisons all that does not measure-up to the required levels of systemic obedience, ignorance, fear, and network-cronyism required for well-functioning socio-economic processes.

2. Universal nihilism is present within the functional and operational moorings of bourgeois-state-capitalism, i.e., the principles of interchangeability, standardization, utility, division, systematization and time-management. Universal nihilism is the by-product of these capitalist principles. And with the ever-narrowing and streamlining of socio-economic processes via these capitalist principles, universal nihilism, in contrast, ever-widens, ever-deepens, and ever-magnifies across the workforce/population.

3. Universal nihilism is present within the 5 properties of neoliberal capitalism art, i.e., ambiguity, entertainment, temperate-moderation, de-politicization and network-connection, it is their sense and meaning. Universal nihilism is embedded in the concept of art-for-art-sake, where sense and meaning is empty, ever-shifting and groundless. Universal nihilism is embedded in the idea that art is open-ended, open to infinite interpretations, or points of views. These capitalist ideas are products of the logic of capitalism, designed to subjugate art into futility and a total inability to influence and/or generate anything, other than, the expression and growth of the universal nihilism increasingly spewing-out of capitalism.

4. Moreover, to transform every (thing) into a digit is to exterminate identity, i.e., the quality that makes every (thing) unique, i.e., individual, and as a result this as well manufactures universal nihilism. This logical necessity for a well-functioning bourgeois-state-capitalism, i.e., the extermination of identity so as to facilitate the exchange of commodities in an effort to accumulate and extract surplus value, in addition generates universal nihilism. The emptying out of individuality, i.e., spirit, from the military-industrial-complex in favor of universal artificiality, enables the accumulation and extraction of surplus value through the elimination of depth, weight, gravity and substance from commodities, commodity-images, people, cultures, services and spectacle happenings. This emptying-out process, within bourgeois-state-capitalism, facilitates the interchangeability, utility, standardization, division, systematization, time-management, and consumption of commodities, commodity-images, people, services, cultures and/or spectacle happenings via trivialization, i.e., post-modern kitsch. This emptying-out process lubricates the socio-economic processes within bourgeois-state-capitalism, accelerating the accumulation and extraction of surplus value via an incessant focus and emphasis on the manufacturing of artificial kitsch, i.e., a manufactures weightlessness of things and people, superficial, mediocre, and bland. The result is a seemingly, impenetrable, glittering, totalitarian façade, constructed on vast amounts of systemically induced, suspensions of disbelief, illusions, sheathing the sense of total emptiness and vacuity beneath the logic of capitalism. This emptiness and vacuity ever-present and produced upon the logic of capitalism is universal nihilism.

-[50]-

50.a) Once detached from all frameworks, frames of reference, sense of identity, other than the logical apparatus of the logic of capitalism, conceptual-commodity-value-management takes root. Conceptual-commodity-value-management is the underlying arbitrariness, randomness, and lack of foundation for any objective value, wage and price determinations, which is allocated to objects, images, people, services and/or spectacle happenings etc., within bourgeois-state-capitalism. The notion of universal nihilism engendered, by the workings of bourgeois-state-capitalism, both by accident and on purpose, enables conceptual-commodity-value-management to take root in the sense that what something or someone is worth, or signifies, is increasingly devoid of underpinnings, i.e., any objective theory of value, price, and wage, other than, the speculative underpinnings of arbitrary mercenary profiteering. Moreover, through the increasing detachment of the workforce/population from any dependable frame of reference and/or logical scaffolding, means that conceptual-commodity-value-management increasingly becomes a lever to subjugate and control the workforce/population. It is increasingly becoming a lever in the sense that as the workforce/population makes advances in wage gains, civic necessities, and liberties, it is simultaneously subdued via arbitrary value manipulations, arbitrary wage machinations, and arbitrary price escalations and depreciations, specifically, value, price, and wage fixing. Because, today, values, wages, and prices, no longer have recourse to any objective basis or abor theory of value for their objective calibrations. Instead, today, values, prices, and wages are increasingly subject to the speculative, mercenary whims of ruling enterprising-networks, i.e., power-blocs, who ruthlessly exercise the logic of capitalism, devoid of empathy or any moral considerations.

50.b) Even, supply and demand is increasingly succumbing to the mechanisms of conceptual-commodity-value-management as conceptual-commodity-value-management increasingly engineers and controls supply and demand via arbitrary value manipulations, wage machinations and arbitrary price determinations thru closely-knit enterprising-networks, i.e., cartels, cabals, associations, unions and/or states etc. As a result, these crony-networks manufacture fluctuations in supply and demand through conceptual-commodity-value-management, subordinating and subjugating the autonomous mechanism of supply and demand to the arbitrary values, wages and price determinations of specific ruling, micro-fascist, oligarchical networks. Together, these ruling enterprising-networks determine the arbitrary price/value/wage of products/commodities/services etc., which are increasingly detached from any rational basis, and are instead, increasingly determined in the minds of those engrossed in the aura of the specific product/commodity/service. Whether, it is the ruling enterprising-networks, themselves, who are totally engrossed in their own grandeur and self-worth, that is, their own arbitrary inflated values, wages and prices, or an unsuspecting public, who is forced to acknowledge these outrageous values, wages and prices, it is increasingly apparent that values, wages and prices are divorced from any objective basis. In effect, values, prices and wages are now subject to the arbitrary mercenary whims of network-collusion, network-cronyism and network-manipulations, specifically, the subjective whims of ruling power-blocs.

50.c) These ruling enterprising-networks, who, devoid of objective underpinnings, increasingly resort to conceptual-commodity-value-management to leverage supply and demand in their favor, in their efforts to satisfy their limitless mercenary impulses, are manufacturing an ever-intensifying universal nihilism. Bewitched by the specific product/commodity/service, these ruling enterprising-networks revolve around, ever tempted to increasingly invest their mental/physical activity in brand-auras as reflections of their individual greatness, the product/commodity/service in question becomes an identity, a brand, a social status, a blessed profession, which embodies a manufactured sacred aura. Likewise, for a select few, this artificial aura fills the empty-void of the self and the universal nihilism manufactured by the socio-economic processes of bourgeois-state-capitalism, and moreover, becomes the arbitrary measuring stick for value, wage, and price determinations. The aura, or the fetish, becomes the arbitrary stimulus of conceptual-commodity-value-management, both for the hollowed-out self of a person and for its commodity-brand-image. The artificially-constructed aura of a commodity, service and/or profession becomes the nexus by which to determine value, prices and wages. Having jettisoned all rational modern labor theories of value in favor of post-industrial, post-modern theories of value and surplus value, these ruling, micro-fascist, oligarchical networks now determine values, wages and prices, within their specific economic branches, based on their own arbitrary notions of self-worth and unmitigated force. Increasingly, with the adoption of post-industrial, post-modern theories of value and surplus value, prices, values, and wages, are increasingly subject to the arbitrary whims of ruling enterprising-networks, i.e., power-blocs, which are able to enclose and control specific markets and specific professions. As a result, prices, values and wages, within a specific market and/or profession, are increasingly subjective, arbitrary and artificially-constructed by ruling, micro-fascist, oligarchical networks. Consequently, what these capitalist networks deem acceptable, pertaining to values, prices and wages, is increasingly exaggerated, irrational, and baseless, lacking any rational foundation, yet, nonetheless, still possesses seeming legitimacy, authenticity, and validity, because, these ruling, micro-fascist, oligarchical networks control, manipulate, and govern, specific economic branches and commodity markets. What is lauded, by these enterprising-networks, as the product of autonomous, market mechanisms, devoid of any conscious planning, rigging and/or design, is in fact, socially-constructed and artificially-manufactured, behind the magical veil of Adam Smith's invisible hand. Values, prices and wages, devoid of any rational basis, are artificially and arbitrarily fabricated sums, which have been reinforced in people's minds by the sheer gravity and weight of the ruling, micro-fascist, oligarchical networks slithering, in and across, the inter-connected stratums of the capitalist monolithic edifice.

50.d) Crushed beneath the logic of capitalism, and bewitched by the alluring aura of a single product/commodity/service etc., always closely tied to the universal nihilism manufactured by bourgeois-state-capitalism, the workforce/population slumbers in perpetual suspension of disbelief. A perpetual suspension of disbelief, crafted by the siren-song of specific ruling capitalist-networks, i.e., power-blocs, revolving around specific products/commodities/services etc., who, covertly, exercise conceptual-commodity-value-management behind the illusory screen of the invisible hand, that is, the mechanism of supply and demand. Dazed and confused by the false-consciousness of the invisible hand, the workforce/population dedicates its creative-power through the medium of products/commodities/services etc., believing no one has systemic mastery over any industry and/or profession, when in fact, the reality is the contrary. The illusion of socio-economic equality, projected by the autonomous mechanism of supply and demand within bourgeois-state-capitalism, and enthusiastically propagated by bourgeois-state-capitalism, is able to cleverly stimulate the workforce/population to produce, to consume, and to accept the given contextual supremacy of the logic of capitalism. The logic of capitalism is able to do this on the basis of the illusory equality that the autonomous market mechanism of supply and demand, magically manifests, namely, the spectacular idea that no one has mastery, or can fully control, socio-economic industries and/or any professions. Consequently, conceptual-commodity-value-management, sheathed by the myth of the autonomous mechanism of supply and demand, seduces the workforce/population, via the seeming freedom this autonomous mechanism manifests, to support the capitalist-system. In fact, in many instances, these seemingly, autonomous market mechanisms, working throughout the marketplace at face-value, dupe the workforce/population, cunningly, to accept, machinated, arbitrary value/wage/price determinations, false-consciousness(es) of all sorts and types. All the while, behind the scenes, these value/price/wage determinations are nothing but the artificial constructs of specific, ruling, micro-fascist, oligarchical networks, seeking only to maximize profit, by any means necessary, at the lowest financial cost, as soon as possible.

50.e) Conceptual-commodity-value-management requires continuous validation, objectification and legitimization in order to solidify its arbitrary price, wage and value determinations. Consequently, there are constant appeals to economists and autonomous free-market mechanisms, such as supply and demand, in order to validate, authenticate, and legitimate, erroneous value, wage and price machinations. Moreover, conceptual-commodity-value-management as well mediates relationships between people, it ranks and files them, arbitrarily, according to the logical necessities of the logic of capitalism. For instance, via the conceptual-commodity-value-management of a select few, micro-fascist networks, movie-stars and professional sport-stars are arbitrarily ranked and filed at higher values, wages, prices, and statuses in relation to medical doctors and laborers, within the military-industrial-complex. They are manufactured and celebrated, by the ruling, micro-fascist, oligarchical networks of capitalism, so as to radiate success onto specific industries and onto bourgeois-state-capitalism, in general. They are manufactured and applauded by the celebratory monologue, that is, bourgeois-state-capitalism, as shinning beckons of talent, perfection, and genius, as outputs of greatness, which could only have emanated from the political-economic framework of bourgeois-state-capitalism. Despite being less educated, less useful, less knowledgeable etc., these star-like constructs are systemic emblems of higher rank and file, who owe their whole manufactured existence to the ideational comprehensive framework of capitalism. These manufactured personalities, who themselves, stimulate obedient personality cults, shape mental and physical activities, processes and behaviors of the workforce/population, which are taught to mimic these mythical creatures in their everyday relations, communications and interactions. These artificial star-like constructs, our social betters, are not the product of autonomous mechanisms, they are the product of conceptual-commodity-value-management. They are artificially designed to engender suspension of disbelief, across the military-industrial-complex, so as to rivet segments of the workforce/population evermore to the logical mechanics of bourgeois-state-capitalism, ad infinitum.

50.f) As values, wages and prices arbitrarily inflate or deflate, due to the machinations of capitalist power-blocs, in turn there is a constant increase in the manifestations of micro-fascism and universal nihilism in the workforce/population and society, in general. It is a micro-fascism and a universal nihilism, in most instances, directed not at the ruling, micro-fascist, oligarchical networks of bourgeois-capitalism, or the logic of capitalism, which is the root cause of the ever-increasing micro-fascism and universal nihilism within everyday life. Instead, it is a micro-fascism and a universal nihilism directed at the workforce/population by the workforce/population, itself. It is a micro-fascism and a universal nihilism directed at the workforce/population by the workforce/population, itself, which has been seduced by the illusory equality, emanating from the seemingly autonomous mechanisms of the marketplace, preaching prosperity through hard-work and honesty, yet, is in actuality the opposite of this. These seemingly, autonomous, market-mechanisms sheath the exploitation, the bias and the deliberate machinations of conceptual-commodity-value-management, orchestrated by capitalist power-blocs. The result is that the workforce/population turns against itself, as individual segments of the workforce/population turn against each other, when, the illusion of capitalist prosperity is unveiled to be completely rigged. Moreover, the ruling, micro-fascist, oligarchical networks of bourgeois-capitalism, having manufactured the disarray, now officiate the micro-skirmishes, cunningly reinforcing, the capitalist socio-economic inequalities, which accumulate and extract surplus value, and slowly, transform everyday life bit by bit into a technocratic, hard-lined military-industrial-complex.

50.g) The point is to generate socio-economic antagonisms so as to exploit, annex and subdue as many insatiable drives for ownership/knowledge of the workforce/population as possible, in service of the logic of capitalism, in order to maximize, the accumulation and the extraction of surplus value, i.e. capitalist profit. In contrast, the antagonistic workforce/population sinks ever-deeper into despair, nihilism, religious delusion and crippling poverty, which is both mental and physical.

-[51]-

51.a) Likewise, universal nihilism lies at the base of any hierarchy constructed by bourgeois-state-capitalism. All hierarchies within the military-industrial-complex are, in essence, unfounded and baseless. They are artificial, arbitrary constructs of the ruling, micro-fascism, oligarchical networks, which themselves are artificial, arbitrary constructs of the logic of capitalism. Therefore, any hierarchy, within bourgeois-state-capitalism, is arbitrary and artificial in the sense that it is completely subjective. Hierarchies are artificial, arbitrary constructs based on the current ideational comprehensive framework holding contextual supremacy at the moment, namely, bourgeois-capitalism. The logic of capitalism holds the central position in society, therefore, it is the organizing principle of society. By controlling the central nodes of decision-making-authority, the ideational comprehensive framework of capitalism has become the central organizing principle of society. It inhabits and holds contextual supremacy for global society, at large. In many instances, it manufactures reality, itself.

51.b) First and foremost, all hierarchies are conceptually and psychologically erected, and established, before they are materially and physically erected and established. The latter comes later, i.e., only later does the conceptual hierarchy acquire a material form as it begins its descent, via mental/physical activity, from the abstract to the concrete. The material manifestation of hierarchy enshrines the conceptual manifestation of hierarchy, meaning its physical form and structure is grounded in its psychological form and structure and nothing else. There is no foundational reason, or concept, why the hierarchies and/or the hierarchy of bourgeois-state-capitalism is the way it is, functions the way it functions, and/or houses such and such seemingly, superior, technocratic-cogs. The only thing holding capitalist hierarchies, or the hierarchy of bourgeois-state-capitalism, together, is fundamentally ideological, i.e., the logical necessities of the logic of capitalism, which pin the mercenary capitalist-enterprise for maximum profit, within structured, corporeal, capitalist hierarchies.

> (Note: The physical manifestation of hierarchy is in fact the enshrinement of psychological, subjective, hierarchical, conceptual-frameworks, localized in the mind, but, realized and actualized in material terms.)

51.c) These hierarchies sustain themselves as networks, because, they are without basis within the military-industrial-complex. Because, hierarchies are without basis, within bourgeois-state-capitalism, they increasingly force themselves and are increasingly forced by one another to increasingly conform to the logic of capitalism and its armature of micro-fascism. Changes in technology, changes in science, changes in the mechanical-workings of socio-economic processes, within bourgeois-state-capitalism etc., invariably change all capitalist hierarchies, since, not changing, increasingly exposes these hierarchies to the universal nihilism sheathed beneath the logical apparatus of capitalism. Namely, it exposes these hierarchies to the basic fact that all hierarchies, within bourgeois-state-capitalism, are founded on nothing substantial, or concrete, other than, the fact that these hierarchical structures are dependent for their legitimacy and authority on the disciplinary and punitive-mechanisms of bourgeois-state-capitalism, specifically, the force and power of the logic of capitalism.

51.d) All hierarchies, within bourgeois-state-capitalism, are founded on false-consciousness. They have no connection to any objective reality other than the artificial reality arbitrarily approved and constructed, by bourgeois-state-capitalism. That is, the man-made superficial reality, which buttresses and secures all the logical necessities for bourgeois-capitalism to retain contextual supremacy. In fact, within the military-industrial-complex, capitalist hierarchies are free from fact, they can play with facts etc., but, they do eventually adopt facts as a means to retain contextual supremacy and legitimacy, but, this takes time. For instance, centuries or decades after the fact, capitalist hierarchies will apologize for wrong doings, wrong doings, they would do all-over again, if the situation was the same, genocide, mass murder, mass starvation etc.

51.e) Because of the universal nihilism embedded within hierarchies, hierarchies seek to continually and factually prove their legitimacy and their reason for being, first to the ruling, micro-fascism, oligarchical networks and, second, to the workforce/population. Consequently, with time, hierarchies manufacture all sorts of reasons for being and all sorts of nemeses in their inherent effort to validate themselves, their legitimacy, their reason for being, including, also, so they can accumulate, centralize and extract surplus value for their own personal development, refinement, and expansion. That is, for the development, refinement, and expansion of bourgeois-state-capitalism. In the end, devoid of underpinning, it is nothing but brute force which sustains all capitalist hierarchies.

51.f) A hierarchy is a collectively formed, stratified, ideational set of false-consciousness(es), ossified into objective, socio-economic processes and modes of being, perceiving, interpreting and action, with the goal of regulating, accumulating and extracting surplus value. The secret of any capitalist hierarchy is that there is no genuine hierarchy. Hierarchy, under bourgeois-state-capitalism, is designed to regiment the workforce/population, for the accumulation and extraction of surplus value. Moreover, hierarchy is a type of mechanism designed, by the logic of capitalism, to maintain, to safeguard, and to celebrate, the ruling, micro-fascist, oligarchical networks, while, at the same time, regulating, accumulating, and extracting surplus value, from the workforce/population. Universal nihilism is the by-product and the foundation of this unrelenting, hierarchical, modus operandi. It is the source by which all capitalist hierarchies, vehemently, function and operate to batter-down all antagonisms, all dissonances and all divergences from the logic of capitalism. Yet, within this antagonistic process, hierarchies in addition multiply antagonisms, dissonances, and divergences to the logic of capitalism, because of the ever-expanding ravages and misery manufactured by the inherent universal nihilism inside capitalist hierarchies. That is, the universal nihilism inherent in the logic of capitalism.

-[52]-

52.a) It is important to note that the military-industrial-complex is not conspiratorial by nature, it is organized and structured according to the logic of capitalism, that is all. The logic of capitalism, coinciding with the logical necessities of bourgeois-state-capitalism, organizes the workforce/population according to specific duties and obligations needed for the accumulation and extraction of surplus value, i.e., for the workings of capitalism. This multi-varied, litany of socio-economic processes, which range in size and magnitude, bring certain similar individuals, who never have met, together, into specific socio-economic networks, ranging from elite governing networks to ordinary mundane underprivileged networks. Consequently, temporary conspiracies do develop, due to close network-proximity, meaning certain privilege networks can momentarily profit from temporary conspiracies, such as oligarchies, cartels, monopolies etc. However, it is the logic of capitalism which invariably always benefits, sometimes in the short-term, but invariably always in the long-term, from the plundering, by capitalist entities, in the service of conspiracies. Primarily, for the most part, there are no conspiracies, only the workings of the logic of capitalism, attempting to extract and accumulate greater levels of surplus value, biological or otherwise. The ruling, micro-fascist, oligarchical networks of capitalism, which appear conspiratorial, and at times are, are more accurately the caretakers of the logic of capitalism, exercising its logical imperatives to the best of their abilities. And because of this, these ruling, micro-fascist, oligarchical networks are at times tempted into conspiracies, however the primary benefactor of any conspiracy is always the logic of capitalism.

52.b) Nevertheless, these elite, micro-fascist, oligarchical networks are merely interchangeable mediums by which the logic of capitalism exercises its logical imperatives and workings through. The actors, entities and/or participants in these capitalist, micro-fascist, oligarchical networks are nothing but interchangeable units. They are the media through which the logic of capitalism works its logical imperatives. They are interchangeable points where the logic of capitalism expresses and disseminates itself upon the workforce/population. And, because these interchangeable singularities enact the logic of capitalism with efficiency, potency, and efficacy, these singular, capitalist-entities are rewarded for their servitude by the logic of capitalism in the sense that these points become reservoirs where capital accrues for their own mercenary, selfish benefits through such mechanisms as conceptual-commodity-value-management etc.

52.c) Above any conspiracy lies the logic of capitalism, the primary motivator and benefactor of all exploitation, indoctrination, extortion and thievery, within the military-industrial-complex.

-[53]-

53.a) All in all, the end of the logic of capitalism maybe futile; notwithstanding, the logic of capitalism can be displaced, dislodged and decentralized to the socio-economic periphery. The logic of capitalism can be dislodged from its central socio-economic position and relegated to the level of an auxiliary secondary in all decision-making-authority. The logic of capitalism is riddled with paradoxes, contradictions and illogicalities inside its logical nucleus. These paradoxes, contradictions and illogicalities increasingly propel the logic of capitalism to abandon its central supremacy in an effort to solve these in-built paradoxes, contradictions and illogicalities. In the process of solving these inherent paradoxes, contradictions and illogicalities, within its logical nucleus, the logic of capitalism increasingly organizes, reinforces and brings forth its logical antithetic substitute. This logical antithetic substitute increasingly flips and inverts the logic of capitalism, right-side up again and inside out. This logical antithetic substitute, which is increasingly emboldened, empowered, and designed to supersede the logic of capitalism, solves the inherent paradoxes, contradictions and illogicalities of the logic of capitalism, by dialectically flipping the capitalist logic, right side up and inside out, into the margins of socio-economic existence. And, via this revolutionary/evolutionary process, the antithetic substitute, i.e., the logic of structural-anarchism, releases the logic of capitalism from its inherent pressures, magnified, intensified, and multiplied, inside the nucleus of its despotic logic. This accumulating pressure is unstoppable, due to the fact the logic of capitalism occupies the central position of contextual supremacy, both in all socio-economic processes and in all epicenters of decision-making-authority. Only, the displacement of the logic of capitalism, i.e., total anarchist revolution, can avert the coming catastrophic meltdown of bourgeois-capitalism. The logic of capitalism must be overthrown, dislodged and demolished by the logic of structural-anarchism.

53.b) Ultimately, only the logical antithetic substitute of capitalism, i.e., the poly-rational logic of structural-anarchism, is capable of re-configuring the military-industrial-complex, according to a new political-economic framework, i.e., the framework of structural-anarchism. This new political-economic framework, which supersedes the instrumental-rationality of capitalism and displaces it to the socio-economic periphery, is the poly-rationality of structural-anarchism. It is only the poly-rationality of structural-anarchism, which can defuse the explosive unstable nature of totalitarian-capitalism. It is only the logic of structural-anarchism, i.e., anarchist communism, which can manufacture an inclusive, political-economic framework, grounded in maximum equality, plurality, autonomy and egalitarianism. Because, the poly-rational logic of structural-anarchism invariably leads to the pragmatic installation of an anarchist federation/patchwork of municipalities, worker-cooperatives and autonomous-collectives.

Section Five:
(Conclusion)

The Logic Of Structural-Anarchism:

(The Political-Economic Framework Of Structural-Anarchism)

54.a) The main objective of the logic of structural-anarchism, or for any pragmatic revolutionary/evolutionary project bearing its name, is the displacement and/or dislodgement of the logic of capitalism, from its central position, within all socio-economic processes, all socio-economic frameworks, and all decision-making-authority, in and across the military-industrial-complex. The main objective is the re-positioning of the logic of capitalism to the socio-economic periphery of society as a secondary or minor consideration/element, within all socio-economic processes and all decision-making-authority. The logic of capitalism can be outmoded and antiquated, via the more intelligent and the more organized, poly-rationality of structural-anarchism, which can render the logic of capitalism obsolete, propelling it to the periphery of all socio-economic processes, frameworks and all decision-making-authority. The logic of structural-anarchism can return the logic of capitalism to its natural state as an auxiliary to the workforce/population, via micro-revolutions of everyday life, i.e., little nonconformist, anti-capitalist, diplomatic insurrections, within the micro-recesses of everyday life, which can escalate into radical social change.

54.b) In consequence, the main objective of the logic of structural-anarchism and its micro-revolutionary project is about overturning the logic of capitalism back onto its feet again and onto the margins of socio-economic existence. The micro-revolutionary project of the logic of structural-anarchism is about inverting the logic of capitalism right-side up again, in its rightful logical position as a marginal appendage of the workforce/population, via microscopic, nonconformist, anti-capitalist insurrections, within the micro-recesses of everyday life. The main objective is returning the logic of capitalism to its rightful logical state as a marginal, auxiliary tool, by which, the workforce/population placates its internal and external logical necessities before those of the logic of capitalism, namely, the instrumental-rationality of socio-economic domination.

54.c) The logical mechanics of structural-anarchism is about realizing poly-rationality, including, the structural-anarchist morality/amorality, which is to satisfy the maximum logical necessities of the workforce/population, by any means necessary, at the lowest financial cost, as soon as possible, while, only satisfying the minimum logical necessities of the logic of capitalism. The pragmatic revolutionary/evolutionary project of the logic of structural-anarchism is 1., to maximize the satisfaction of the basic logical necessities of the workforce/population, by any means necessary, at the lowest financial cost, as soon as possible. 2., To only fulfill the minimum basic maintenance requirements of the logic of capitalism, and 3. To maximize poly-rationality in and across the structural-anarchism-complex, i.e., the federation of municipalities, cooperatives and autonomous-collectives. This is the logical fulcrum and revolutionary/evolutionary engine of the logic of structural-anarchism, namely, its platform over and above the logic of capitalism. And, the means by which the logic of structural-anarchism intends to realize this project, is through the strategic and tactical concept of micro-revolution(s). Micro-revolution is a type of logical vortex-catch-22, which can engulf the sum of the soft-totalitarian-state via an ever-increasing, logical escalation of miniature revolutions, within the micro-recesses of everyday life, capable over time to fuse into one, generalized, universal anachist revolution.

54.d) It is this simple poly-rational nucleus at the center of the logic of structural-anarchism that can engender, and already has engendered, innumerable, rudimentary, structural-anarchism transformations, i.e., micro-revolutions, in the micro-recesses of everyday life, that is, the socio-economic processes of bourgeois-state-capitalism. At times and in certain spaces, these rudimentary transformations, which deviate from the logic of capitalism, are temporary. And at times and in certain spaces, these rudimentary transformations, which deviate from the logic of capitalism, are more permanent. Notwithstanding, it is this logical revolutionary/evolutionary engine, housed within the logic of structural-anarchism, subverting the supremacy of the logic of capitalism, in minute ways and in microscopic spaces, in favor of poly-rationality, autonomy, and open-participatory-democracy, which is persistently pointing to a new political-economic framework, namely, the political-economic framework of structural-anarchism-complex. In fact, this micro-revolutionary/evolutionary process is slowly unveiling, and unfolding, the poly-rationality of structural-anarchism. That is, an ideational comprehensive framework, both conceptual and material, which embodies within its poly-rational logic a new socio-economic framework, based on anarcho-socialist modes of production, and anarcho-socialist relations of production, namely, a new basis and context of decision-making-authority.

54.e) This new political-economic framework based on the poly-rationality of structural-anarchism, which rears its head and common sense, now and then, is a form of socio-economic organization which is: 1., more conducive to the logical necessities of the workforce/population than is bourgeois-state-capitalism. Because, the logic of structural-anarchism is more intelligent and more inclusive of varying ideational comprehensive frameworks, while, bourgeois-state-capitalism is not. And, 2., the poly-rationality of structural-anarchism is a form of socio-economic organization, which is, as well, more conducive for the accumulation and extraction of surplus value, than is, bourgeois-state-capitalism, due to the fact that surplus value becomes poly-rational and collective property, namely, a means for ameliorating the socio-economic conditions for every segment of the workforce/population. The political-economic framework of structural-anarchism is more conducive to the logical necessities of the workforce/population, and the accumulation and extraction of multi-varied surplus value than is bourgeois-state-capitalism, because, the poly-rationality of structural-anarchism organizes capital, productive forces and relations of production to benefit all, instead of the few.

54.f) In effect, the logic of structural-anarchism is able to incorporate higher levels of the insatiable drive for ownership/knowledge than the logic of capitalism, because, it is poly-rational instead of uni-rational. Thus, ultimately, it is able to spread ownership/knowledge, among every portion of the workforce/population, by enlarging the definition of what constitutes productivity, communal ownership and capital. The result is the maximum fulfillment of the basic maintenance requirements for the workforce/population and the minimum fulfillment of the basic maintenance requirements of the instrumental-rationality of capitalism. As a result, a greater sum of the workforce/population is more apt to participate in the communal accumulation and extraction of surplus value, that is, multi-varied anarcho-capital, when, surplus value belongs to all, is shared by all, and guaranteed to all, in relative equal measure.

54.g) The communal ownership of capital, property, knowledge, socio-economic processes, and decision-making-authority, in and across the structural-anarchism-complex, by all, in relative equal measure, will energize the development of an anarcho-socialist mode of production, consumption, and distribution. Since, everyone will possess a genuine, vested-interest in all socio-economic processes and decision-making-authority, in and across the structural-anarchism-complex. All for one and one for all in relative equal measure is the motto. This means the abolition of private property.

54.h) In short, the logic of structural-anarchism is an ideational comprehensive framework, programmed to seize all capitalist modes of production, consumption, and distribution, so as to re-engineer all capitalist forces of production and all capitalist relations of production, upon a poly-rational, anarcho-socialist mode of production, thus abolishing capitalist exploitation and capitalist domination. The point is to redesign the capitalist mode of production in its entirety, according to new anarcho-socialist relations, new productive relations, and new productive forces, namely, a new poly-rational mode of production. That is, an anarcho-socialist mode of production and anarcho-socialist relations of production, consumption, and distribution.

54.i) In fact, the logic of structural-anarchism is fundamentally based on engineering anarcho-socialist relations of production, consumption, and distribution, out of the anarcho-socialist mode of production, consumption and distribution, and vice versa. In contrast to capitalist relations, anarcho-socialist relations are grounded in socio-economic guarantees, basic civil rights, limited-horizontal-order, open-participatory-democracy and poly-rationality, that is, in general, pragmatic egalitarianism. Wherefore, universal salary caps, a universal income grid and a universal value/price grid, for all professions, commodities, services etc., shall organize relations and any socio-economic mode of production, consumption and distribution upon an anarcho-egalitarian basis.

54.j) The point is to place definitive limits and caps on all profit accumulation, extraction, and exploitation, so as to maximize equality, plurality and equal-opportunity, for all. Ultimately, the objective is to push every socio-economic process, every organization and every decision-making-authority to its limit, via an anarcho-socialist mode of production, an anarcho-socialist set of relations, and the full-implementation of an open-participatory-democracy. That is, an open-participatory-democracy set to maximize the basic maintenance requirements of the workforce/population, without resorting to any radical capitalist exploitation, repression and/or organization etc. The structural-anarchism-complex is not founded upon instrumental-rationality, which stems from modern Enlightenment thinking and inevitably leads again and again to totalitarianism. Instead, the structural-anarchism-complex is founded upon poly-rationality, that is, a multiple set of multi-level, multi-variable rationalities, which incorporate a multiplicity of points of views, within all decision-making-authority, and the overall, open-participatory-democracy.

55.a) Above all, the workforce/population is the nodular point and nexus, which
embodies within itself all revolutionary/evolutionary capabilities, deviations and
forces able to lead to the radical and total transformation of society. These
revolutionary/evolutionary capabilities, deviations and forces are housed in
the constitution and in the composition of the workforce/population. Hence, why the logic
of capitalism and its material manifestation, the military-industrial-complex, incessantly
attempt to truncate its deviations, appropriate its capabilities, and/or transform its
forces, i.e., its revolutionary/evolutionary manifestations, into a substantial
capitalist machine in the service of profit and the ideational comprehensive framework of
capitalism. In this regard, the workforce/population is both, simultaneously, the nexus and
engine of radical social change and the nexus and engine of capitalist development.
Moreover, these revolutionary/evolutionary capabilities, deviations, and forces, housed
within the workforce/population, can erupt in all sorts of explosive, transformative ways,
which can totally be spontaneous, unpredictable and catastrophic. As a result, the
workforce/population is the nodular lever and the fulcrum for any new political-economic
framework, ideational comprehensive framework, and universal transformation, such as
the logic of structural-anarchism. Consequently, the insatiable drive for
ownership/knowledge of the workforce/population, localized in the micro-recesses of
everyday life, are the microscopic war-zones of the antithetic, anti-capitalist,
substitute, the logic of structural-anarchism versus the logic of capitalism.

55.b) In fact, the workforce/population is the fiery crucible of all, antagonistic,
political-economic frameworks, vying for contextual supremacy and
decision-making-authority over the logic of capitalism, i.e., the central organizing
principle. The insatiable drive for ownership/knowledge of the workforce/population, is the
starting point and the focal point for any revolutionary/evolutionary project, whether, it
is marxist-communism or something more revolutionary and insurrectionary like
anarchist-communism, namely, the logic of structural-anarchism.

56.a) The force of structural-anarchism, as the antithetic substitute to the logic of capitalism,
is poly-rationality, which is not necessarily geared towards armed-revolution, but,
instead, towards variation and horizontalism, devoid of any dominance hierarchy. Its main
objective is the stimulation of nonconformist, anti-capitalist forms of production,
reproduction, consumption and distribution, full of resistance, creativity, and resilience,
within the current networks of bourgeois-state-capitalism. Its main objective is
poly-rationality, i.e., new forms of thinking and doing things, anything goes, namely,
anything, which is antagonistic to the political-economic framework of
neoliberal, bourgeois-state-capitalism. That is, anything, which is positive, unyielding,
and seeks to override the logic of capitalism, anything, which seeks to install an
anti-capitalist form of socio-economic relations, an anti-capitalist form of socio-economic
organization, which is more egalitarian, more inclusive, more participatory, more
intelligent, and more poly-rational, than, the instrumental-rationality of capitalism.

> (Note: In fact, the instrumental-rationality of capitalism draws its creative-power
> and revolutionary capabilities from the logic of structural-anarchism,
> namely, the poly-rationality of structural-anarchism.)

56.b) The force of the logic of structural-anarchism is its notion that radical social
change is something that begins very small in the micro-recesses of everyday
life, within the workforce/population. The workforce/population is the focal point and the
starting point, but out of the workforce/population, radical social change can intensify,
magnify and/or expand into lasting, trans-formative, socio-economic revolution, a universal
anarchist revolution. The pragmatic revolutionary/evolutionary project of the logic of
structural-anarchism has the mechanism of micro-revolution/micro-insurrection/micro-refusal
at its nexus. This is its engine for radical social change and for an all-encompassing,
poly-rational, egalitarian, political-economic framework.

56.c) Micro-revolutions are microscopic insurrections in the private and public spheres
of everyday life, which at first glance seem innocuous, innocent, and banal that
can nonetheless instill a solid sense of autonomy and liberty in any solitary
individual. Enabling him or her to slightly sense and possibility envision an
egalitarian time and place without the dominance of totalitarian-capitalism,
where there is less socio-economic disparities and a veritable antithetic
substitute the central position of contextual supremacy. That is, an antithetic substitute
able to decentralizes, horizontalizes, and democratizes the soft-totalitarian-forces of the

status quo and the logic of capitalism, transforming these potent forces into a more intelligent, more egalitarian, open-participatory-democracy etc.

56.d) For the logic of structural-anarchism, micro-revolutions of everyday life are the positive means for radical social change. Micro-revolutions are the means for annexing the physical/mental means of production, consumption, and distribution, from the logic of capitalism, even if it is only innocuous and/or temporary. A micro-revolution can be such a thing as Rosa Parks annexing an unreachable bus-seat so as to subvert the status quo. Micro-revolutions can be such things as alternative book clubs, where socialist and revolutionary ideas are discussed. Micro-revolutions can be brief moments in certain spaces, which can briefly transform these short time-periods and small spaces into emancipatory moments and movements against the logic of capitalism. Even the notion of taking a bike to work instead of an S.U.V. can be radical, if extended over a long enough period of time and space. These miniature acts are micro-revolutionary, if they deliberately run contrary to the micro-dictatorships of the automobile, oil/gas companies and such ideas as the petrol-state. Even, if only temporary, these deliberate, conscious acts are in essence micro-refusals against the ideational comprehensive framework of capitalism. These micro-revolutionary acts, following the poly-rationality of structural-anarchism, are lines of thought, expressing a conscious/unconscious demand for radical social change, namely, a demand for a new organizing principle capable of redistributing socio-economic resources, more equitably, in and across the stratums of everyday life. Micro-revolutions are such things as occupy movements, insurrections, Mondragon-types of cooperatives, open-file sharing, general wild-cat strikes, socially conscious graffiti, books, and urban guerrilla gardening movements, which stealth-like, beautify decaying public spaces with greenery and new forms of life and collectivism beyond the logic of capitalism etc.

56.e) Although mostly temporary, micro-revolutions have the ability to build upon themselves into a genuine, large-scale trans-formative anarchist revolution that can multiply, mutate, and expand into the decentralization, horizontalization, and/or the substitution of the logic of capitalism. When in their immediate revolutionary/evolutionary process, micro-revolutions allow the antithetic substitute, against the logic of capitalism, the opportunity to centralize, to reorganize and to supervise momentarily the microscopic socio-economic processes and networks of the military-industrial-complex. Micro-revolutions are the counter-cultural and anti-capitalist, political-economic choices we make everyday, which upset and/or temporarily, transform the status quo and the exploitative capitalist relations engendered by the logic of capitalism. Whether, temporary or permanent, micro-revolutions are the engines for a generalized, nonconformist, anti-capitalist, insurrectionary anarchist revolution. Micro-revolutions, or micro-insurrections, are always fermenting deep within the military-industrial-complex, ready to blow-up the logic of capitalism.

-[57]-

57.a) Micro-revolutions are manufactured by the poly-rationality of structural-anarchism, which runs contrary to the instrumental-rationality of capitalism. Moreover, micro-revolutions are energized via a particular structure of feeling or spirit, a structure of feeling or spirit, which outlines and sheathes micro-revolutions and, in general, the logic of structural-anarchism, inside a certain revolutionary/evolutionary commonsense, poly-rationality, shared by all anarcho-participants. This structure of feeling, or spirit, which outlines and sheathes micro-revolutions, is manufactured and fueled by micro-revolutions themselves and, in general, by the logic of structural-anarchism, itself. This structure of feeling, or spirit, is best described as the armature of micro-revolutionism. The armature of micro-revolutionism is an anarchist morality/amorality. And, ultimately, the armature of micro-revolutionism is the antithetic substitute to the armature of micro-fascism; and in fact, micro-revolutionism runs contrary to the armature of micro-fascism, both on purpose, and as a means towards something totally new and poly-rational, namely, the structural-anarchism-complex.

57.b) In general, the armature of micro-revolutionism is the zeitgeist and the gestalt of the post-capitalism age, where all functions and all operations within the socio-economic formation, the structural-anarchism-complex, are increasingly designed and constructed to realize:

a humane age, where there is an emphasis on organizing socio-economic processes and decision-making-authority within society to better serve, with the greatest capacity, and in greatest numbers, the logical necessities of the workforce/population. For the armature of micro-revolutionism, all that is of consequence is the poly-rationality of structural-anarchism, the needs of the workforce/population in the greatest numbers, and the preservation, refinement and development of the anarcho-socialist mode of production, including, any decision-making-authority that aligns according to the logic of structural-anarchism. Consequently, the logic of structural-anarchism limits and eliminates all bourgeois-capitalist developments, intellectual and/or physical, which might threaten, upset, and/or run-counter, the anarchist federation/patchwork of municipalities, cooperatives and autonomous-collectives, while, encouraging those anarcho-socialist developments, which augment and buttress the structural-anarchism-complex and poly-rationality, in general. In sum, micro-revolutionism is the underlying revolutionary spirit, i.e., structure of feeling, unifying segments of the workforce/population vis-à-vis anarcho-socialist organizations and limited horizontal-orderings. That is, horizontal-orderings which invariably liberate, stimulate and/or generate, the free flow of information, institutional transparency, individual privacy, forward-thinking knowledges, pragmatic egalitarianism and open-participatory-democracy. That is, a pragmatic egalitarianism, grounded in poly-rationality, capable of overriding the instrumental-rationality of capitalism, temporarily and permanently. Once freed from the contextual supremacy of bourgeois-state-capitalism, the logic of structural-anarchism, via its armature of micro-revolutionism, empowers the independent, self-governing nature of the workforce/population, so as to re-organize society along the guidelines of an anarchist open-participatory-democracy. Specifically, the anarchist federation/patchwork of municipalities, cooperatives and autonomous-collectives, where, all types and forms of capital are shared by all, guaranteed to all and benefit all, in relative equal measure.

57.c) The logic of structural-anarchism, via its armature of micro-revolutionism, is intelligence which strives to enhance general intelligence, i.e., poly-rationality. Its purpose is positive radical social change, progress, and anarcho-socialist, intellectual/material relations and developments. It is about stimulating, within the micro-recesses of everyday life, heterogeneity, autonomy, free thinking, critical thinking, inclusion, institutional transparency, open-participatory-democracy, and real post-modernism. That is, poly-rationality, a more intelligently organized political-economic framework for the workforce/population called: the structural-anarchism-complex. In sum, it strives to make the world less divided, more post-modern, and more pragmatically egalitarian, but not completely egalitarian, as small differences are a basic maintenance requirement of the workforce/population.

57.d) Unlike the logic of capitalism, the logic of structural-anarchism embodies as a principle the idea of limited private ownership, namely, a small sum of guaranteed personal property. The logic of structural-anarchism values limited private ownership because limited private ownership, or a small sum of personal property, is a necessary component of a well-functioning, pragmatic, egalitarian, workforce/population. It is a necessary component for individual well-being and a healthy identity. Where, the logic of structural-anarchism takes issue with the logic of capitalism is its idea of unlimited private ownership, which, according to the logic of structural-anarchism must be radically limited, restrained, and re-organized in order to fully maximize equality and the basic maintenance requirements of the workforce/population. And, contrary to the logic of pure communism, the logic of structural-anarchism understands that to have no private ownership, whatsoever, is as well detrimental to individual well-being and a well-adjusted identity. For the logic of structural-anarchism, a well-functioning, pragmatic, egalitarianized workforce/population and socio-economic formation, requires limited private ownership, that is, protected small sums of personal property, since, this is a stimulus for the growth of anarcho-socialist relations and anarcho-socialist modes of production, consumption and distribution.

-[58]-

58.a) In consequence, as the replacing antithetic gestalt, zeitgeist, and structure of feeling, the armature of micro-revolutionism attempts to hardwire the logic of structural-anarchism into the mental and the physical circuits, systems, and processes of the military-industrial-complex. It attempts to transform the military-industrial-complex in part and/or as a whole, into the anarchist federation/patchwork of municipalities, cooperatives and autonomous-collectives. Micro-revolutionism is the pragmatic poly-rationale, gestalt and structure of feeling of the logic of structural-anarchism, which rears its head, from time to time, in and across the stratums of the military-industrial-complex, in various forms, resulting in micro-skirmishes with the logic of capitalism. The logic of structural-anarchism, via the armature of micro-revolutionism, is programmed to permeates the stratums of the military-industrial-complex. As a result, the armature of micro-revolutionism is present and operational wherever, and whenever, deviation is ingenuity, intelligence is disobedience and pragmatic egalitarianism favors open-participatory-democracy etc. In fact, these poly-rational maxims, comprised inside the armature of micro-revolutionism, lead to the formation of horizontal-networks and limited, temporary, horizontal-hierarchies, namely, the egalitarian, poly-rational, standards of the structural-anarchism-complex. Indeed, the armature of micro-revolutionism is utilized to measure the level of compliance of the workforce/population in relation to the poly-rationality of structural-anarchism. Finally, the armature of micro-revolutionism outlines the anti-capitalist escalator, which leads directly to the federation of municipalities, cooperatives and autonomous-collectives, that is, the structural-anarchism-complex:

The Armature of Micro-Revolutionism

```
[Intelligence]----------------------------------------------------------[Deviation]
|  \                                                                        /|
|   x---------------------------[Micro-Revolutionism]---------------------x |
|   |\                                                                    /| |
|   | \------------------------------------------------------------------/ | |
|   | [The Federation of Municipalities, Cooperatives and Autonomous-Collectives ] | |
|   | /------------------------------------------------------------------\ | |
|   |/                                                                    \| |
|   x---------------------------[Micro-Revolutionism]---------------------x |
| /                                                                        \|
[Communal-Dialogue]--------------------------------------------[Anti-Capitalist-Synergy]
```

This framework/armature is the means by which the anarchist federation/patchwork of municipalities, cooperatives and autonomous-collectives governs the structural-anarchism-complex, manufactures its self-governing workforce/population, controls the logic of capitalism, disseminates the poly-rationality of structural-anarchism, and accumulates and extracts surplus value, for the benefit of all by all. All movements up or down any necessary, yet, limited horizontal-hierarchies, within the structural-anarchism-complex, by members of the workforce/population is measured and analyzed by the inherent, systemic armature of micro-revolutionism, which safeguards, augments and supports the logic of structural-anarchism and the ruling anarchist federation/patchwork of municipalities, cooperatives and autonomous-collectives, i.e., the best representatives and best embodiments of the poly-rationality of structural-anarchism.

58.b) 1. Synergy is the means by which the anarchist federation of municipalities, cooperatives and autonomous-collectives, organizes anarcho-socialist relations in the favor of all and for the benefits of all by all. Synergy is the interaction or cooperation of two or more organizations, or segments of the workforce/population, so as to produce and manifest a combined influence and effect greater than the sum of their separate individual parts. Voluntary, mutual-aid, cooperative synergy is the means by which the logic of structural-anarchism overrides the parameters of the military-industrial-complex in favor of an inclusive, transparent, poly-rational, open-participatory-democracy, namely, the structural-anarchism-complex. Voluntary, mutual-aid, cooperative synergy is the means by which the bourgeois-capitalist status quo is detonated, revolutionized and re-organized into the anarchist federation of municipalities, cooperatives and autonomous-collectives. Voluntary, mutual-aid, cooperative synergy is the transparent glass ceiling smashed to pieces in favor of intelligence over obedience, where illusions of career advancement are replaced by genuine anarcho-socialist relations, anarcho-socialist productive forces and, in general, an anarcho-socialist mode of production, producing vast amounts of pragmatic egalitarianism, while, creating the limited horizontalized-institutions needed for the structural-anarchism-complex.

2. Deviation is the means by which the anarchist federation of municipalities, cooperatives and autonomous-collectives measures and determines intelligence, creativity and ingenuity in relation to the acceptable, poly-rational standards of the structural-anarchism-complex. Positive deviation is intelligence, creativity and ingenuity in the sense that deviation is a pragmatic sign of the evident independence and innate egalitarianism of the workforce/population. The way certain segments of the workforce/population express their poly-rationality indicates their level intelligence, ingenuity and revolutionary consciousness.

3. Dialogue is the means by which the anarchist federation of municipalities, cooperatives and autonomous-collectives, determines respect for its form of rule and the level of open-participatory-democracy. Dialogue fixes the workforce/population to the anarchist federation of municipalities, cooperatives and autonomous-collectives. Dialogue focuses the workforce/population in service of the logic of structural-anarchism. As well, dialogue eliminates the plethora of capitalist exploitative relationships from the structural-anarchism-complex. Positive dialogue enables the poly-rationality of

structural-anarchism to expand, to intensify, and to refine itself, ad infinitum, maximizing the pragmatic egalitarianism of open-participatory-democracy housed in the structural-anarchism-complex. Finally, positive dialogue is focused not necessarily on consensus, but it can be, its primary focus is cooperative-synergy and horizontal-organization, with a certain set of limited, temporary, horizontal-hierarchies, which are capable of maximizing the basic maintenance requirements of the workforce/population, while, extinguishing the dictates of the logic of capitalism. The anarchist federation of municipalities, cooperatives and autonomous-collectives, i.e., the structural-anarchism-complex, utilizes positive dialogue to loosely regiment and instruct autonomous segments of the workforce/population to horizontally organize themselves into an open-participatory-democracy, namely, a pragmatic egalitarian, high-tech., fully-automated, poly-rational, post-industrial, post-modern, structural-anarchism-complex.

4. Intelligence is poly-rationality. It is the means by which the anarchist federation of municipalities, cooperatives and autonomous-collectives determines rank and file based on creativity, ingenuity, positive dialogue and constructive critique. The goal is to develop an anarchist federation/patchwork of independent free thinkers capable of open-participatory-democracy, mutual respect and mutual-aid synergy, sharing in and benefiting from the total sum of surplus value embodied in the structural-anarchism-complex, in relative equal measure. Intelligence is communally profitable in the sense that it is capable of increasingly revolutionizing the socio-economic processes of the structural-anarchism-complex, according to poly-rationality, thus, maximizing the accumulation and extraction of multi-varied surplus value in the service and benefit of all by all. What makes the logic of structural-anarchism superior to the logic of capitalism is that it is a more intelligent political-economic framework and socio-economic formation. That is, its ideational comprehensive framework constructs more intelligent socio-economic modes and processes in the service and benefit of all by all, through poly-rationality, thus, its superiority and its inherent, pragmatic egalitarianism, collectivism and post-modernism. The logic of structural-anarchism structures its socio-economic formation more intelligently than the logic of capitalism, due to the fact that it utilizes greater segments of the workforce/population, via its inclusive, armature of micro-revolutionism, which magnifies poly-rationality and collectivism. The logic of structural-anarchism, via the armature of micro-revolutionism, engineers maximum dialogue, cooperative synergy, intelligence and creative deviation by the fact that it includes greater portions of the workforce/population within decision-making-authority, via the installation of poly-rationality and an open-participatory-democracy.

58.c) The armature of micro-revolutionism contrary to the armature of micro-fascism is designed to short-circuit instrumental-rationality, while, engendering poly-rationality. The armature of micro-revolutionism engenders poly-rational, anarcho-socialist structures and modes of production, namely, limited horizontal-hierarchies and poly-rational, socio-economic processes housed within a structural-anarchism-complex. The armature of micro-revolutionism insulates the logic of structural-anarchism, i.e., the anarchist federation of municipalities, cooperatives and autonomous-collectives, from the logic of capitalism, permitting the poly-rationality of structural-anarchism to be welded to the workforce/population, thus, overriding the instrumental-rationality of capitalism through plurality, equality, and multi-variable post-modernity.

58.d) The armature of micro-revolutionism is temperate, sobering, poly-rationality, processing human material through the horizontalized-decentralized-networks of the structural-anarchism-complex, with conscience, with thoughtfulness, and with only the preservation, expansion and legitimacy of the workforce/population, i.e., the anarchist federation of municipalities, cooperatives and autonomous-collectives, as its end.

58.e) The armature of micro-revolutionism is the logical process of being, thinking, saying, and acting, according to the basic maintenance requirements of the workforce/population, i.e., the logic of structural-anarchism, that is, poly-rationality. In essence, the armature of micro-revolutionism is pragmatic egalitarianism empowered with poly-rational purpose, fashioning a structural-anarchism-complex into a plural, streamlined, organic, hi-tech, generative, open-participatory-democracy, namely, a plural, multi-varied, socio-economic patchwork, stitched freely together via the poly-rationality of structural-anarchism.

58.f) The armature of micro-revolutionism is exactly what the logic of structural-anarchism and its material manifestation, the structural-anarchism-complex, require in order to construct, maintain, and expand, the anarchist federation of municipalities, cooperatives and autonomous-collectives. This open-democratic-system of socio-economic deviations, cooperative synergies, poly-rational intelligences, and dialogic communication, empowers the development of open-participatory-democracy, whereupon, the forces of production, the relations of production, comprised in a general anarchist mode of production, are shared by all, benefit all, and are guaranteed to all. The point is a free, affluent, critical-thinking, poly-rational, workforce/population, antagonistic to the totalitarian logic of capitalism and all exploitative capitalist apparatuses; which nonetheless, embodies a structure of feeling, i.e., a zeitgeist, that fuels an expansionary pragmatic egalitarianism, resulting in a poly-rational structural-anarchism-complex.

-[59]-

59.a) The logic of structural-anarchism is the next rational and evolutionary/revolutionary stage of political-economic development and socio-economic development. The logic of structural-anarchism is the next rational and evolutionary/revolutionary step, due to the fact that its ideational comprehensive framework is a more intelligently organized socio-economic formation, which invariably, augments the workings of all socio-economic processes by increasing the levels and parameters of open-participatory-democracy and by democratizing surplus value, i.e., ownership/knowledge, in service and benefit of all by all. The logic of structural-anarchism is logically programmed to decentralize, horizontalize and democratize hierarchies, institutions, and decision-making-authority, in and across the military-industrial-complex into a loose federation of municipalities, cooperatives and autonomous-collectives, i.e., communes, grounded on poly-rationality.

59.b) The logic of structural-anarchism is a political-economic framework, i.e., ideational comprehensive framework, which augments the socio-economic processes for capital extraction and capital accumulation, while organizing these socio-economic processes into cooperatives, autonomous-collectives and municipalities, where workers and citizens of the federation are simultaneously the owners of surplus value, the users of surplus value and the means for the accumulation and/or extraction surplus value, that is, multi-varied, anarchist surplus value. By organizing socio-economic processes more intelligently and manufacturing more intelligent equality, throughout the structural-anarchism-complex, via cooperatives, autonomous-collectives and municipalities, the logic of structural-anarchism increases initiative and participation within its poly-rational, socio-economic processes, whose golden fruits are enjoyed by all, in relative equal measures.

59.c) By serving the logical necessities of the workforce/population, more intelligently, and with greater pragmatic egalitarianism, the logic of structural-anarchism is able to overcome the unlimited artificial scarcity, competition, privatization, radical specialization, and the radical financial disparities, manufactured by the military-industrial-complex and the logic of capitalism. In contrast to the logic of capitalism, the logic of structural-anarchism is increasingly becoming more in-tuned with the march of real history, since, the logic of structural-anarchism improves socio-economic processes and communal management, much better, by emphasizing open-participatory-democracy, collectively-shared property, heterogeneity and poly-rationality.

59.d) The logic of structural-anarchism is the greater leveling of socio-economic disparities within society. The logic of structural-anarchism is an extension of the leveling processes, taking place in the cultural sectors, where every cultural expression is as equal as another, every culture is as equal as another, every art-form is as equal as another, and every individual is as equal as another. The logic of structural-anarchism is this cultural-equalization-process applied to the political-economic framework of bourgeois-state-capitalism. However, the logic of structural-anarchism is not about total political-economic equalization, it is about curtailing political-economic disparities. It is, first and foremost, about minimizing political-economic extremes, minimizing economic disparities, and minimizing political disparities, between various sectors of the workforce/population, both financially and politically, founded on basic, anarcho-socialist, financial guarantees and poly-rationality.

59.e) The structural-anarchism-complex is a stateless federation, meaning the political sphere is an open-participatory-democracy, without political parties, revolving around municipal governing bodies, whereupon the institutional-administration of daily life is an administration of things, people and services, exercised by cyclical experts, officials, and professionals, who no longer answer to a federal and state/provincial government, but instead, to municipalities, who themselves, only answer to their specific, municipal citizenry.

59.f) As a result, the political-economic framework of structural-anarchism does acknowledge some economic differences as a necessary element of a healthy economy, but that financial disparities need not be so extreme as they are now under the logic of capitalism. For example, it is irrational for a sport star, whose profession is not truly necessary for the maintenance and progression of socio-economic processes, to be making such an astronomical amount of capital in comparison to another profession, a profession that is necessary to the maintenance and progression of socio-economic processes. A more intelligently organized society, poly-rational society, would limit and/or cap the amount of capital/income a sport athlete can make in relation to other professions within its societal parameters. It is not to say that a sport athlete cannot make more capital/income, but that this financial disparity of capital/income should not be so extreme as to be toxic and parasitic to socio-economic equality, democracy, and the overall community. The political-economic framework of structural-anarchism is designed to place salary caps on all professions, especially those professions whose income greatly out weigh their utility and/or functionality in ameliorating socio-economic processes. The ideational comprehensive framework of structural-anarchism is about limited hierarchy, both politically, economically and financially etc.

59.g) All in all, the point of the political-economic framework of structural-anarchism is to manufacture a more intelligently organized society, where the workforce/population is allowed to grow and develop in limited hierarchical formats, like an orchestra and/or a revolving assembly, that is, free, horizontal, communal formats, which maximize poly-rationality and, most importantly, open-participatory-democracy.

–[60]–

60.a) It is important to note that the political-economic framework of structural-anarchism is not antithetic to the idea of the state, contrary to most anarchist philosophies. For the ideational comprehensive framework of structural-anarchism, it is the question of what type of stateless-organizational-form will maximize open-participatory-democracy, individual autonomy and poly-rationality. If the current state-organizational-form is unacceptable and flawed, then what type of stateless-organizational-form can minimize socio-economic oppression, in-humaneness and/or exploitation, while, maximizing individual autonomy, equality, open-participatory-democracy, and poly-rationality? What kind of system can maximize the greatest general happiness and liberty for the greatest number? According to the logic of structural-anarchism, the answer is the federation of municipalities, cooperative and autonomous-collectives, grounded in poly-rationality.

(Note: Injustice, inequality, financial disparity and/or exploitation, can never be totally eliminated from social existence, via any state and/or any political-economic-framework, whatever the organizational-form of that framework and/or state. It is a question of what political-economic framework and/or state, or lack thereof, can best minimize injustice, inequality, financial disparity and/or exploitation. The political economic framework of structural-anarchism, once established, will always be a work in progress, whose ideational comprehensive framework and material manifestation, i.e., the federation of municipalities, cooperatives and autonomous-collectives, will perpetually require poly-rational adjustments, rethinking, and reforms in order to continually ameliorate its open-participatory-democracy. The difference however between the logic of structural-anarchism and the logic of capitalism is that socio-economic reforms and logical adjustments are easier, faster, and less drastic, across the structural-anarchism-complex than across military-industrial-complex. The reason is because the structural-anarchism-complex is based on poly-rationality while the military-industrial-complex is based on unitary, instrumental-rationality.)

60.b) For the political-economic framework of structural-anarchism, the state is a natural and necessary outcome/outgrowth of the workforce/population, engineered to placate its basic maintenance requirements. The state is a manifestation of intellectual and material activity, and was initially organized to satisfy the logical necessities of the workforce/population. Only, later was the state subjugated by the ruling, micro-fascist, oligarchical networks in service of the logic of capitalism. Only, later was the state corrupted in service of the logic of capitalism, manipulated by the logic of capitalism to do its bidding, to satisfy its mercenary demands, and to empower the greedy interests of its ruling, micro-fascist, oligarchical networks. Only, later was the state slowly stripped of its reach, its influence, and its capacities, by the logic of capitalism, and downgraded to the level of a common bureaucratic means in service of the instrumental-rationality of capitalism, programmed solely to lay the groundwork for the unlimited accumulation and extraction of surplus value, that is, capitalist profit. The state, subjugated by the logic of capitalism, is a coercive, despotic, killing machine, fundamentally driven by the accumulation and extraction of surplus value. Whether, soft or hard-line, the capitalist state is a soul-sucking, instrumental-rational apparatus, breeding truncated degenerates of all types and kinds, who cling to its unyielding, rotten, institutional machinery in order to discipline and punish any departures from the bourgeois-capitalist status quo. For the bourgeois-capitalist-state, in the final analysis, might equals right. And, might obliterates all that stands in the way of bourgeois-capitalist progress and capitalist objectives, namely, the instrumental-rationality of bourgeois-capitalism.

60.c) For the political-economic framework of structural-anarchism, the state is a type of technology, which in itself, is neither good nor bad, it is those who wield its authority, which transform the state into a mechanism of death, capital, discipline, punishment, and absolute obedience. Under the logic of structural-anarchism, the state can be more intelligently organized and reconfigured towards nobler ends and egalitarian principles, that is, poly-rationality. However, the bourgeois-capitalist-state must first be demolished, since, the anarchist federation is stateless. The anarchist federation only relies on the administration of things, services, and people, through municipalities, worker-cooperatives and autonomous-collectives or communes. The federation is stateless in the sense that it does not sanction political-representation, it sanctions solely referendums on all major civic decisions, directly via the municipal citizenry, itself, where each represents him or herself. As a result, certain segments of the state will be abolished such as the federal and provincial/state levels of the governing apparatus, because these detached, abstract apparatuses are outgrowths of the logic of capitalism and instrumental-rationality. These detached, abstract apparatuses, both the federal and the provincial/state apparatuses, enshrined in the logic of capitalism and vice versa, are in actuality composites of a litany of exploitative, socio-economic relationships, namely, the capital/labor relation at the center of the military-industrial-complex, disguised in a multitude of forms, infecting all the stratums of everyday life. These master/slave relationships of various forms and types are appearances only, appearances concealing the logic of capitalism within their scaffolding, namely, the capital/labor relationship at the center of capitalist production, consumption and distribution, dominating and exploiting the workforce/population and nature, via instrumental-rationality. Consequently, these federal, state/provincial abstractions are too disconnected, from the workforce/population and the socio-economic base of society, and as a result, these abstractions will have to be abolished so that decision-making-authority can return back from which it came and sprang, i.e., municipalities. Municipalities, loosely knitted together into a poly-rational federation, are all that is required to maximize the workings of an open-participatory-democracy founded on poly-rationality. Only certain federal and provincial institutions that are absolutely necessary for the basic maintenance requirements of the workforce/population will be allowed to endure, but only under the decision-making-authority of municipalities, and not any federal and/or provincial electoral/governing body. Due to the fact that, these detached, abstract apparatuses have always only served the mercenary ends of the instrumental-rationality of capitalism, cloaked in the dogma of bourgeois-capitalist populism.

60.d) For the political-economic framework of structural-anarchism, the stateless state is a logical necessity in order to maximize satisfaction of the basic maintenance requirements of the workforce/population. For the political-economic framework of structural-anarchism it is the current hierarchical and representational form of statehood, organized according to the logic of capitalism, which has warped its structures, its objectives, and its basic workings. Change its central logic, i.e., the instrumental-rationality of capitalism, and the state, founded on another operational logic, i.e., the poly-rationality of structural-anarchism, can be rehabilitated, reorganized, and re-established, on a more viable premise, a more intelligent, poly-rational, organizational-form, namely, the federation of municipalities, cooperatives and autonomous-collectives, devoid of any useless federal, and/or provincial/state apparatuses.

(Note: Changing the material conditions of society via physical activity inevitably changes the ideational conditions of society in the immediate sense, including the state. Vice versa, changing the ideational conditions of society, via mental activity, eventually, changes the material conditions of society in the long-term, including the state. However, ideational changes take longer to influence change in the material conditions of society, due to the fact that ideas are incorporeal and abstract. They require longer time-frames to objectify and become solid, concrete manifestations and/or processes.)

60.e) In general, the political-economic framework of structural-anarchism would not and could not do away with some sort of state-organizational-form, due to the fact that to do away with all state-organizational-forms, or any type of authority, is utterly detrimental to the logical necessities of the workforce/population. Devoid of any robust, state-organizational-form, inevitably validates the current excesses of the military-industrial-complex, i.e., the logic of capitalism, resulting in the demolition of society, to such an extreme, as to reduce civilization to pure chaos, pure competitive warfare and/or a pure kleptocracy. This would be a political-economic stage, where might equals right, every time, and where marauding nomadic bands of despotic barbarians, pillage and destroy without end. Under a new organizing-principle, derived from a new centralized logic, akin to the logic of structural-anarchism, the state would undergo a total transformation, reorganization, and reconfiguration, under new poly-rational imperatives, which would abolish federal/state/provincial institutions in favor of municipalities, that is, a collective administration of things, people and services. This is the poly-rational apparatus advocated by the ideational comprehensive framework of structural-anarchism.

-[61]-

61.a) The displacement and dislodgement of logic of capitalism as the central primary logic within socio-economic processes will bring forth a series of micro-groupings across the military-industrial-complex, which will eventually come to comprise the structural-anarchism-complex, a complex of multi-varied ideational comprehensive frameworks, founded on poly-rationality. These cooperative constellations will handle the same modes of production, consumption and distribution, as before, but according to a new system of relations, which organize socio-economic relations, differently, along the lines of a different, ideational comprehensive framework. Moreover, federal and provincial/state decision-making-authority will be re-distributed at the level of municipalities, more specifically, municipal subsets housed in co-operatives and autonomous-collectives. The federal and provincial electoral/governing bodies will be abolished, while absolutely necessary federal and provincial institutions will be reformed and made subservient to the decision-making-authority of all municipalities. Due the fact that the federal and provincial/state organizational-forms are direct manifestations derived from the municipal base, via the instrumental-rationality of capitalism in order to dominate and exploit the workforce/population. These federal and provincial/state abstractions were directly derived from municipalities because municipalities comprise the source of all decision-making-authority. These federal and provincial/state organizational-forms are made to constantly remain aloof and increasingly detached from the everyday needs of the workforce/population so as to facilitate the maximization of capitalist profit, by any means necessary, at the lowest financial cost, as soon as possible. These capitalist organizational abstractions, directly engineered, via the logic of capitalism, are only designed to satisfy the minimum necessary requirements of the workforce/population. In reality, these capitalist organizational abstractions are in fact designed, by the logic of capitalism, to fashion ever-increasing, socio-economic disparity and financial detachment in order to free the logic of capitalism from all unnecessary fetters, preventing the accumulation and extraction of surplus value. The logic of capitalism must not get bogged-down in the daily existence and/or the incessant details of the workforce/population, hence, the establishment of the federal, provincial/state, electoral/governing bodies, by the logic of capitalism. In this regard, via these capitalist organizational abstractions, the logic of capitalism divorces itself as best it can from all existential considerations, other than, the maximization of capitalist profit. Consequently, the logic of capitalism manufactured the federal and provincial/state apparatuses, out of municipalities, in order to ever-increasingly divorce itself from the socio-economic base and the municipal base, i.e., the workforce/population, which circulates, proliferates, and propagates, within the micro-recesses of municipalities. Finally, the logic of capitalism manufactured the federal and provincial/state apparatuses, out of municipalities, to annex the decision-making-authority flowing from municipalities, which it increasingly sees, and has always seen, as antagonistic to its endless pursuit for the unlimited accumulation, centralization and extraction of surplus value. That is, the unlimited capitalist profits, accumulated, centralized and extracted, directly from the unstoppable, sweaty, secretions of the workforce/population.

61.b) As a result, the logic of structural-anarchism is founded on the idea of eliminating and abolishing the abstractions of the provincial/state and federal forms of representation in order to empower and reinvest decision-making-authority in municipalities from which it came and sprang. The logic of structural-anarchism is founded on the idea that: 1. The workforce/population is the primary locus of decision-making-authority, which primarily organizes its existence into municipalities; hence, municipalities are the best embodiments of this decision-making-authority, in the sense that, municipalities are the basic democratic-apparatuses of decision-making-authority and poly-rationality. And 2., the workforce/population, naturally hardwired for connection, inevitably participates in cooperatives, autonomous-collectives, and municipalities, due to the fact, these organizational-forms are the best means for satisfying its basic maintenance requirements.

61.c) Notwithstanding, the glue that interweaves the federation of municipalities, co-operatives and autonomous-collectives, together, locally, provincially and nationally, into a flexible, well-functioning, open-participatory-democracy is the mutual agreement between all citizens to participate, within the parameters of a poly-rational, structural-anarchism-constitution. Akin to the constitutions of bourgeois-state-capitalism (with various major structural and systemic changes), a structural-anarchism-constitution outlines an anarcho-socialist system of administration, including basic civil rights, concerning all citizens. However, in contrast to the constitutions of bourgeois-state-capitalism, a structural-anarchism-constitution empowers municipalities, with primary decision-making-authority, via the elimination of the federal and provincial/state, electoral/governing bodies, in favor of only the municipal, electoral/governing bodies. Together, united by an overarching structural-anarchism-constitution, municipalities are empowered to govern both a set of absolutely necessary, federal and provincial institutions, as well as, their own specific, individual, municipal institutions. Finally, and more importantly, in contrast to the constitutions of bourgeois-state-capitalism, a structural-anarchism-constitution is comprised of a secondary charter/bill of civil rights, i.e., a charter/bill of socio-economic guarantees. This crucial charter/bill of socio-economic guarantees is both the pivot and the engine, propelling society out of the military-industrial-complex, i.e., bourgeois-state-capitalism, towards the political-economic framework of structural-anarchism, that is, the structural-anarchism-complex. Due to the fact, this additional charter/bill of socio-economic guarantees is designed to flip the logic of capitalism on its head, right-side up again, as an appendage of the workforce/population, thus inaugurating, the logic of structural-anarchism into the central position of socio-economic control as the socio-economic, organizing principle of society. The charter/bill of socio-economic guarantees is designed: 1. to empower cooperatives and autonomous—collectives in their socio-economic relationships with municipalities. 2. The charter/bill of socio-economic guarantees is designed to municipalize the total sum of capital, property and authority between all citizens of the federation. And 3., the charter/bill of socio-economic guarantees is designed to fulfill the fundamental socio-economic birth-right of all citizens, namely, to have and to possess, basic socio-economic guarantees, regardless of race, age, gender, class, rank and/or file etc. This is poly-rationality in action.

61.d) The logic of structural-anarchism and its political-economic framework, i.e., its ideational comprehensive framework, is meant to engender and to establish:

(The 26-Theses Charter/Bill of Socio-Economic-Guarantees)

1. This charter/bill guarantees the abolition of both federal and provincial/state organizational-forms of electoral representation in favor of a federation of municipalities, co-operatives and autonomous-collectives, municipalities functioning on a short-term rotational and electoral basis, by citizens and for citizens, who are further organized in cooperatives and/or autonomous-collectives. All specific, municipal, administrative positions are to be contained to specific duties and tasks, and subject to a yearly, nomination process. This includes the ability by the citizenry of the federation to annul and recall all administrators, at any time, during a specific administrative mandate. Decision-making-authority resides with the people, not with administrators, whose only authority pertains to the administration of specific duties and tasks on behalf of the citizenry of the federation, such as administrating a power-plant etc. In addition, any small group will have the right to seccession from any autonomous-collective, or commune, so as to start their own collective or individual commune, under specific conditions, corresponding to the anarchist constitution and the charter/bill of socio-economic-guarantees.

2. This charter/bill guarantees that all municipal nominated branches of government will rely on referendums in order to enact policy. Decision-making-authority, either locally, provincially and/or nationally, will be based on all citizens within the federation, participating together via referendums. In addition, under the federation of municipalities, cooperatives and autonomous-collectives, necessary national institutions will no longer answer to provincial or federal elected branches disconnected from the socio-economic base; instead, they will answer to the organizational-form of the socio-economic base, i.e., municipalities themselves, and/or, in general, the federation of municipalities, cooperatives and autonomous-collectives, itself. Furthermore, these institutions will be horizontalized and non-hierarchical, as much as possible.

3. This charter/bill guarantees the abolition and dissolution of political parties in an effort to encourage regular citizens to participate in politics. No group or party shall collude in an effort to limit political choice.

4. This charter/bill guarantees term limits on all civil servants, academics, administrators, judges, logics etc., in order to promote socio-economic change, rotation, and general political-economic involvement for all citizens. All power to the anarchist federation and its citizens in relative equal measure.

5. This charter/bill guarantees that the ownership/knowledge of all surplus value and property is in essence the collective property of all citizens and is to be shared by all citizens. As a result, the capital/labor relation is to be abolished in order to permit a new and more efficient, pluralist, anarcho-socialist mode of production to develop and takeover the sum of societal production, consumption and distribution.

6. This charter/bill guarantees the right of each citizen to limited property, i.e., ownership/knowledge and the basics of life, i.e., food, shelter, water, education etc. It is one of the grounding premises of the federation of municipalities, cooperatives and autonomous-collectives that for individual well-being, limited property is a necessity, while, unlimited private ownership/knowledge and/or private property is not. Everyone has rightful claim to the means of life, since, human and societal progress and development demands it.

7. This charter/bill guarantees to increase all socio-economic parameters within society into an open-participatory-democracy, founded on full automation, artificial intelligence, and poly-rationality. Only within the political-economic framework of structural-anarchism can full automation and artificial intelligence be controlled and be effectively, liberating. The logic of capitalism and capitalist social relations transform these technological forces into forces for ever-increasing exploitation and enslavement. In contrast, under the poly-rationality of structural-anarchism, and various anarcho-socialist modes and relations, these technological forces are regulated and transformed into emancipatory mechanisms for the amelioration of the federation and its citizenry. For the logic of structural-anarchism, the way by which technological forces are utilized is based on what citizens of the federation request via referendums and direct participatory action. The point is a litany of use-values, more free-time, and collectivist goods over capitalist individualist commodities.

8. This charter/bill guarantees the transformation of all heavy industry and/or multi-national industries into cooperatives, where workers self-manage themselves, and share in the successes of their industry and/or company, along with the federation of municipalities, cooperatives and autonomous-collectives itself, which as well benefit from the spoils of industry.

9. This charter/bill guarantees the abolition and dissolution of mega-corporations and mega-unions in favor of small, horizontalized, cooperative, micro-industries and collectivist entrepreneurial-ships. Limits are to be placed on size so as to limit influence and encourage open-participatory-democracy and non-hierarchical horizontalism, namely, anarchist poly-rationality. Initially, after the anarchist revolution, the market is to be subordinated and subdued to a decentralized planned and shared economy. However, the goal is to eventually wither all market economies into a fully decentralized set of planned and shared economies. Whereupon, the goal is anarchist shared-abundance and no longer artificial capitalist scarcity.

10. This charter/bill guarantees the severing of all political relations with any monarchy. A structural-anarchism-state is a republic, i.e., a type of republic, functioning as an autonomous governing body and organized by citizens for citizens into municipalities, cooperatives and autonomous-collectives.

11. This charter/bill guarantees the right to work to all citizens, that is, the right to work, regardless of market fluctuations and labor-fluctuations, if citizens so choose. That is, the right to refuse unemployment in favor of work. The right to a job, if one desires such. The right to the means of production, consumption and distribution, regardless of social standing. However, the ultimate goal is to reduce the work-day, for all, in order to encourage self-exploration, leisure and self-amelioration.

12. This charter/bill guarantees the right to a living salary for all citizens of the federation of municipalities, cooperatives and autonomous-collectives, regardless of employment or unemployment, background, education, gender, race and/or culture etc. Salary is to be allocated in relative equal measure, depending on one's job and one's specific personal situation. Those doing complex jobs are to receive slightly more than those who do simple jobs and/or refuse to work.

13. This charter/bill guarantees limits on how much income an individual or group can make via salary caps on all professions, services and individual earnings, via a UNIVERSAL INCOME GRID. Remuneration shall be determined and based by the stress, difficulty, and complexity of the specific job and work, which is an incalculable measurement, meaning, it is at best an educated guess. Consequently, every few years the universal income grid shall be subject to readjustments by the citizenry of the anarchist federation. In addition, this charter/bill guarantees the re-distribution of wealth, when income and wealth inadvertently exceed salary caps. And, finally, any legal tender and/or remuneration notes shall have a time-limit, wherefore, any legal tender and/or remuneration notes shall be spent by a certain date and time, or be declared null and void. The point is to eliminate money-hoarding.

14. This charter/bill guarantees the abolition of wealth and financial inheritance.

15. This charter/bill guarantees the prohibition of the requirement of references when applying for a job so as to abolish the centrality of network-cronyism, i.e., network-affiliation, as a basic factor to any employment opportunity.

16. This charter/bill guarantees the right to a home and free transportation for all citizens, due to the fact that a home and free transportation are basic maintenance requirements for the workforce/population.

17. This charter/bill guarantees economic protection during sickness, old age, unemployment, and/or accident to all citizens.

18. This charter/bill guarantees the heavy taxation of organized religions and churches, regardless of spiritual belief. The federation of municipalities, cooperatives and autonomous-collectives is a secular atheist organizational-form, devoid of deities, thus, it strives for total societal secularism.

19. This charter/bill guarantees the right to quality medical treatment and quality medicines, free of charge, i.e., a federated health care and drug plan, for all citizens of the federation.

20. This charter/bill guarantees free education for all citizens as education is a basic maintenance requirement for any poly-rational, well-informed citizenry.

21. This charter/bill guarantees free and equal access to the means of physical and mental production, consumption and distribution, by any municipality, cooperative and/or autonomous-collective within the federation, including its citizenry.

22. This charter/bill guarantees environmental protection and solid independent scientific observations, study of the environment and the decommissioning of all atomic-nuclear-power-stations, coal-stations etc., in favor of renewable energy sources etc., The intent is to achieve a healthy equilibrium between society and nature via clean and green energy, full automation and artificial intelligence.

23. This charter/bill guarantees the limited and gradual demolition of surveillance mechanisms and surveillance institutions in order to fundamentally reduce all institutional capacities for total surveillance. In contrast, this charter/bill guarantees that all institutions be reconstructed and re-conceptualized for maximum institutional transparency and the servicing of the anarchist citizenry.

24. This charter/bill guarantees the municipalization of the credit and banking system. That is, the collectivization of the credit and banking-system, so as to alleviate and lessen credit and money pressures on all socio-economic processes and entities with the goal of eventually eliminating credit, debt-slavery and money-hoarding, altogether. The point is: 1. to abolish usury, interest on capital, and the interest rate in order to eventually eliminate and/or significantly reduce the centrality of financial quantifiable capital within socio-economic processes, both mental and physical processes. And 2., the point is to eliminate and/or significantly reduce profiteering by fostering the exchange of goods, commodities and services at their individual cost of production, or if this is not possible, at a cost equitably determined by the federation and its citizenry. Consequently, a UNIVERSAL PRICE GRID FOR GOODS AND SERVICES is to be established, wherefore, goods and services are to be priced affordably and equitably for the citizen of federation. Ultimately, the goal is to eliminate, or spread-out, effectively, capital and eliminate debt, while, equalizing and maximizing accessibility to socio-economic resources for all.

25. This charter/bill guarantees the dissolution and abolition of large-scale businesses and institutions in favor of small, streamlined cooperatives spread-out in and across the anarchist federation. The point is to construct cooperatives and autonomous-collectives, i.e., communes, akin to the Mondragon-Cooperative so as to maximize efficiency and democratic-participation, in and across the federation and the stratums of everyday life for all citizens.

26. This charter/bill guarantees the downsizing of the professional military and all professional police-forces within the federation of municipalities, cooperatives and autonomous-collectives in favor of a small, well-educated, pool of rotational full-time specialists, including a large-scale pool of volunteer reservists, if and/or when socio-economic conditions deteriorate and/or breakdown. Moreover, the judicial-system is to be re-organized and re-conceptualized according to the logical necessities of the poly-rationality of structural-anarchism, specifically, according to the logical necessities of the federation of municipalities, cooperatives and autonomous-collectives, instead of bourgeois-capitalist elites. The point is sharing, collectivism, equality and autonomy.

61.e) According to the political-economic framework of structural-anarchism, the federal level and the provincial/state level of decision-making-authority are useless appendages, designed by the logic of capitalism to further its mercenary objectives, and whose real source of influence in fact derives from municipalities. Federal and provincial/state decision-making-authority is a micro-fascist abstraction, constructed by the instrumental-rationality of capitalism, so as to better manage, discipline, and punish the workforce/population, according to the logical necessities for the accumulation and extraction of surplus value, that is, capitalist profit-making.

61.f) Under the logic of capitalism and its material manifestation, the military-industrial-complex, federal and provincial/state governing-apparatuses have turned against municipalities and the workforce/population in order to safeguard and expand the logic of capitalism, namely, the horrors of instrumental-rationality. Micro-fascism is the disease of instrumental-rationality, whose locus is found in federal, administrative-power-structures and provincial/state-power-structures. It is from these two points of pure abstraction that the micro-fascism bacterium of so-called, instrumental-rationality, socio-economically germinates and socio-economically emanates, infecting all the creative, autonomous, socio-economic networks of municipalities, including the workforce/population. Removing these two disconnected points of pure political-economic abstraction, will inevitably enhance intelligent organization, social justice, egalitarianism, autonomy, and poly-rationality, within all the compartments and stratums of everyday life, including the workforce/population, ultimately, leading to the formation of the structural-anarchism-complex.

-[62]-

62.a) With the abolition of the federal and provincial/state, organizational-electoral-form, micro-city-states, i.e., municipalities, will play a greater role in directing local, provincial/state, national, and international policies, including all political-economic objectives. This can only serve local municipalities more intelligently, efficiently and cooperatively. These micro-city-states, i.e., municipalities, are composites of cooperatives and autonomous-collectives, a mash-up of various, specific, segments of the workforce/population, vying for decision-making-authority, yet united and over-arched, by the underlying, poly-rationality of structural-anarchism enshrined in the structural-anarchism-constitution and its charter/bill of socio-economic guarantees. The logic of structural-anarchism asserts that micro-city-states are more in-tuned with the workforce/population, due to the fact that municipalities are regional-entities, meaning there is less abstraction between the workforce/population, the stratums of everyday life and decision-making-authority. Devoid of the governmental abstractions, manufactured the logic of capitalism, micro-city-states, i.e., municipalities, empowered by the logic of structural-anarchism, have greater vested interests in the safeguard, the welfare, and the amelioration of their specific regions, including knowing the particular strengths and weaknesses of their specific regions, specifically, their workforce/population. As a result, this can only maximize the satisfaction of needs, and happiness, for the greatest number, within the municipal compartments of the structural-anarchism-complex.

62.b) The program objective, for the political-economic framework of structural-anarchism, is a federation of municipalities, cooperatives, and autonomous-collectives, founded on the basic organizing-principles of collectivism, intelligence, respect, institutional transparency, individual privacy, and an overall open-participatory-democracy, enshrined within the poly-rational, parameters of civic human rights and socio-economic guarantees.

-[63]-

63.a) The logic of structural-anarchism in relation to Marxism has many diverging points:

Contra-Marx: The logic of capitalism is inherent in the insatiable drive for ownership/knowledge, in fact, it is a product of the insatiable drive for ownership/knowledge, thus, it can be displaced but not totally destroyed.

63.b) Contra-Marx: The workforce/population cannot totally do away with the logic of capitalism, because, the logic of capitalism is inherent in the insatiable drive for ownership/knowledge. Notwithstanding, the logic of capitalism can be marginalized, displaced, and dislodged from its centralized contextual supremacy, namely, as the basic organizing principle of socio-economic relations, socio-economic processes, and in general, society. The logic of capitalism can be returned to its rightful place as an appendage and/or a minor consideration within decision-making-authority of the workforce/population. This is the basic revolutionary/evolutionary premise of the logic of structural-anarchism.

63.c) Contra-Marx: The logic of structural-anarchism = poly-rationality, i.e., a rational multiplicity/plurality, focused on decentralization, while, Marxism = instrumental-rationality, i.e., a rational unity/totality, focused on centralization.

63.d) Contra-Marx: There is no such thing as materialism in the sense that materialism is first and foremost a type of conceptualism, i.e., a type of concept, which has the added characteristic of physicality.

63.e) Contra-Marx: Everything is abstract, conceptual to the end; reality, materiality, is but variations in degrees of conceptual-abstraction, meaning that materialism is a form of conceptualism grasped in the mind as a concept that has corporeality. Materiality is a conceptual idea that humans increasingly define and refine with exactitude the more humans experience the pluralities of sensations that comprise this conceptual idea that has a material quality.

63.f) Contra-Marx: It is true that Marx encapsulated intellectual activity as a component of material labor, i.e., a type of material labor. When Marx speaks about material labor he also includes within his analysis immaterial/mental labor. However, what Marx failed to realize is that materiality itself is wholly conceptual. The sum total of the physical world is comprise of concepts, i.e., it is a linguistic totally. The world is a language from alpha to omega, from the infinitely small to the infinitely large. The world is a unified language comprised of infinite micro-languages. Science is the study, discovery and understanding of micro-languages, those languages that possess a material component. Yes, materiality exists but it is a type of concept, it is conceptual first and foremost. The material world is a language we as humans can experience with our senses, but this experience contrary to popular belief is conceptual through and through. Conceptuality is the inescapable fact of our species, the human condition and the sum total of existence, i.e., animals, nature, reality etc. We cannot step outside conceptuality, nothing is beyond concepts, concepts whether material or immaterial construct the world and permit the human species to master and to comprehend the world.

63.g) <u>Contra-Marx</u>: History is the march of conceptualism rather than materialism. History is the by-product of mental/physical activity working on itself and on nature, struggling with itself and with nature in an effort to master and comprehend nature and itself. Materialism is only an aspect of the march of conceptualism; notwithstanding, both usually progress and develop, hand in hand, in a dialectical manner, without any end-point to the process. History is not the result of class struggle, it is the result of general antagonism.

63.h) <u>Contra-Marx</u>: Marxism is an ideological framework, i.e., an ideational comprehensive framework, that despite its claims, is a ready-made ideological machine automated with a sequence of answers and solutions to all socio-economic phenomena, which ultimately ends with the statement: "The bourgeoisie/capitalists are at fault and to blame for all socio-economic ills and suffering". Marxism allots blame in human terms to a particular entity/class, which comes to be seen from the Marxist lens as the epicenter of malice, i.e., the bourgeoisie, the human embodiment of the logic of capitalism and/or capital. In contrast, for the logic of structural-anarchism, it is the logic of capitalism, which is at fault, the bourgeoisie/capitalist is but a medium through which the logic of capitalism enacts its imperatives. In fact, there is no bourgeoisie/capitalist, par excellence, there is only a set of ruling, micro-fascist, oligarchical networks, which embody and enact the instrumental-rationality of capitalism. This is not necessarily a class as these ruling, micro-fascist, oligarchical networks reside and exercise their influence, in and across the stratums of the military-industrial-complex, in various fashions, not strictly through class. These ruling, micro-fascist, oligarchical networks do not necessarily exercise their influence from the top down, i.e., vertically, although they do on certain occasions, they, in fact, tend to exercise their influence from side to side, i.e., horizontally, from a harden, instrumental center towards a loose poly-rational periphery.

-[64]-

64.a) <u>Contra-Marx</u>: For the logic of structural-anarchism, species-being is not some ephemeral empty concept, but is, specifically, the insatiable drive for ownership/knowledge, within all living entities. The notion of the insatiable drive for ownership/knowledge surpasses Marx's species-being analysis in the sense that it specifies a specific definition of what species-being is. What it consists of and what it is comprised of, namely, what species-being embodies in its most accurate and precise make-up. The insatiable drive for ownership/knowledge is species-being, that is, the mechanism within all living entities, which manufactures value, i.e., all sorts of forms and types of capital, which are then seized from it, by the logic of capitalism. For example, the species-being of snake, i.e., the insatiable drive for ownership/knowledge of a snake, is a specific type of entity, which interprets, perceives, acts, and is, in the world, according to a very distinct and unique mode of being, perceiving, interpreting and acting. It has an original insatiable drive for ownership/knowledge. The snake manufactures a specific type of capital, specific to the characteristics of its species-being, namely, its insatiable drive for ownership/knowledge. That is its species-being is always unfolding in a specific manner, it is always attempting to understand, conquer, and own, greater portions of its specific environment in order to manufacture greater portions of its specific surplus value, both to survive and thrive, i.e., so it can increase its influence in the world, replicate itself in the world, and magnify its species-being, in general, via its mercenary impulses. The same logic applies for the human species, whose species-being is a specific insatiable drive for ownership/knowledge. Like the snake, the human species is unable but to accumulate and extract its own specific forms of surplus values, which permit the human species, this species-being, both as a collective and as an individual, to expand, intensify, and refine, its dominion over the globe. As a result, the logic of structural-anarchism refines the Marxist concept of

species-being, by giving it a more stringent definition and procedural
definition, including expanding the concept of species-being, beyond the human
species, that is, by incorporating all living entities, within the concept.

64.b) <u>Contra-Marx</u>: For the logic of structural-anarchism, surplus value, i.e., capital,
is a far more complex notion than it is for Marx. For the logic of
structural-anarchism, capital is all the sorts of extras and
surpluses, which the workforce/population, mentally and physically, produces
consumes, and distributes, over and above, its basic maintenance
requirements. Capital can be both material and/or immaterial, measurable
and/or immeasurable etc. Capital can be emotional. Capital can be conceptual.
And capital can be a reservoir of human energy slated for human reproduction
etc. Hence why, according to logic of structural-anarchism, all matter is in
essence and substance multi-varied capital. Contrary to Marx, the logic of
structural-anarchism puts forward the notion that humans, from womb
to tomb, are inescapably engaged in the mental/physical production of all
sorts of surplus values. It is la raison d'être of the insatiable drive for
ownership/knowledge found in nature and human existence. The production of
surplus value cannot be bottled-up. It is the essence and substance of
species-being. Surplus values can only be disregarded, depending on the
particular ideational comprehensive framework, meaning, certain ideational
comprehensive frameworks fetishize certain types of surplus values, i.e.,
capitals, like the logic of capitalism, which only acknowledges, financial
quantifiable capital, i.e., capitalist profit, measureable wealth and private
property.

64.c) <u>Contra-Marx</u>: It is the fundamental premise of the logic of structural-anarchism
that production, i.e., the modern industrial factory, housing a specific
capitalist mode of production, comprised of particular productive forces and
relations of production, is no longer the nexus of the manufacturing of
capitalist surplus value, i.e. capitalist profit. Although, the modern
industrial factory continues to produce financial, quantifiable capital,
production has moved outside the modern industrial factory, whereupon, every
moment in a humans' life is engaged in capitalist production. This new
capitalist mode of production is post-industrialism, post-modernism and
post-Fordism. In the age of post-industrial, post-modern,
bourgeois-state-capitalism, capitalist surplus value is accumulated and
extracted from all stratums of everyday life, both private and public, mental
and physical. The military-industrial-complex has shed the parameters of the
old, modern, industrial factories and now is an all-encompassing totality,
set to bleed the workforce/population, dry, in all the micro-recesses of
everyday life. All creative-powers, which ameliorate the systemic-processes
of bourgeois-state-capitalism are value producing. In this regard,
contrary to Marx, surplus value is today both measurable and immeasurable,
conceptual and material etc., as the well-spring of surplus value can
originate from anywhere, within the stratums of military-industrial-complex.
No longer does labor-power, i.e., the insatiable drive for ownership/knowledge
of the workforce/population, need to be tied to the modern industrial factory
in order to produce and influence value, price and wage. In the
post-industrial, post-modern age, all sorts of unquantifiable, creative forces
produce and influence value, price and wage-determinations, free of all modern
scientific quantification. In fact, within post-industrial, post-modern,
bourgeois-state-capitalism, all humans are, conscious and/or unconscious,
means of capitalist production, consumption and distribution. All humans,
consciously and/or unconsciously, are involved in one way or another
in capitalist production, capitalist consumption and capitalist distribution,
whatever form this may take. All humans, whether involved in direct production
of capitalist profit, or not, ameliorate and augment, the efficiency,
efficacy, and potency of the socio-economic processes of
bourgeois-state-capitalism, in all sorts of predictable and unpredictable
ways. History demonstrates this. Consequently, all sorts of unpaid
creative-powers, devoid of wage, which ameliorate, streamline, and develop,
the socio-economic processes of bourgeois-state-capitalism are always active,
in and across the stratums of the military-industrial-complex, manufacturing
value. Moreover, all sorts of unpaid creative-powers, continue to function and
operate, without monetary recognition and/or acknowledgment. The reason is
the duplicitous, mercenary aims of the military-industrial-complex, whose
ideational comprehensive framework, the logic of capitalism, has always
functioned and operated on some form of zero-wage work, i.e., unpaid
creative-power, in one manner or another. Thus, we must overthrow capitalism.

64.d) <u>Contra-Marx</u>: Socially necessary labor-time is no longer the primary basis for determining value, price, wage and/or surplus value. The relation between necessary labor-time, i.e., the labor-time necessary to reproduce the worker as an efficient labor-power via an average time-segment of commodity-production, and surplus labor-time, i.e., the unpaid labor-time beyond the reproduction of the worker as an efficient labor-power, is no longer properly applicable within post-industrial, post-modern, bourgeois-state-capitalism. Labor-time is no longer the basis of value, price, wage, and surplus value determinations.

64.e) <u>Contra-Marx</u>: Although, Marx's labor theory of value and surplus value continues to persist in various peripheral corners of the world, these theories are increasingly being usurped by the theory of conceptual-commodity-value-management. The theory of conceptual-commodity-value-management is founded on the notion that value, wage, and price are, in essence, conceptual and arbitrary, based on what the workforce/population is, conceptually and theoretically, forced to pay for a product/commodity/service. As a result, value, price, and wage increasingly have nothing to do with labor-time. They have no recourse to the amount of labor or the socially necessary labor-time, needed to produce something. In short, force and power decide.

64.f) <u>Contra-Marx</u>: Today, wage, price, and value determinations are increasingly the result of conceptual-commodity-value-management, i.e., arbitrary value, wage, and price determinations derived from price, wage, and value manipulations and machinations, by ruling, micro-fascist, oligarchical networks, which hold market power and productive power under their autocratic control. According to the theory of conceptual-commodity-value-management, these ruling, micro-fascist, oligarchical networks, which have cornered a market, a production sphere, a commodity, a service, and/or a profession etc., in some shape or form, arbitrarily set values, wages, and prices, according to what they deem an acceptable number and level of profit. This is purely based on the vagaries of their mercenary whims. These ruling, micro-fascist, oligarchical networks are able to set values, wages, and prices, according to their own arbitrary standards, because together, they are capable of enforcing, either through monopoly, cartels, power-blocs and/or regulatory disciplinary-mechanisms, these artificially constructed values, wages and prices.
In short, value, wage, and price determinations are increasingly derived from the arbitrary whims of ruling, micro-fascist, oligarchical networks, because of force, rather than, any scientific quantifiable labor-time.

64.g) <u>Contra-Marx</u>: Whatever, a capitalist entity, a capitalist power-bloc and/or a capitalist-network can get away with in the marketplace is legitimate and valid. And, what something, or someone, is worth is a matter of conceptual-perception. That is,a set of conceptual-perceptions artificially constructed and manipulated by the ruling, micro-fascist, oligarchical networks, namely, those capitalist-networks which have cornered specific commodity-markets, production-spheres, professions, and/or services etc. These ruling, micro-fascist, oligarchical networks manufacture artificial needs for specific professions, commodities, and/or services, because, they govern large swathes of the economic sphere, political sphere, the legal-system, and the capitalist-state. In effect, these ruling, micro-fascist, oligarchical networks, fused together under the logic of capitalism, have short-circuited the coercive laws of competition, for themselves, while, imposing these very same coercive laws of competition unto the workforce/population, in a more intense form. As a result, these ruling, micro-fascist, oligarchical networks are, in essence, able to exercise plutocratic rule over specific professions, markets, production spheres, commodities, and services etc., thus, enabling them to set prices, values and wages according to their own arbitrary whims.

64.h) <u>Contra-Marx</u>: To various degrees, micro-fascist, oligarchical networks have hijacked politics and the economy. To such an extent, that price, value, and wage, today, are no longer determined by socially necessary labor-time or labor, but instead, these items are increasingly determined by the vagaries of conceptual-commodity-value-management. That is, arbitrary and artificially, constructed value, price and wage, founded on the domination of conceptual-perception by these ruling, micro-fascist, oligarchical networks. For instance, the arbitrary values, wages, and prices of sport stars, images, artworks, services, professions, IPOs, medicines, real estates etc., or any other material and/or immaterial product, is fabricated by conceptual-commodity-value-management, i.e., value/price/wage machinations, rather than, any exact amount of labor-time, which might have went into a productive labor process. Of course, the cost of production may provide a basis for the minimum price, value, and wage, for a material and/or immaterial product or service, but, this does not set the parameters for value, wage and price determinations, when price, wage, and value are conceptually based upon, what the public is, theoretically, able to pay, and arbitrarily accept.

64.i) <u>Contra-Marx</u>: The theory of conceptual-commodity-value-management, explains huge mark-ups, sudden price escalations, monopoly price fixes, artwork prices, image prices, radical salary hikes, sport-star salaries, corporate salaries, and all sorts of immaterial commodity prices. Notwithstanding, all of these socially constructed, arbitrary price, wage, and value determinations have nothing to do with labor-time and/or Marx's law of value. Conceptual-commodity-value-management is a means to: 1. exploitatively extract and accumulate greater amounts of surplus value from the workforce/population. 2., it is a means to intensify and concentrate capital into fewer and fewer hands, augmenting control, wealth, and decision-making-authority, in a tiny set of ruling, micro-fascist, oligarchical networks. And 3., conceptual-commodity-value-management is a means to intensify, refine, and expand, the regimentation of the workforce/population, according to the logical necessities of the logic of capitalism.

(<u>Note</u>: Bourgeois economists are the oracles of conceptual-commodity-value-management. Many times, they set the basic standards and artificial parameters, for arbitrary prices, values, and wages, pertaining to the arbitrary whims of the ruling, micro-fascist, oligarchical networks, which snake throughout the military-industrial-complex.)

-[65]-

65.a) <u>Contra-Marx</u>: According to the logic of structural-anarchism, Marxism, namely, the current history of Marxism is this:

There have been historical mistakes on Marxism's part, say the Marxists, but, Marxism will correct its methods and its dictatorship, so believe and have faith in the Marxist philosophy and religion, i.e., historical-materialism. Marxist communism will refine itself and eventually lead to a global communist revolution, which will bring forth a more civilized global society, by eliminating suffering, injustice, and the exploitation of humans by other humans. According to the logic of structural-anarchism, socialist utopias cannot be achieved, in material terms, they are ideals to work towards only, despite, knowing full well that such communist-ideals can never be fully realized. They are at best guiding principles to ameliorate socio-economic conditions. Moreover, it is important to note that the many, various, Marxist revolutionary projects, which have come to pass, have resulted in socio-economic systems that have been far more coercive, disciplinary, punitive and deadly than bourgeois-state-capitalism. Another Marxist totalitarian-dictatorship is no longer feasible. And consequently, such authoritarian communist-ideals must be jettisoned in favor of something new, something more concrete, that is, an open-participatory-democracy solidified on a anarcho-socialist-constitution, civic human rights, and tangible, socio-economic guarantees.

65.b) <u>Contra-Marx</u>: The logic of structural-anarchism does not base any socio-economic transition to a post-capitalism society on the idea of the dictatorship of the proletariat, which inevitably leads to hardline-totalitarianism. The logic of structural-anarchism bases any socio-economic transition to a post-capitalism society on the idea of a structural-anarchism-constitution, civic human rights and a set of tangible socio-economic guarantees. The structural-anarchism-constitution and the charter/bill of socio-economic guarantees can safeguard against totalitarianism and as well facilitate the implementation of the federation of municipalities, cooperatives and autonomous-collectives with a pragmatic and legal framework based on a sound constitution, civic human rights and a set of tangible socio-economic guarantees.

65.c) <u>Contra-Marx</u>: Antagonism is at the center of human existence, including any socio-economic formation, whatever it may be. Therefore, antagonism can never be abolished or superseded. Antagonism is a fact of life. It is omnipresent and always manifests in different forms. Contrary to Marx, antagonism is not class oriented; it manifests in all sorts of ways and manners. It maybe possible to curtail and severely limit class antagonism, as Marxists argue, but, general antagonism is a fact of history and the unfolding of history, which constantly requires organization, demolition and re-organization.

-[66]-

66.a) <u>Contra-Marx</u>: Marx's two class analysis of the capitalist society, that between the bourgeois-capitalist and the proletariat, is no longer applicable. Post-industrial, post-modern, bourgeois-state-capitalism is no longer divided between two economic classes of citizens. In fact, post-industrial, post-modern, bourgeois-state-capitalism is highly complex and divided into a multitude of groupings based on all sorts of things, principles and/or values.

66.b) <u>Contra-Marx</u>: Post-industrial, post-modern, bourgeois-state-capitalism is multi-varied and predominantly classless, despite, being highly hierarchical and supporting a capitalist state-finance-corporate-aristocracy. Post-industrial, post-modern, bourgeois-state-capitalism is a society highly diversified and fragmented. It is a society organized into a multitude of relational constellations, which mutate and change frequently, based on time and space. Post-industrial, post-modern, bourgeois-state-capitalism is full of subcultures, counter-cultures, and/or dominant cultures, which are increasingly fluid and ever-changing. Yet, these groupings are always dominated and encapsulated by the logic of capitalism, i.e., the soft-totalitarian-state. Only, the logic of capitalism ties these relational constellations, together, by overarching and underlying these multi-varied groupings. In effect, the logic of capitalism forces these multi-varied groupings, both softly and severely, to conform to the capitalist imperative of maximum profit. It is in this regard that the logic of capitalism has been able to fashion, itself, into a soft-totalitarian-state.

66.c) <u>Contra-Marx</u>: Any simplified two class analysis of society is obsolete. The bourgeoisie/capitalists are today employed in all sorts of managerial roles and consumer roles etc., sometimes subordinate, sometimes equal, and sometimes superior. Proletariat-unions are investors, stock-owners, and managers, whose roles change and admix with bourgeois-capitalists, in different areas and in various manners, in and across the military-industrial-complex. The working class can vote as can the bourgeoisie, both can take part in municipal, provincial/state, and federal governments, and both, in certain spaces and time-periods, govern state of affairs, while, the other is temporarily in a subservient position.

66.d) <u>Contra-Marx</u>: The old Marxist revolutionary subject is in tatters and, in many instances, is no more. Notwithstanding, there are societal divisions; however, these divisions are not necessarily based on class. According to the logic of structural-anarchism, the primary divisions in society are those between administrative-micro-fascist-technocrats, i.e., the a vast array of truncated elite bureaucrats, buttressing the ruling, micro-fascist, oligarchical networks and the logic of capitalism, and in constrast, the innovative, micro-revolutionist- praxiacrats. That is, the vast array of marginalized, middle-class pragmatists, locked into the subordinated networks and structures of bourgeois-state-capitalism. A praxiacrat is the anti-thesis of the technocrat, it is those highly specialized entities, which exercise the armature of micro-revolutionism, consciously and/or unconsciously, in an attempt to temporarily, or permanently, subvert the logic of capitalism, namely, the military-industrial-complex. The praxiacrat is engaged in the praxis of exercising, practicing, and realizing, the poly-rationality of structural-anarchism, in and across the micro-recesses of everyday life. A praxiacrat can come from any stratum of the military-industrial-complex, any stratum of everyday life. He or she is not necessarily class based, or class focused. He or she exists, interacts, and struggles in a multitude of relational constellations, in and across the stratums of the military-industrial-complex in the name of radical plurality, radical equality and pragmatic egalitarianism. He or she is in essence a poly-rational entity.

66.e) <u>Contra-Marx</u>: Of course, it is true as Marx theorized that there is an oligarchy governing society, but this oligarchy is in fact a set of many networks, devoid of personnel. It is a logic. It is the logic of capitalism, which organizes social relations and the forces of production into a dominant complex of productive modes. There is more interaction and communication between governing groupings and subservient groupings than Marx initially conceived. Moreover, the way these ruling, micro-fascist, oligarchical networks are organized is more nuanced and multi-dimensional. These ruling capitalist-networks exercise their force and influence in a seemingly uncoordinated group fashion, which, cunningly, conceals the ruling unity and central logic tying them together. These ruling, micro-fascist, oligarchical networks, at times and in certain spaces, blend so effectively with subservient networks that both networks lose all distinctions, pertaining to the ruled and the ruling. When such melding takes place between the ruled and the ruling, which occurs more and more, what governs society is no longer people, or a specific class, but, a ruling logic, namely, a ruling logical apparatus. In these unified instances, it is an ideational comprehensive framework which governs the way of life and logical order of things, not people. The ruled and ruling becomes so intertwined that freewill vanishes and totalitarian-fascism sets-in, infecting the micro-recesses of everyday life and the workforce/population, itself. In essence, this unification process is the materialization of the logic of capitalism at every level of socio-economic existence. Wherein, the logic of capitalism now fuses and snakes throughout the socio-economic fabric of the society, determining all aspects of mental and physical being, perceiving, interpreting, and acting, pertaining the workforce/population and the agents of capitalism.

66.f) <u>Contra-Marx</u>: Decision-making-authority within post-industrial, post-modern, bourgeois-state-capitalism is exercised not necessarily in a top-down manner, although, this continues manner of decision-making-authority continues to persist. In contrast, instead, today decision-making-authority is primarily exercised from the bottom-up and from the periphery towards a totalitarian center. Decision-making-authority is exercised through a governing logic, which is imprinted upon and embedded in all sorts of processes, procedures, networks, structures, machines, practices and/or bureaucracies etc., including human beings. In fact, humans are the unsuspecting carriers and applicators of the ruling logic. This ruling logic, at times and in certain spaces, blends so seamlessly with everyday behaviors, everyday conversations, and everyday perceptions, coercing people, that these unsuspecting people believe this ruling logic to be synonymous with their personal, individual, self-identity. This is the mystical kernel in the logic of capitalism in the sense that it manufactures religious zeal and fanaticism for profit-making, ad nauseam.

-[67]-

67.a) The fundamental dichotomy in and across the stratums of the military-industrial-complex is not between classes, i.e., bourgeoisie and proletariat, as everyone has become a worker in whatever position he or she maybe stationed, in and across, the stratums of bourgeois-state-capitalism. In fact, the fundamental dichotomies in and across the stratums of the military-industrial-complex are between bureaucratic-technocrats, i.e., instrumental-rationality and reform, and anarcho-praxiacrats, i.e., poly-rationality and revolution. It is between those that prevent social change and intellectual advancement, at any cost, via instrumental-rationality, and those that stimulate social change and intellectual advancement, at any cost, via poly-rationality. This is the fundamental revolutionary dichotomy within the capitalist system. It is here, where decision-making-authority is most localized and in need of antagonism. It is here, where micro-revolutionary entities and micro-fascism entities, embedded in all sorts of socio-economic groupings and processes, both in the private sector and public sector, vie for contextual supremacy and morsels of decision-making-authority. It is here, where the capitalist system will be blasted out of existence. It is the bureaucratic-technocrats, i.e., the embodiments of the logic of capitalism, versus the anarcho-praxiacrats, i.e., the embodiments of the logic of structural-anarchism, which continually, manifest during the socio-economic breakdowns of bourgeois-state-capitalism, that personify the underlying clash between the poly-rationality of structural-anarchism and the instrumental-rationality of capitalism.

67.b) Although, formless and undefined in many instances, in contrast to the micro-fascism networks of the bureaucratic-technocrats, the anarcho-praxiacrats develop revolutionary consciousness and revolutionary/evolutionary force through their daily micro-skirmishes with the armature of micro-fascism set-up by the ruling, micro-fascism, oligarchical networks. Through these miniature micro-skirmishes, in and across, the military-industrial-complex, the anarcho-praxiacrats refine themselves and their poly-rational praxis into an ever-increasing set of micro-revolutionary networks, in contrast to and antagonistic to, the logic of capitalism. Through this revolutionary/evolutionary process, the anarcho-praxiacrats establish themselves as the best representatives and/or embodiments of the antithetic substitute and replacement to the logic of capitalism.

67.c) Praxiacrats are formed via a the growing sense of nihilism. That is, by the sense and the concrete examples, which practically demonstrate that the existing institutions of bourgeois-state-capitalism have ceased to adequately respond to the problems and the critical socio-economic crises, burgeoning within everyday life. Namely, the critical socio-economic conditions, these senile capitalist-institutions, themselves, have in part engendered and in part have been created to solve. Micro-revolutions of everyday life strive to transform the political-economic institutions of bourgeois-state-capitalism in ways that these very institutions forbid, poly-rationality. Therefore, the triumph of the logic of structural-anarchism, its praxiacrats, and all micro-revolutions, is based on establishing a new set of institutions for an outdated set, i.e., to completely abandon the institutions of bourgeois-state-capitalism in order to reformulate these institutions along poly-rational lines, the poly-rational necessities of a structural-anarchism-complex.

67.d) It is crisis or breakdown alone, which weakens institutions and ideational comprehensive frameworks; and as bourgeois-state-capitalism is prone to systemic malfunctions of all types and kinds, its institutions are continually weakened via the socio-economic assaults of incessant, socio-economic breakdowns. As a result, increasing segments of the workforce/population are increasingly being flung-out from the socio-economic processes of bourgeois-state-capitalism, specifically, from economic life, itself, and forced to live in the urban and suburban wasteland of bourgeois-state-capitalism. Due to this, the disconnected insatiable drives for ownership/knowledge of the workforce/population are increasingly behaving in erratic fashions, in and across the stratums of the military-industrial-complex, prompting, the multiplication of disciplinary-mechanisms and punitive-mechanisms, in and across everyday life. Only, when a rash of socio-economic breakdowns, deepen, will society inherently divide into two antagonistic counter-logics, on a general societal scale, i.e., the instrumental-rationality of capitalism versus the poly-rationality of structural-anarchism. Only, when socio-economic breakdowns, deepen, will bourgeois-state-capitalism polarize between two great factions, i.e., those individuals and groupings, which seek to defend the current, senile, collection of technocratic, capitalist institutions, and those individuals and groupings, which seek to implement a new collection of anarcho-socialist institutions. These two factions are not classes in the Marxists sense, as these factions amass proponents from all the stratums of the military-industrial-complex, regardless of economic origins. In contrast to Marxist thinking, these two factions have a tendency to divide along the ideational comprehensive framework of capitalism, i.e., instrumental-rationality, and along the ideational comprehensive framework of structural-anarchism, i.e., poly-rationality.

– [68] –

68.a) The logic of structural-anarchism is a pragmatic philosophy and a pragmatic political-economic framework based on the specific, pragmatic, socio-economic formation of the federation of municipalities, cooperatives and autonomous-collectives. The workings of structural-anarchism are about realizing its central logical nucleus, i.e., to satisfy the maximum logical necessities of the workforce/population, by any means necessary, at the lowest financial cost, as soon as possible, while, only satisfying the minimum logical necessities of the logic of capitalism. The logic of structural-anarchism is programmed to decentralize, horizontalize, and democratize, socio-economic processes, technologies, and decision-making-authority, by establishing poly-rationality as the foundation-stone for all socio-economic formations and all socio-economic processes.   The principle is that:

> The decentralization, horizontalization, and democratization of socio-economic processes, relations, ideational comprehensive frameworks, technologies, modes of production, and decision-making-authority, via a series of intensifying, expanding micro-revolutions, will eventually result in a new socio-economic, organizational-formation, superior to bourgeois-state-capitalism, by the very fact, this new formation is an open-participatory-democracy. That is, an open-participatory-democracy, which empowers, emboldens, and galvanizes the formation of a vast anarchist federation of municipalities, cooperatives and autonomous-collectives, based on poly-rationality. Whereupon, its anarcho-communist economy will function and operate akin to a cooperative series of dynamic-formations, strategically-engineered to maximize equality, autonomy, institutional transparency, privacy, and the full-satisfaction of human needs. And, whose political apparatus, or multiplex, will inspire the maximization of an all-inclusive, democratic-participation at the municipal level, via a structural-anarchism-constitution, civic human rights, and an all-important set of socio-economic guarantees, for all citizens. Specifically, referendums on all essential policies and economic issues will serve as the primary tool of the open-participatory-democracy and, specifically, the structural-anarchism-complex.

(<u>Note</u>: The political-economic framework of structural-anarchism is the maximum limit, and socio-organizational formation, capable of supporting maximum liberty, equality, and individual autonomy, within a cohesive, organized, egalitarian, lawful whole, without descending into unstructured lawless anarchy, and/or a hard-line, coercive, totalitarian dictatorship. Its fail-safe or linchpin is poly-rationality.)

68.b) The logic of structural-anarchism is not Utopian idealism, but, a pragmatic, practical-oriented, political-economic framework, grounded in a poly-rational logic and a pluralist praxis of everyday life. That is, a pragmatic egalitarianism, which unifies, multi-varied, ideational comprehensive frameworks in a diverse patchwork, stitched freely together, by the poly-rationality of structural-anarchism. The logic of structural-anarchism is a micro-revolutionary, post-modern project, which attempts to lessen the socio-economic divisions, artificial scarcity, capitalist competition, and universal nihilism, within the present-day, capitalist system, including after, or when, this totalitarian system malfunctions, breakdown, and detonates sky-high.

(Note: The structural-anarchism-complex is the reformulation, the reorganization, and the reconstruction of the capitalist system, in general, into an open-participatory-democracy, where the logic of capitalism is returned from where it came and sprang as a secondary proxy, subsumed within the workforce/population. The only logic capable of absorbing, reorganizing, and dislocating the instrumental-rationality of capitalism, from its contextual supremacy, is the poly-rationality of structural-anarchism.)

68.c) The logic of structural-anarchism is not a contradiction in itself, i.e., an oxymoron, as some might think, in the sense that the notion of structure seems to contradict the notion of anarchy, i.e., the idea that by definition anarchism cannot have a structure because it is seemingly anti-structure. However, to the contrary, real anarchism is about structuring, socio-economic modes, relations, processes, and society, as a whole, along different, more intelligent, democratic lines than what bourgeois-state-capitalism has permitted and accomplished to date, hence, the appropriate terminology of structural-anarchism.

68.d) Structural-anarchism is a political-economic framework and a poly-rational form of praxis, which is about constructing, demolishing, and reconstructing, mental/physical activity according to a different organizational principle, i.e., poly-rationality, so as to maximize liberty, equality, and open-participatory-democracy for the greatest number. The logic of structural-anarchism is about a new anarcho-socialist mode of production. That is, it is about new anarcho-socialist forces of production and new anarcho-socialist relations of production in combination with new anarcho-socialist modes of consumption and distribution. Consequently, the logic of structural-anarchism calls for a more intelligently organized society, a poly-rational society, where, the principles of intelligence, dialogue, creative deviation, and synergy, i.e., a collectivist rationality, between equal citizens, plays a predominant role in societal, decision-making-authority.

-[69]-

69.a) Where culture is increasingly becoming anarchic, plural, cooperative, collectivist, and poly-rational, politics and economics are increasingly becoming unified, fanatical, and totalitarian. In politics and economics, differences, deviations, and diversities are increasingly being streamlined into a unitary, political-economic framework, founded on the logic of capitalism, where, there is only one-way of doing things and only one-way of thinking about things, specifically, the maximization of profit.

69.b) Today, the workforce/population is both, a mental and/or physical, producer, distributer and consumer within bourgeois-state-capitalism, regardless of race, gender, age and/or class etc., but, this is all, since, they cannot be anything else without courting disaster, discipline and punishment. Today, the workforce/population is always in a moment of capitalist production, consumption and distribution, both mentally and physically, whereupon, the capitalist imperative for the maximization of profit, governs everything, including, all aspects of human existence. The workforce/population must work, both physically and mentally, in service of the logic of capitalism, across the military-industrial-complex. Any socio-economic deviations, from this fundamental imperative, activate the totalitarian, punitive-mechanisms and judicial-processes of the military-industrial-complex, i.e., instrumental-rationality, which gradually and/or immediately stifle, regiment, and/or eliminate, such socio-economic deviations, depending on the poly-rational transgression. The logical apparatus of bourgeois-state-capitalism does this, because the logic of capitalism, is in essence at war, with everything and everyone, in its constant efforts to maximize capitalist profit, by any means necessary, at the lowest financial cost, as soon as possible. Humans are always locked into power-struggles with capitalism.

69.c) The ideational comprehensive framework of capitalism is a technocratic machine, both material and conceptual, where all questions have their black and white answers, yes and no procedures, where all social-ills have their easy-fix solutions and scapegoats. The ideational comprehensive framework of capitalism is all-knowing and seeks to be all-encompassing, its fundamental logic, i.e., instrumental-rationality, is autocratic and is one of the many paths towards conceptual, material, despotic-totalitarianism. The ideational comprehensive framework of capitalism is the bewitchment and subjugation of poly-rational intelligence into mono-rationality, a mono-rationality engineered in service of particular, capitalist delusions, false-consciousness, and exploitative, mercenary, profit-making opportunism. The instrumental-rationality of capitalism is its own greatest weapon in the sense that its extremely myopic, reductive, imperative for profit, which has limited flexibility, is the manner by which the logic of capitalism batters-down all antagonisms over an extended period of time and/or space. In fact, the ideational comprehensive framework of capitalism perpetually reinforces itself, materially and conceptually, ad nauseam. Profit and power, are the spells by which the workforce/population are continuously seduced, manipulated, and programmed, by capitalist instrumental-rationality, into a litany of false-beliefs, false-consciousness, and capitalist, socio-economic processes. That is, material capitalist processes designed to interminably proceed towards socio-economic totalitarianism, specifically, the pure despotism of neoliberal, totalitarian-capitalism, regardless if they intend to or not. The prime directive is forever to maximize capitalist profit, by any means necessary, at the lowest financial cost, as soon as possible, that is, to integrate everything and everyone within the universal domination of instrumental-rationality.

– [70] –

70.a) The post-modern project is not complete. The fundamental meta-narrative of capitalism continues to persist and bewitch the sum of humanity. The reason for this is that post-modernism has yet to fully-discover and realize its motor force, anarchism. In fact, post-modernism is anarchism and anarchism is post-modernism, but, the meta-narrative of bourgeois-capitalism has divorced post-modernism from its engine, anarchism. Consequently, bourgeois-capitalism has turned post-modernism into bourgeois post-modernism. It has de-fanged post-modernism. As a result, post-modernism must re-establish its connection with its motor force, anarchism, so as to attain full-maturity and development.

70.b) If the post-modern condition is defined by the incredulity towards meta-narratives, then, the meta-narrative of capitalism is the last great bastion of the Enlightenment and its two-faced ideal of human equality, absolute knowledge, and civic emancipation. Indeed, the meta-narrative of capitalism, the crown-jewel of the Enlightenment, continues to prosper and enslave, both mentally and physically, the rational human spirit, with dreams of material and immaterial luxury, opulence, and egalitarian abundance, which as always, are items manufactured on material and conceptual exploitation, enslavement, and the immiseration of the workforce/population.

70.c) The meta-narrative of bourgeois-capitalism radiates disaster triumphant in the name of the Enlightenment. Therefore, the post-modern project is not over as it has yet to reach its real revolutionary zenith, structural-anarchism, whereupon, even the Enlightenment meta-ideals of bourgeois-capitalism and its reductive instrumental-rationality, shall be overthrown in the name of real equality, namely, socio-economic equality, plurality and poly-rationality. That is, a vast, multi-dimensional, network/federation of political-economic variations and poly-rational differences, stitched loosely together, like patchwork, via the logic of structural-anarchism. This radical, post-modern revolution is an anarchist revolution, without grand-narratives, demanding, the end of all grand-narratives. The post-modern anarchist revolution is the radical application of the post-modern incredulity towards meta-narratives to the last standing meta-narrative of the Enlightenment, bourgeois-capitalism. So far, the post-modern project has not gone far enough. It has not reached its Nth degree, structural-anarchism and the destruction of bourgeois-capitalism. Post-modernism has not realized its full-blown capacities, the overthrow of the last grand mythology, bourgeois-capitalism. That is, the lethal dissolution of the Enlightenment via the lethal dissolution of its last standing meta-narrative, i.e., the meta-narrative of bourgeois-capitalism, the logic of capitalism.

70.d) Anarchism is the engine of post-modernism and post-modernism is the spirit of anarchism in the sense that both are the zenith and apex of radical social change, radical plurality, radical equality, and pragmatic-egalitarianism in its purest form. Consequently, anarchism and post-modernism are synonymous. Anarchism and post-modernism are synonymous in the sense that post-modernism is epistemological anarchism in thought-form, i.e., narrative-form, and anarchism is pragmatic post-modernism in active-form, i.e., methodological-form. Specifically, anarchism is post-modernism operating on the ground, working in and across the micro-recesses of everyday life, physically attempting to demolish the totalitarian unity of bourgeois-capitalism into a post-modern, socio-economic plurality. Likewise, post-modernism is anarchism operating in theory, working in and across the micro-recesses of everyday life, mentally attempting to demolish the totalitarian unity of bourgeois-capitalism into an anarchist, socio-economic heterogeneity. In short, anarchism and post-modernism are synonymous in the sense that they have similar foundations, namely, radical equality, radical plurality and a radical antipathy towards meta-narratives, including the meta-narrative of bourgeois-capitalism.

70.e) Anarchism is pragmatic demolition, that is, the post-modern critique actualized in material-form, while, post-modernism is theoretical demolition, that is, the anarchist critique actualized in conceptual-form. Both anarchism and post-modernism champion plurality, heterogeneity, and egalitarianism, among all micro-narratives. Anarchism is the methodology of post-modernism and post-modernism is the epistemology of anarchism, hence, why both are synonymous with each other, i.e., two sides of the same coin, two peas in the same pod, wherein, the goal for both is to maximize a plurality of small narratives, whereupon, none is favored over another. Consequently, both post-modernism and anarchism strive for the revolutionary implementation of radical egalitarianism in and across the sum of everyday life via conceptual and physical acts of demolitionism and the general-strike.

70.f) Any revolution, that is, any post-modern anarchist revolution, is about the structural alteration of the capitalist system. Any revolution, that is, any post-modern anarchist revolution, is the result of the multiplying incongruities between the structures of the capitalist system and the growing demands for economic-financial equality, namely, the collective sharing of socio-economic resources by all, in relative equal measure.

70.g) The logic of structural-anarchism is about the radical structural alteration of bourgeois-state-capitalism; hence, the term "structural" within the political philosophy of structural-anarchism. Namely, the logic of structural-anarchism is a political philosophy hell-bent on realizing a structural-anarchism-complex. That is, a federation/patchwork of municipalities, worker-cooperatives and autonomous-collectives, sharing all, in relative equal measure, within the parameters of an open-participatory-democracy. The point is to construct a fully-developed, poly-rational, socio-economic, pragmatic-egalitarianism.

70.h) Any revolution's success, micro and/or macro, partial and/or total, is determined by the amount of free thinking, creativity, autonomy, equality, plurality, and open-participatory-democracy, it generates. And, also, by the extent that it improves everyday life and everyday living conditions for the greatest number.

70.i) From this premise, any revolution that takes place, micro and/or macro etc., including any post-modern anarchist revolution, would have to be more intelligent, more egalitarian, and more poly-rational, than bourgeois-state-capitalism. It would have to be a revolution, or a series of micro-revolutions, which makes society more collectively participatory, more intelligently organized and, as a result, a society more economically equal and egalitarian. This is the criteria for any successful revolution(s), micro and/or macro etc., specifically, any post-modern anarchist revolution.

70.j) From this premise, the primary objective of any revolution, micro and/or macro etc., including any post-modern anarchist revolution, must be the leveling-down of socio-economic, hierarchical, capitalist disparities, through the re-organization of ownership/knowledge, surplus value, and modes of production, along more democratic-horizontal-lines. Therefore, what is required is a gestalt switch, a gestalt switch, where all the senile, political-economic institutions of bourgeois-state-capitalism are demolished and re-constructed, according to the logic of structural-anarchism.

70.k) Successful revolutions are those revolutions, micro and/or macro etc., including any post-modern anarchist revolution, which improve the everyday lives of citizens, specifically, by significantly augmenting the decision-making-authority of all citizens and civic-participants over their private and public spheres.

-[71]-

71.a) From these tiny private and public spheres, micro-revolutions blossom into new states of consciousness, i.e., structures of feeling, and new socio-economic formations, new clusters of ideational comprehensive frameworks, with the inclusive, poly-rationality of structural-anarchism stationed on the center-point as the singular, unifying ideational comprehensive framework, namely, the new organizing principle for all logics. Micro-revolutions permit solitary singularities to feel part of a movement, even, if these poly-rational singularities may not directly be part of any mass movement. It is in micro-recesses of everyday life, beneath, the highly obdurate stratums of the military-industrial-complex that the seeds of radical social change, germinate. And, thus, it is in the micro-recesses of everyday life where microscopic insurrections have the most influence. Radical molecular alterations in the micro-spheres of everyday life have the capacity within them to reverberate in and across the obdurate stratums of the military-industrial-complex and smash them to pieces, whereupon, nothing is left but pure anarchism.

71.b) Mass movements are always the aftershocks of these hidden, perpetual micro-revolutions, which every so often spark, within the micro-recesses of everyday life, radical social change, in reaction and in revolution to the ineptitude of senile capitalist institutions. These perpetual combustions and molecular upsurges of life-affirming force, which ever-mushroom throughout the micro-spheres, are the fuel of radical, grassroots, social change, and any socio-economic transformation. By working collectively and poly-rationally, these life-affirming, revolutionary/evolutionary forces, ever-emanating from the workforce/population, might be eventually, assembled to erect a new poly-rational set of horizontal institutions, i.e., anarcho-socialist institutions, whose edifice, the structural-anarchism-complex, will be built upon the antiquated apparatuses, mechanisms, and processes of bourgeois-state-capitalism. Of course, the structural-anarchism-complex will be devoid of the logic of capitalism and structured according to a new, poly-rational, set of relations and mode of production, consumption and distribution etc., namely, a poly-rational, set of anarcho-socialist relations and modes, functioning and operating, according to new set of socio-economic parameters, designed horizontally in line with the logic of structural-anarchism etc.

– [72] –

72.a) Enjoying contextual supremacy, the central-operating-code of capitalism is omnipresent, meaning, the workforce/population has no external and what appears external is always a product of the universal capitalist code, just as what appears internal is always a product of the universal capitalist code, thus, the secret of the capitalist machine, the logic of capitalism. Codes voiding codes, codes encoding codes, itself, ad infinitum, and the will to power is contained in this made-made shell designed by bourgeois-capitalism. The military-industrial-complex, the soft-totalitarian-state, is the current artificial context of the will to power, i.e., the insatiable drive for ownership/knowledge. Yet, the insatiable drive for ownership/knowledge, housed in the workforce/population and nature, will have other socio-economic formations, more intelligent, and more refined than post-industrial, post-modern, bourgeois-state-capitalism. As, the logical process of this poly-rational drive is radical social change, collectivism, and continual, revolutionary refinement. Consequently, all socio-economic formations, archaic, and incapable of real radical social change, will decay, pass away to the grave and the dustbin of history.

(The will to power, intrinsic in the workforce/population and/or nature, is the elementary means of a revolutionary process out of capitalism, grounded all types of species-being. This reative-power strives for radical equality and heterogeneity.)

72.b) The will to power, the insatiable drive, simultaneously and ubiquitously, centralized and decentralized, is intrinsic from the infinitesimal to the colossal, and vice versa. The will to power is a force, fashioned and designed to centralize, decentralize, and refine itself, ad infinitum, without expenditure or accumulation, without stop or start, without set quantity or quality, but ideally, only as one generalized, serialized, sequence of revolution(s) and evolution(s) of the same, basic, form and structure. Henceforth, the insatiable drive for ownership/knowledge is perpetually constructing, demolishing, and re-constructing, itself, into a new man-made shell, an oscillating synthesis of ruling, dynamic-formations, anarcho-communism, with the poly-rationality of structural-anarchism at the controls. Ultimately, nothing can get in its way, since, the structural-anarchism-complex is the next step, the next stage, the next age, beyond the outmoded bric-à-brac, that is, bourgeois-state-capitalism, the soft-totalitarian-state.

72.c) The reason is, the logic of structural-anarchism is more poly-rational, more refined, more democratic, thus, more egalitarian. The poly-rationality of structural-anarchism is the limit of equality, liberty, efficiency, collectivity, and open-participatory-democracy, short of spiraling into total anarchy. As a result, the structural-anarchism-complex is better equipped to sate the basic maintenance requirements of the workforce/population and nature. This includes all the highly-developed, anarcho-socialist modes and relations, currently multiplying in and across the stratums of everyday life, requesting autonomy, equality, heterogeneity, decision-making-authority, and basic socio-economic guarantees.

72.d) So the basic truth of Structural-Anarcho-Political-Economics:

A will to power, within nature and human existence, whose singular, plural, unrelenting purpose, if it is to have one, is radical social change, the continuous, spatio-temporal refinement of structural-organization, its own fundamental essence, poly-rationality. The will to power, both general and specific, both unanimously material and conceptual, at once, here, now, forever, irreversibly speeds towards new historical transformations and new socio-economic formations, anarcho-communism, ad infinitum etc...

72.e) Real history is the unfolding of the will to power, a convergence of mental and physical forces and/or logics, pitted against one another in a multiplicity of fluctuating, antagonistic and/or mutual-aid relationships, vying for contextual supremacy. Real history is a fiery molten crucible, anarchy, buried deep, beneath manufactured pseudo-history and superficiality, ever-ready to explode, unfold, by way of the revolutionary rabble. Purged and purified of all capitalist modes or relations, real history will glisten, glisten through a new logical system and paradigm. And, any small impetus can germinate and activate the universal anarchist revolution. So, make haste praxiacrat, rabble-rouser, grab history, own it, and bend it to your will, lest, history slips between your fingers into something other, something false, something that will wield real history against you from above.

72.f) All told, the self-inflicted global-suicide of totalitarian-capitalism lies behind the blazing eyes of millions marching together, arm in arm over its cold metallic corpse, smashed to pieces, under the militant boot of structural-anarchism, commanding, <u>IMMEDIATE DEMOLITIONIST-ACTION AND THE GENERAL-STRIKE</u>!!!